The Role of Representatives of Minority Shareholders in the System of Corporate Governance

European University Studies

Europäische Hochschulschriften

Publications Universitaires Européennes

Series II **Law**

Reihe II Rechtswissenschaft

Série II Droit

Volume/ Band **5909**

Wenjia Yan

The Role of Representatives of Minority Shareholders in the System of Corporate Governance

In the Context of Corporate Governance in the US, EU and China

PL ACADEMIC RESEARCH

Bibliographic Information published by the Deutsche Nationalbibliothek
The Deutsche Nationalbibliothek lists this publication in the Deutsche Nationalbibliografie; detailed bibliographic data is available in the internet at http://dnb.d-nb.de.

Zugl.: Hamburg, Univ., Diss., 2016

D 18
ISSN 0531-7312
ISBN 978-3-631-70005-1 (Print)
E-ISBN 978-3-631-70006-8 (E-PDF)
E-ISBN 978-3-631-70007-5 (EPUB)
E-ISBN 978-3-631-70008-2 (MOBI)
DOI 10.3726/b10758

PL Academic Research is an Imprint of Peter Lang GmbH.
Peter Lang – Frankfurt am Main · Bern · Bruxelles · New York · Oxford · Warszawa · Wien

This publication has been peer reviewed.

www.peterlang.com

Acknowledgements

The writing of this dissertation is the first significant academic challenge that I have faced. Without the support of the following people, this study would not have been completed. For this I owe them my deepest gratitude.

First of all, I would like to express my deepest sense of gratitude to Professor Heribert Hirte at Hamburg University, who undertook the task of acting as my supervisor despite his many other academic commitments and political affairs. He supported me throughout my thesis with his patience and knowledge while allowing me to work in my own way. His wisdom, knowledge and commitment to the highest standards inspired and motivated me. I attribute the level of my Doctor degree to his encouragement and effort. I am also thankful for the excellent example that he has provided as a successful professor. As a beginner in the field of academic research of law, I feel so lucky that I experienced four years with him at Hamburg University.

I would also like to thank Xiaodan Zhang, my husband, who is also a PhD candidate in Law, without whom this effort would have been worth nothing. He is not only my husband, but also my career partner. His serious attitude towards academic research and toughness have significantly influenced and encouraged me. When I encountered difficulties in the process of dissertation writing, he always stood by my side and supported me by saying "I believe in you".

Finally, I would like to take this opportunity to express the profound gratitude to my beloved parents and grandmother for their love and continuous support, both spiritually and materially. They always support, encourage and believe in me, as well as so unselfishly care for me. Their contribution to me is so tremendous that words cannot fully express my gratitude to them.

This dissertation is dedicated to my family.

Contents

Abbreviation

ABA	American Bar Association
AG	Aktiengesellschaft
AktG	Aktiengesellschaftsrecht
BetrVG	Betriebsverfassungsgesetz
CEO	Chief Executive Officer
CSRC	China Securities Regulatory Commission
DAX	Deutscher Aktienindex
DGCL	Delaware General Corporation Law
EC	European Commission
ECFR	European Company and Financial Law Review
e.g.	for example
EU	European Union
GCGC	German Corporate Governance Code
GDP	Gross Domestic Product
GEM	Growth Enterprise Market
GmbH	Gesellschaft mit beschränkter Haftung
i.e.	it is
IRRC	Investor Responsibility Research Center Institute
MBCA	Model Business Corporate Act
Medef	Mouvement des entreprises de France
MitbestG	Mitbestimmungsgesetz
NASDAQ	National Association of Securities Dealers Automated Quotations
NDPTCA	North Dakota Publicly Traded Corporation Act
NPC	National People's Congress
NYSE	New York Stock Exchange
PLCs	Public Listed Companies
RMB	Ren Min Bi
RPTs	Related-party Transactions
SASAC	State-owned Assets Supervision and Administration Commission of the State Council
SEC	Securities Exchange Commission
SETC	State Economic and Trade Commission
SOEs	State-owned Enterprises
TFEU	Treaty on the Functioning of the European Union
UCLA	University of California, Los Angeles
US	United States
USA	United States of American
UK	United Kingdom of Great Britain and Northern Ireland

VBL	Versorgungsanstalt des Bundes und der Länder
WpÜG	Gesetz zur Regelung von öffentlichen Angeboten zum Erwerb von Wertpapieren und von Unternehmensübernahmen
ZGR	Zeitschrift für Unternehmens- und Gesellschaftsrecht
ZHR	Zeitschrift für das gesamte Handels- und Wirtschaftsrecht

Bibliography

Literatures

A. Sorkin: "Germany's Blackstone Deal Swats Down "Locust" Talk". *New York Times*, April 24th, 2006.

Adolf, A. Berle / Gardiner, C. Means: *The Modern Corporation and Private Property*. Transaction Publishers: 1991.

Agrawal, Anup / Knoeber, Charles R.: "Firm Performance and Mechanisms to Control Agency Problems Between Managers and Shareholders". *Journal of Financial and Quantitative Analysis*, Vol. 31, No. 3, 9.1996, pp. 377–397.

Aguilera R. / Jackson G.: "The cross-national diversity of corporate governance Dimensions and determinants". *Academy of Management Review*, Vol. 28, No. 3, 2003, pp. 447–465.

AktG.

Alchian A.A. / Demsetz H.: "Production, Information Costs and Economic Organization". *American Economic Review*, Vol. 62, No.5, 1972, pp. 777–795.

Alchian, Armen / Demsetz, Harold: "Production, Information Costs, and Economic Organization". *American Economic Review*, Vol. 62, No. 5, 12.1972, pp. 777–795.

ALI Principles of Corporate Governance: *Analysis and Recommendations* § 2.01 cmt. f (1994).

Allen W.: "Ambiguity in Corporation Law". *Delaware Journal of Corporate Law*, Vol. 22, 1997, pp. 894–903.

Allen, William T. / Jacobs, Jack B. / Strine, Leo E. Jr.: "Function over Form: A Reassessment of Standards of Review in Delaware Corporation Law". *The Business Lawyer*, Vol. 56, No. 4, 8.2001, pp. 1287–1321.

Allen, William T.: "Independent Directors in MBO Transactions: Are They Fact or Fantasy?" *The Business Lawyer*, Vol. 45, No. 4, 8.1990, pp. 2055–2063.

Altman, Ken: *Current Corporate Governance Trends in Germany*, 14.5.2010, retrieved 12.7.14, from http://blogs.law.harvard.edu/corpgov/2010/05/14/current-corporate-governance-trends-in-germany/.

American Bar Association – Committee on Corporate Laws: *Guidelines for the Unaffiliated Director of the Controlled Corporation.*

American Bar Association: *Business Law Section.*

American Bar Association: *The Business Lawyer*, Vol. 45, No. 1, 11.1989, pp. 429–440.

Andrade, Gregor / Mitchell, Mark / Stafford, Erik: "New Evidence and Perspectives on Mergers". *Journal of Economic Perspectives*, Vol. 15, No. 2, Spring 2001, pp. 103–120.

Aspen Institute: *Overcoming Short-Termism: A Call for a More Responsible Approach to Investment and Business Management*, 2009, retrieved 15.05.2014, from http://www.aspeninstitute.org/sites/default/files/content/docs/business%20and%20society%20program/overcome_short_state0909.

Axley, Ralph E.: "The Case Against Cumulative Voting". *Wisconsin Law Review*, Vol. 1950, No. 2, 1950, pp. 278–287.

Bagley, Constance E. / Page, Karen L.: "The Devil Made Me Do It: Replacing Corporate Directors' Veil of Secrecy with the Mantle of Stewardship". *San Diego Law Review*, Vol. 36, No. 4, 1999, pp. 897–946.

Bainbridge, Stephen M.: "Director Primacy: The Means and Ends of Corporate Governance". *Northwestern University Law Review*, Vol. 97, No. 2, Winter 2003, pp. 547–618.

Bainbridge, Stephen M.: "Independent Directors and the ALI Corporate Governance Project". *George Washington Law Review*, No. 61, Vol. 4, 1992–1993, pp. 1034–1083.

Bainbridge, Stephen M.: "The Business Judgment Rule as Abstention Doctrine". *Vanderbilt Law Review*, Vol. 57, No. 1, 2004, pp. 83–134.

Bainbridge, Stephen M.: "The Politics of Corporate Governance: Roe's Strong Managers, Weak Owners". *Harvard Journal of Law & Public Policy*, Vol. 18, No. 1–10, 1995, pp. 671–737.

Bainbridge, Stephen M.: *A Critique of the NYSE's Director Independence Listing Standards.* UCLA School of Law, Research Paper No. 02–15, 2002, retrieved 15.7.2014, from http://www.ssrn.com/abstract_id=317121.

Bainbridge, Stephen M.: *Corporate Governance after the Financial Crisis.* Oxford University Press: 5.2012.

Bainbridge, Stephen M.: *The New Corporate Governance in Theory and Practice.* Oxford University Press: 7.2008.

Baird, Douglas G. / Henderson, M. Todd: "Other People's Money". *Stanford Law Review*, Vol. 60, No. 5, 2008, pp. 1309–1343.

Balotti, R. Franklin / Hanks, James J. Jr.: "Rejudging the Business Judgment Rule". *The Business Lawyer*, Vol. 48, No. 4, 1993, pp. 1337–1353.

Barontini R. / Caprio L.: "The Effect of Family Control on Firm Value and Performance: Evidence from Continental Europe". *European Financial Management*, Vol. 12, No. 5, 2006, pp. 689–723.

Baums, Theodor / Scott, Kenneth E.: "Taking Shareholder Protection Seriously? Corporate Governance in the United States and Germany". *The American Journal of Comparative Law*, Vol. 53, No. 1, 2005, pp. 31–75.

Bayer, Walter / Hoffmann, Thomas: „AG-Report: Aktienrecht in Zahlen, Drittelbeteiligung der Arbeitnehmer im Aufsichtsrat". *Sonderteil Der Zeitschrift Die Aktiengesellschaft*, 2010.

Baysinger Barry D. / Butler Henry N.: "Revolution Versus Evolution in Corporation Law: The ALI's Project and the Independent Director". *George Washington Law Review*, Vol. 52, No. 4&5, 1984, pp. 557–581.

Bebchuk, Lucian A. / Kraakman, Reinier / Triantis, George: "Stock Pyramids, Cross-Ownership and Dual Class Equity: The Mechanisms and Agency Costs of Separating Control from Cash-Flow Rights". In: Morck R. (ed.): *Concentrated Corporate Ownership*. NBER: 2000, pp. 445–460.

Bebchuk, Lucian A. / Roe, Mark J.: "A Theory of Path Dependence in Corporate Ownership and Governance". *Stanford Law Review*, Vol. 52, No. 1, 11.1999, pp. 127–170.

Bebchuk, Lucian A. / Weisbach, Michael S.: "The State of Corporate Governance Research". *The Review of Financial Studies*, Vol. 23, No. 3, Corporate Governance, 3.2010, pp. 939–961.

Bebchuk, Lucian A.: "A Rent-Protection Theory of Corporate Ownership and Control". In: National Bureau of Economic Research: *Working Paper 7203*, 1999, retrieved 12.3.2013, from http://www.nber.org/papers/w7203.

Bebchuk, Lucian A.: "Letting Shareholders Set the Rules". *Harvard Law Review*, Vol. 119, No. 6, 2006, pp. 1784–1813.

Bebchuk, Lucian A.: "Limiting Contractual Freedom in Corporate Law: The Desirable Constraints on Charter Amendments". *Harvard Law Review*, Vol. 102, No. 8, 6.1989, pp. 1820–1860.

Bebchuk, Lucian A.: "The Case for Increasing Shareholder Power". *Harvard Law Review*, Vol. 118, No. 835, 2005, pp. 833–914.

Bebchuk, Lucian A.: "The Myth of the Shareholder Franchise". *Virginia Law Review*, Vol. 93, No. 675, 2007, pp. 675–732.

Becht, Marco / Röell, Ailsa: "Blockholdings in Europe: An International Comparison". *European Economic Review*, Vol. 43, No. 4–6, 1999, pp. 1049–1056.

Belcredi, Massimo / Bozzi, Stefano / Di Noia, Carmine: "Board elections and shareholder activism: the Italian experiment, Boards and Shareholders in European Listed Companies: Facts, Context and Post-crisis Reforms". In: Belcredi, Massimo / Ferrarini, Guido (eds.): *International Corporate Law and Financial Market Regulation*. Cambridge University Press: 2.2014, pp. 1–66.

Benoit, Bertrand: "German Deputy Still Targets "Locusts"". *Financial Times*, 14.2.2007.

Berglof, Eric / Peroti, Enrico: "The Governance Structure of the Japanese Financial". *Kei retsu*, Vol. 36, No. 2, 10.1994, pp. 259–284.

Berliner Morgen post 26.10.2009.

Berliner, Martin Peltzer / von Werder, Axel: „Der "German Code of Corporate Governance (GCCG)" des Berliner Initiativkreises". *Die Aktiengesellschaft: AG*, Vol. 46, 2001, pp. 1–15.

Bertrand, Marianne / Mehta, Paras / Mullainathan, Sendhil: "Ferreting Out Tunneling: An Application to Indian Business Groups". *The Quarterly Journal of Economics*, Vol. 117, No. 1, 2.2002, pp. 121–148.

Bertrand, Marianne / Schoar, Antoinette: "The Role of Family in Family Firms". *Journal of Economic Perspectives*, Vol. 20, No. 2, 2006, pp. 73–96.

Betriebsverfassungsgesetz, 1952.

Bhagat, Sanjai / Black, Bernard: "The Non-Correlation Between Board Independence and Long-Term Firm Performance". *Journal of Corporation Law*, Vol. 27, No. 2, Winter 2002, pp. 231–273.

Bhagat, Sanjai / Black, Bernard: "The Uncertain Relationship Between Board Composition and Firm Performance". *The Business Lawyer*, Vol. 54, No. 3, 5.1999, pp. 921–963.

Bhagat, Sanjai / Brickley, James A.: "Cumulative Voting: The Value of Minority Shareholder Voting Rights". *Journal of Law and Economics*, Vol. 27, No. 2, 1984, pp. 339–366.

Bisconti A.: "The Double Bottom Line: Can Constituency Statutes Protect Socially Responsible Corporations Stuck in Revlon Land?". *Loyola of Los Angeles Law Review*, Vol. 42, No. 3, 2009, pp. 765–806.

Black, Bernard S. / Kraakman, Reinier: "A Self-enforcing Model of Corporate Law". *Harvard Law Review*, Vol. 109, No. 8, 1996, pp. 1911–1982.

Black, Bernard S.: "Shareholder Activism and Corporate Governance in the United States". *New Palgrave Dictionary of Economics and the Law*, Vol. 3, 1998, pp. 459–465, 462.

Black, Bernard S.: "The Value of Institutional Investor Monitoring: The Empirical Evidence". *UCLA Law Review*, Vol. 39, No. 4, 1992, pp. 895–940.

Blair, Margaret M. / Stout L.: "Director Accountability and the Mediating Role of the Corporate Board". *Washington University Law Quarterly*, Vol. 79, No. 2, 2001, pp. 403–448.

Blair, Margaret M.: *Ownership and Control: Rethinking Corporate Governance for the Twenty-first Century*. Washington, D.C.: Brookings Institution: 1995.

Block, Dennis J. / Maimone, Michael J. / Ross, Steven B.: "Duty of Loyalty and the Evolution of the Scope of Judicial Review, The Scope of Judicial Review". *Brooklyn Law Review*, Vol. 59, No. 1, 1993–1994, pp. 65–106.

Boatright, John R.: "Employee Governance and the Ownership of the Firm". *Business Ethics Quarterly*, Vol. 14, No. 1, 1.2004, pp. 1–21.

Boatright, John R.: "Fiduciary Duties and the Shareholder-Management Relation: Or, What's so special about Shareholders?". *Business Ethics Quarterly*, Vol. 4, No. 4, 10.1994, pp. 393–407.

Bolton, Patrick / Samama, Frédéric: "L-Shares: Rewarding Long-term Investors". *ECGI Finance Working Paper* No. 342/2013.

Bolton, Patrick / Becht, Marco / Röell, Alisa: "Corporate governance and control". In: Constantinides G.M. / Harris M. / Stulz R. M. (eds.): *Handbook of the Economics of Finance*. Elsevier: 1st Edition, Vol. 1, chapter 1, 2003, pp. 1–109.

Borokhovich, Kenneth A. / Parrino, Robert / Trapani, Teresa: "Outside Directors and CEO Selection". *Journal of Financial and Quantitative Analysis*, Vol. 31, No. 3, 9.1996, pp. 337–355.

Borowski, Irwin: "Corporate Accountability: The Role of the Independent Director". *Journal of Corporation Law*, Vol. 9, No. 3, 1984, pp. 455–472.

Bottomley, Stephen: *The Constitutional Corporation*. Ashgate Publishing, Ltd.: 1.1.2007.

Bowes, Harlowe E. / De Bow, Ledlie A.: "Cumulative Voting at Elections of Directors of Corporations". *Minnesota Law Review*, Vol. 21, No. 4, 1937, pp. 351–370.

Branson, Douglas M.: "The Rule That Isn't a Rule – The Business Judgment Rule". *Valparaiso University Law Review*, Vol. 36, No. 3, 2002, pp. 631–651.

Branson, Douglas M.: "The Very Uncertain Prospect of "Global" Convergence in Corporate Governance". *Cornell International Law Journal*, Vol. 34, No. 2, 2001, p. 321–362.

Bratton, William / McCahery, Joseph A.: "Comparative Corporate Governance and the Theory of the Firm: The Case Against Global Cross Reference". *Columbia Journal of Transnational Law*, Vol. 38, No. 2, 1999, pp. 213–298.

Bratton, William W.: "Self-Regulation, Normative Choice, and the Structure of Corporate Fiduciary Law". *The George Washington Law Review*, Vol. 61, No. 4, 1993, pp. 1084–1129.

Brudney, Victor: "Contract and Fiduciary Duty in Corporate Law". *Boston College Law Review*, Vol. 38, No. 4, 1997, pp. 595–665.

Brudney, Victor: "The Independent Director: Heavenly City or Potemkin Village?". *Harvard Law Review*, Vol. 95, No. 3, 1982, pp. 597–659.

Bruno, Sabrina: "Directors' Versus Shareholders' Primacy in U.S. Corporations Through the Eyes of History: Is Directors' Power "Inherent"?". *European Company and Financial Law Review*, 2012, pp. 421–445.

Cahn, Andreas / Donald, David C.: *Comparative Company Law: Text and Cases on the Laws Governing Corporations in Germany, the UK and the USA*. Cambridge: July 2010.

CalPERS: *CalPERS Investments* 5.5.2014, retrieved 12.7.2014, from http://www.calpers.ca.gov/index.jsp?bc=/investments/home.xml.

Castanias, Richard P. / Helfat, Constance E.: "Managerial and Windfall Rents in the Market for Corporate Control". *Journal of Economic Behavior & Organization*, Vol. 18, No. 2, 7.1992.

Cernat, Lucian: "The Emerging European Corporate Governance Model: Anglo-Saxon, Continental, or still the Century of Diversity?". *Journal of European Public Policy*, Vol. 11, No. 1, 2004, pp. 147–166.

Charreaux, Gerard / Desbrières, Philippe: "Corporate Governance: Stakeholder Value Versus Shareholder Value". *Journal of Management and Governance*, Vol. 5, No. 2, 2001, pp. 107–128.

Cheffins, Brian R.: "Corporate Law and Ownership: A Darwinian Link?". *University of New South Wales Law Journal*, Vol. 25, No. 2, 6.2002, pp. 346–388.

Chen, Victor Zitian / Li, Jing / Shapiro, Daniel M.: "Are OECD-prescribed "good corporate governance practices" really good in an emerging economy?". *Asia Pacific Journal of Management*, Vol. 28, No. 1, 2011, pp. 115–138.

Chhaochharia, Vidhi / Grinstein, Yaniv: "CEO Compensation and Board Structure". *The Journal of Finance*, Vol. 64, No. 1, 2.2009, pp. 231–261.

China Securities Regulatory Commission / State Economic and Trade Commission: *Code of Corporate Governance for Listed Companies in China*, 7.1.2001.

China Securities Regulatory Commission: *Guidelines for Articles of Association of Chinese Listed Companies*, 16.3.2006.

China Securities Regulatory Commission: *Guiding Opinions on the Establishment of Systems of Independent Directors in Listed Companies*, 16.8.2001.

China Securities Regulatory Commission: *Measures for the Administration of the Takeover of Listed Companies*, 15.3.2012.

China Securities Regulatory Commission: *Report on the Development of Chinese listed corporate governance*, 2010.

China State Council: *Some Opinions of the State Council on Promoting the Reform, Opening and Steady Growth of Capital Markets*, 31.1.2004.

Choi, Stephen J.: "Law, Finance and Path Dependence: Developing Strong Securities Markets". *Texas Law Review*, Vol. 80, No. 7, 2002, pp. 1657–1728.

Choi, Stephen: "Proxy Issue Proposals: Impact of the 1992 SEC Proxy Reforms". *Journal of Law, Economics, & Organization*, Vol. 16, No. 1, 4.2000, pp. 233–268.

Claessens, S. / Djankov, S. / Lang L.H.P.: "The separation of ownership and control in East Asian corporations". *Journal of Financial Economics*, Vol. 58, No. 1–2, 2000, pp. 81–112.

Clark, Gordon L.: "Financial Valuation of the German Model: The Negative Relationship Between Ownership Concentration and Public Market Returns, 1997–2001". *Economic Geography*, Vol. 81, No. 1, 2005, pp. 11–29.

Clark, Robert Charles: *Corporate Law*. New York: Aspen Publishers, 1986.

Clarke B.: "Takeover Regulation: Through the Regulatory Looking Glass". *German Law Journal*, Vol. 8, No. 4, 2007, pp. 381–426.

Clarke, Donald C.: "Nothing but Wind? The Past and Future of Comparative Corporate Governance". *American Journal of Comparative Law*, Vol. 59, No. 1, 2011, pp. 75–110.

Clarke, Donald C.: "The Independent Director in Chinese Corporate Governance". *Delaware Journal of Corporate Law*, Vol. 31, No. 1, 2006, pp. 125–228.

Claussen, Carsten P. / Bröcker, Norbert: „Corporate-Governance-Grundsätze in Deutschland – nützliche Orientierungshilfe oder regulatorisches Übermass?". *Die Aktiengesellschaft: AG*, Vol. 45, No. 11, 2000, pp. 481–491.

Cleland, Alan S. / Bruno, Albert V.: "Building value: Customer and shareholder". *Strategy & Leadership*, Vol. 25, No. 3, 1997, pp. 22–28.

Coffee, John C. / Schwartz, Donald E.: "The Survival of the Derivative Suit: An Evaluation and a Proposal for Legislative Reform". *Columbia Law Review*, Vol. 81, No. 2, 3.1981, pp. 261–336, 316–318.

Coffee, John C.: "A Theory of Corporate Scandals: Why the US and Europe Differ". *Oxford Rev of Economic Policy*, Vol. 21, No.2, 2005, pp. 198–211.

Coffee, John C.: "Beyond the Shut-Eyed Sentry: Toward a Theoretical View of Corporate Misconduct and an Effective Legal Response". *Virginia Law Review*, Vol. 63, No. 7, November, 1977, pp. 1099–1278.

Coffee, John C.: "Racing towards the Top: The Impact of Cross-Listings and Stock Market Competition on International Corporate Governance". *Columbia Law Review*, Vol. 102, No. 7, 11.2002, pp. 1757–1831.

Coffee, John C.: "The Future as History: The Prospects for Global Convergence in Corporate Governance and Its Implications". *Northwest University Law Review*, Vol. 93, No. 3, 1999, pp. 641–785.

Coffee, John C.: "The Rise of Dispersed Ownership: The Roles of Law and the State in the Separation of Ownership and Control". *Yale Law Journal*, Vol. 111, No. 1, 10.2001, pp. 1–82.

Cohn, Stuart R.: "Demise of the Director's Duty of Care: Judicial Avoidance of Standards and Sanctions through the Business Judgment Rule". *Texas Law Review*, Vol. 62, No. 4, 1983, pp. 591–638.

Cole, Arthur T. Jr.: "Legal and Mathematical Aspects of Cumulative Voting". *Supreme Court Library Queensland*, Vol. 2, No. 3, 3.1950, pp. 225–244.

Commission of the European Communities: *Communication from the Commission to the Council and the European Parliament, Modernizing Company Law and Enhancing Corporate Governance in the European Union – A Plan to Move Forward*, 21.5.2003.

Committee on Corporate Law, Other Constituency Statutes: "Potential for Confusion". *The Business Lawyer*, Vol. 45, No. 4, 1990, pp. 2253–2271.

Company Law of the People's Republic of China, amended in 2013.

Conac, Pierre-Henri / Enriques, Luca / Gelter, Martin: "Constraining Dominant shareholders' self-dealing: The legal framework in France, Germany and Italy". *European Company and Financial Law Review,* Vol. 4, No. 4, 2007, pp. 491–528.

Cools, Sofie: "The Dividing Line Between Shareholder Democracy and Board Autonomy: Inherent Conflicts of Interest as Normative Criterion". *European Company and Financial Law Review,* Vol. 11, No. 2, 2014, pp. 258–296.

Copeland T. / Koller T. / Murrin J.: *Valuation, Measuring and Managing, McKinsey & Company Inc.* 5th Edition, 26.7.2010.

Corporate Governance Committee: *Belgium Corporate Governance Code,* 12.3.2009.

Corporations and Private Property: "A Conference Sponsored by the Hoover Institution". *Journal of law and economics,* Vol. 26, No. 2, 6.1983, pp. 395–427.

Cotter, James / Palmiter, Alan / Thomas, Randall: "ISS Recommendations and Mutual Fund Voting on Proxy Proposals". *Villanova Law Review,* Vol. 55, No. 1, 55, 2010, pp. 1–56.

Cotter, James F. / Shhdasani, Anil / Zenner, Marc: "Do Independent Directors Enhance Target Shareholder Wealth During Tender Offers?". *Journal of Financial Economics,* Vol. 43, No. 2, 1997, pp. 195–218.

Cox, James D. / Munsinger, Harry L.: "Bias in the Boardroom: Psychological Foundations and Legal Implications of Corporate Cohesion". *Law and Contemporary Problems,* Vol. 48, No. 3, Summer 1985, pp. 83–135.

Cox, James D.: "Searching for the Corporation's Voice in Derivative Suit Litigation: A Critique of Zapata and the ALI Project". *Duke Law Journal,* Vol. 1982, No. 6, pp. 959–1011.

Cox, James D.: "The Paradoxical Corporate and Securities Law Implications of Counsel Serving on the Client's Board". *Washington University Law Quarterly,* Vol. 80, No. 541, 2002, pp. 541–567.

Cronqvist, Henrik / Nilsson, Mattias: "Agency Costs of Controlling Minority Shareholders". *The Journal of Financial and Quantitative Analysis,* Vol. 38, No. 4, 12.2003, pp. 695–719.

CSMAR Solution: *Takeover and Restructure Database,* retrieved 25.6.2013, from http://www.gtarsc.com/.

Cubbin, John / Leech, Dennis: "The Effect of Shareholding Dispersion on the Degree of Control in British Companies: Theory and Measurement". *Economic Journal,* Vol. 93, No. 370, 1983, pp. 351–369.

Cull, Robert / Xu, Lixin Colin: "Institutions, Ownership, and Finance: The Determinants of Profit Reinvestment among Chinese Firms". *Journal of Financial Economics,* Vol. 77, No. 117, 2005, pp. 117–146.

Cyril Moscow: "The Representative Director Problem". *Insights,* 6.2002.

Dahya, Jay / Karbhari, Yusuf / Xiao, Jason Zezong / Yang, Mei: "The Usefulness of the Supervisory Board Report in China". *Corporate Governance: An International Review*, Vol. 11, No.4, 2003, pp. 308–321.

Daily, Catherine M. / Dalton, Dan R.: *Board of Directors Leadership and Structure: Control and Performance Implications.* Max M. Fisher College of Business: Ohio State University, 1994.

Dallas, Lynne L.: "The Multiple Roles of Corporate Boards of Directors". *San Diego Law Review*, Vol. 40, No. 3, 2003, pp. 781–820.

Dalton, Dan R. / Daily, Catherine M. / Ellstrand, Alan E. / Johnson, Jonathan L.: "Meta-Analytic Reviews of Board Composition, Leadership Structure, and Financial Performance". *Strategic Management Journal*, Vol. 19, No. 3, 1998, pp. 269–290.

Davies P. / Schuster, Edmund – Philipp / Van de Walle de Ghelcke, Emilie: "The Takeover Directive as a Protectionist Tool?". In: Bernitz, Ulf / Ringe, Wolf-Georg (eds.): *Company Law and Economic Protectionism: New Challenges to European Integration.* Oxford University Press: 2010, p. 105–157.

Davies, Paul L. / Hopt, Klaus J.: "Corporate Boards in Europe – Accountability and Convergence". *American Journal Comparative Law*, Vol. 61, No. 2, 2013, pp. 301–375.

Davies, Paul: "Employee Representation and Corporate Law Reform: A Comment from the United Kingdom". *Comparative Labor Law and Policy Journal*, Vol. 22, No. 1, 2000, pp. 135–148.

Delaware General Corporation Law: *Delaware Code*, Title 8 Chapter 1.

DeMott, Deborah A.: "Reweaving the Corporate Veil: Management Structure and the Control of Corporate Information". *Law and Contemporary Problems*, Vol. 41, No. 3, 1980, pp. 183–221.

Demsetz, Harold / Lehn, Kenneth: "The Structure of Corporate Ownership: Causes and Consequences". *Journal of Political Economy*, Vol. 93, No. 6, 1985, pp. 1155–1177.

Demsetz, Harold: "The Structure of Ownership and the Theory of the Firm". *Journal of Law and Economics*, Vol. 26, No. 2, Corporations and Private Property: A Conference Sponsored by the Hoover Institution, 6.1983, pp. 375–390.

Deutsche Bundesbank Eurosystem: *Statistic Über Wertpapierinvestments*, 2012, retrieved 15.7.2014, from http://www.bundesbank.de/Redaktion/DE/Downloads/Service/Meldewesen/Bankenstatistik/Depotstatistik/berichtsschema_statistik_wertpapierinvestments.pdf?__blob=publicationFile.

DG Internal Market: *Study on Monitoring and Enforcement Practices in Corporate Governance in the Member States.* EU Commission: 23.9.2009.

Directive 2003/6/EC of the European Parliament and of the Council of 28 January 2003 on insider dealing and market manipulation (market abuse).

Directive 2003/71/EC of the European Parliament and of the Council of 4 November 2003 on the prospectus to be published when securities are offered to the public or admitted to trading and amending Directive 2001/34/EC.

Directive 2004/109/EC of the European Parliament and of the Council of 15 December 2004 on the harmonization of transparency requirements in relation to information about issuers whose securities are admitted to trading on a regulated market and amending Directive 2001/34/EC.

Directive 2004/39/EC of the European Parliament and of the Council of 21 April 2004 on markets in financial instruments amending Council Directives 85/611/EEC and 93/6/EEC and Directive 2000/12/EC of the European Parliament and of the Council and repealing Council Directive 93/22/EEC.

Directive 2005/56/EC of the European Parliament and of the Council of 26 October 2005 on cross-border mergers of limited liability companies.

Directive 2007/63/EC of the European Parliament and of the Council of 13 November 2007 amending Council Directives 78/855/EEC and 82/891/EEC as regards the requirement of an independent expert's report on the occasion of merger or division of public limited liability companies.

Directive 2009/109/EC of the European Parliament and of the Council of 16 September 2009 amending Council Directives 77/91/EEC, 78/855/EEC and 82/891/EEC, and Directive 2005/56/EC as regards reporting and documentation requirements in the case of mergers and divisions.

Directive 2013/34/EU of the European Parliament and of the Council of 26 June 2013 on the annual financial statements, consolidated financial statements and related reports of certain types of undertakings, amending Directive 2006/43/EC of the European Parliament and of the Council and repealing Council Directives 78/660/EEC and 83/349/EEC.

Dodd, Graham / Warner, Jerold: "On Corporate Governance: A Study of Proxy Contests". *Journal of Financial Economics*, Vol. 11, No. 1, 1983, pp. 401–438.

Donaldson, T., Preston L.E.: "The stakeholder theory of the corporation Concepts, evidence and implications". *Academy of Management Review*, Vol. 20, No. 1, 1995, pp. 65–91.

Donaldson, William H.: *Speech by SEC Chairman: 2005 CFA Institute Annual Conference*, 8.5.2005, retrieved 15.6.2014, from http://www.sec.gov/news/speech/spch050805whd.htm.

Dooley, Michael / Veasey, E. Norman: "The Role of the Board in Derivative Litigation: Delaware Law and the Current ALI Proposals Compared". *Business Lawyer*, Vol. 44, No. 2, 1989, pp. 503–542.

Dooley, Michael P.: "Two Models of Corporate Governance". *The Business Lawyer*, Vol. 47, No. 2, 2.1992, pp. 461–527.

Dougherty C.: "The Buzz on German Private Equity". *The Economist International Herald Tribune,* 20.10.2006.

Drucker, Peter F.: *Management: Tasks, Responsibilities, Practices.* Harper & Row Management Library, 1974.

Du Plessis, Jean J. / Hargovan, Anil / Bagaric, Mirko: *Principles of Contemporary Corporate Governance.* Cambridge University Press: 2nd Edition, 2011.

Duchin, Ran / Matsusaka, John G. / Ozbas, Oguzhan: "When are Outside Directors Effective?". *Journal of Financial Economics,* Vol. 96, No. 2, 5.2010, pp. 195–214.

Dunn, William: "Pattern Recognition Receptors: Doubling Up for the Innate Immune Response". *Cell Press,* Vol. 111, No. 7, 12.2002, pp. 927–930.

Dutch Corporate Governance Code, drafted by Tabaksblat Committee, revised by the Frijns Committee in 12.2008.

Easterbrook, Frank / Fischel, Daniel: "Voting in Corporate Law". *Journal of Law and Economics,* Vol. 26, No. 2, 1983, pp. 395–427.

Easterbrook, Frank H. / Fischel, Daniel R.: "Corporate Control Transactions". *Yale Law Journal,* Vol. 91, No. 4, 1982, pp. 698–737.

Easterbrook, Frank H. / Fischel, Daniel R.: "The Corporate Contract". *Columbia Law Review,* Vol. 89, No. 7, Contractual Freedom in Corporate Law, November, 1989, pp. 1416–1448.

Easterbrook, Frank H. / Fischel, Daniel R.: "The Proper Role of a Target's Management in Responding to a Tender Offer". *Harvard Law Review,* Vol. 94, No. 6, 1981, pp. 1161–1204.

Easterbrook, Frank H. / Fischel, Daniel R.: *The economic structure of corporate law.* Harvard University Press: 1991.

Easterbrook, Frank H. / Fischel, Daniel R.: *The Economic Structure of Corporation Law.* Harvard University Press: Cambridge, Mass, 1991, pp. 36–39.

ECGF Statement: *Statement of the European Corporate Governance Forum on Related Party Transactions for Listed Entities,* of 10.3.2011.

Editors, Law Review: "Cumulative Voting: Removal, Reduction and Classification of Corporate Boards". The University of Chicago Law Review: Vol. 22, No. 3, Spring 1955, pp. 751–759.

Eisenberg, Melvin A.: "The Duty of Care of Corporate Directors and Officers". *University of Pittsburgh Law Review,* Vol. 51, No. 4, 1990, pp. 945–972.

Eisenberg, Melvin A.: "The Legal Roles of Shareholders and Managers in Corporate Decision-making". *California Law Review,* Vol. 57, No. 1, 1969, pp. 1–181.

Eisenberg, Melvin Aron: "Legal Models of Management Structure in the Modern Corporation: Officers, Directors, and Accountants". *California Law Review,* Vol. 63, No. 2, 1975, pp. 375–439.

Elson, Charles M. / Gyves, Christopher J.: "The Enron Failure and Corporate Governance Reform". *Wake Forest Law Review,* Vol. 38, No. 3, 2003, pp. 855–884.

Enriques L. / Gatti M.: "EC Reforms of Corporate Governance and Capital Markets Law: Do They Tackle Insiders' Opportunism?". *Northwestern Journal of International Law and Business*, Vol. 28, No. 1, 2007, pp. 1–45.

Enriques L. / Gatti M.: "Is There a Uniform EU Securities Law After the Financial Services Action Plan?" *Stanford Journal of Law, Business & Finance*, Vol. 14, No. 1, 2008, pp. 43–81.

Enriques, Luca / Volpin, Paolo: "Corporate Governance Reforms in Continental Europe". *Journal of Economic Perspectives*, Vol. 21, No. 1, 2007, pp. 117–140.

Enriques, Luca: "Bad Apples, Bad Oranges: A Comment from Old Europe on Post-Enron Corporate Governance Reforms". *Wake Forest Law Review*, Vol. 38, No. 3, 2003, pp. 911–935.

Enriques, Luca: "The law on company Directors' self-dealing: A comparative analysis". *International and Comparative Corporate Law Journal*, Vol. 2, No. 3, 2000, pp. 297–333.

Ernst & Young: *Wem gehört der DAX? Analyse der Aktienärsstruktur der DAX-Unternehmen*, 27.4.2012, retrieved 15.7.2014, from http://www.handelsblatt.com/finanzen/boerse-maerkte/boerse-inside/boersenindex-wem-der-dax-gehoert/8187798.html.

European Commission: *Commission Recommendation of 15 February 2005 on the role of non-executive or supervisory directors of listed companies and on the committees of the (supervisory) board (2005/162/EC).*

European Commission: *Communication from the Commission to the European Parliament and the Council on Long-Term Financing of the European Economy*, 27.3.2014.

European Commission: *EU Action Plan of European Company Law and Corporate Governance – a modern legal framework for more engaged shareholders and sustainable companies.*

European Commission: *EU Green Paper on Long-Term Financing of the European Economy*, 25.3.2013.

European Commission: *Feedback Statement Summary of Responses to the Commission Green Paper on the EU Corporate Governance Framework*, 5.11.2011.

European Commission: *Green Paper: The EU corporate governance framework*, 5.4.2011.

European Commission: *Proposal for a Directive of the European Parliament and of the Council amending Directive 2007/36/EC as regards the encouragement of long-term shareholder engagement and Directive 2013/34/EU as regards certain elements of the corporate governance statement.*

European Commission: *Proposal for a Directive of the European Parliament and of the Council on Takeover Bids*, 10.2002.

European Commission: *Report of the Reflection Group on the Future of EU Company Law*, 4.2011.

European Commission: *Report on the application by the Member States of the EU of the Commission Recommendation on the role of non-executive or supervisory directors of listed companies and on the committees of the (supervisory) board*, 13.7.2007.

European Parliament, Council of the European Union: *Directive 2007/36/EC of the European Parliament and of the Council of 11 July 2007 on the exercise of certain rights of shareholders in listed companies.*

Evaluation of Corporate Governance in Top 100 PLCs of China in 2012, retrieved 15.1.2013, from http://wenku.baidu.com/view/74f36a20a5e9856a561260d6.html.

Faccio M. / Lang L.H.P.: "The Ultimate Ownership of Western European Corporations". *Journal of Financial Economics*, Vol. 65, No. 3, 2001, pp. 365–395.

Fahlenbrach, Rüdiger / Low, Angie / Stulz, René M.: "Why do Firms Appoint CEOs as Outside Directors?". *Journal of Financial Economics*, Vol. 97, No. 1, 7.2010, pp. 12–32.

Fairfax L.: "Easier Said Than Done? A Corporate Law Theory for Actualizing Social Responsibility Rhetoric". *Florida Law Review*, Vol. 59, No. 4, 9.2007, pp. 771–828.

Fairfax L.: "The Rhetoric of Corporate Law: The Impact of Rhetoric on Corporate Norms". *Journal of Corporation Law*, Vol. 31, No. 3, 2006, pp. 875–718.

Fama E.F. / Jensen M.C.: "The separation of ownership and control". *Journal of Law and Economics*, Vol. 26, No. 2, 1983, pp. 301–328.

Fama, Eugene F. / Jensen, Michael C.: "Agency Problems and Residual Claims". *Journal of Law & Economics*, Vol. 26, No. 2, 6.1983, pp. 327–349, 329.

Fama, Eugene: "Agency Problems and the Theory of the Firm". *The Journal of Political Economy*, Vol. 88, No. 2, 1980, pp. 288–307.

Feinerman, James V.: "New Hope for Corporate Governance in China?". *The China Quarterly*, No. 191, 9.2007, pp. 590–612.

Ferran, Eilis: *Building an EU Securities Market.* Cambridge University Press: 2004.

Ferrarini G. / Giudici P.: "Financial Scandals and the Role of Private Enforcement: The Parmalat Case". In: Armour, John / McCahery, Joseph (eds.): *After Enron: Improving Corporate Law and Modernising Securities Regulation in Europe and the US*". Oxford University Press, 2006, pp. 159–213.

Ferrarini, Guido / Filippelli, Marilena: "Independent directors and controlling shareholders around the world". *ECGI Working Paper* N. 258/2014, 5.2014.

Ferrarini, Guido A. / Moloney, Niamh: "Executive Remuneration in the EU: The Context for Reform". *Oxford Review Economic Policy*, Vol. 21, No. 2, 2005, pp. 304–323.

Ferreira M. / Matos P.: "The Colors of Investors' Money: The Role of Institutional Investors around the World?". *Journal of Financial Economics*, Vol. 88, No. 3, 2008, pp. 499–533.

Ferreira, Daniel / Kirchmaier, Tom: "Corporate Boards in Europe: size, independence and gender diversity". In: Belcredi, Massimo / Ferrarini, Guido (eds.): *Boards and shareholders in European listed companies: facts, context and post-crisis reforms.* International Corporate Law and Financial Market Regulation. Cambridge University Press: 2.2014, pp. 191–223.

Fich, E.M.: "Are some outside directors better than others? Evidence from director appointments by Fortune 1000 firms". *Journal of Business,* Vol. 78, No. 5, 2005, pp. 1943–1971.

Fisch, Jill E. / Gentile, Caroline M.: "The Qualified Legal Compliance Committee: Using the Attorney Conduct Rules to Restructure the Board of Directors". *Duke Law Journal,* Vol. 53, No. 2003, pp. 517–584.

Fisch, Jill E.: "Taking Boards Seriously". *Cardozo Law Review,* Vol. 19, No. 1–2, 1997–1998, pp. 265–290.

Fisch, Jill E.: "The New Federal Regulation of Corporate Governance". *Harvard Journal of Law & Public Policy,* Vol. 28, 2004, pp. 39–50.

Fisch, Jill E.: "The Overstated Promise of Corporate Governance – Corporate Governance: Promises Kept, Promises Broken by Jonathan Macey". *The University of Chicago Law Review,* Vol. 77, No. 2, Spring 2010, pp. 923–958.

Fischel, Daniel R.: "The Business Judgment Rule and the Trans Union Case". *The Business Lawyer,* Vol. 40, No. 4, 8.1985, pp. 1437–1455.

Fischel, Daniel R.: "The Corporate Governance Movement". *Vanderbilt Law Review,* Vol. 35, No. 6, 1982, pp. 1259–1292.

Fitting, Karl / Wlotzke, Otfried / Wißmann, Hellmut / Koberski, Wolfgang / Kleinsorge, Georg / Freis, Gerhild: *Mitbestimmungsrecht Kommentar.* Verlag Franz Vahlen: 4th Edition, 2011.

Fleischer A. / Sussman A.R. / Lesser H.: *Takeover Defense.* Prentice Hall Law & Business: 4th Edition, 1990.

Fogel, Eric M. / Geier, Andrew M.: "Strangers in the House: Rethinking Sarbanes-Oxley and the Independent Board of Directors". *Delaware Journal of Corporate Law,* Vol. 32, No. 1, 2007, pp. 33–72.

Freeman, R. Edward: "Stockholders and Stakeholders: A New Perspective on Corporate Governance". *California Management Review (pre-1986),* Vol. 25, No. 3, p. 88.

French Corporate Governance Code: *Mouvement des entreprises de France (Medef),* amended in 6.2013.

Friedman E. / Johnson S. / Mitton T.: "Propping and Tunneling". *Journal of Comparative Economics,* Vol. 31, No. 4, 12.2003, pp. 732–750.

Friedman M.: "The Social Responsibility of Business is to Increase its Profits". *New York Times Magazine,* 13.9.1970, Section 6, p. 33.

Gan Peizhong: "Lun Wanshan Woguo Shangshi Gongsi Zhili Jiegou zhong de Jianshi Zhidu" [Discussions on Improving the Supervisory Board in the Corporate Governance System of China]. *China Legal Science,* 2001, No. 5, p. 84.

Geens, Koen: "Corporate boards in Belgium". In: Davies, Paul / Hopt, Klaus / Nowak, Richard / van Solinge, Gerard (eds.): *Corporate Boards in Law and Practice.* Oxford University Press: 2013.

Gelfond, Sebastian: "Reevaluating the Duties of Target Management in a Hostile Tender Offer". *Boston University Law Review,* Vol. 60, No. 3, 1980, pp. 403–473.

Gelter M.: "Why Do Shareholder Derivative Suits Remain Rare in Continental Europe?". *Brooklyn Journal of International Law,* Vol. 37, No. 3, 2012, pp. 843–892.

German Corporate Governance Code, The Commission (Regierungskommission Deutscher Corporate Governance Kodex), 26.5.2010.

Gevurtz, Franklin A.: "The Business Judgment Rule: Meaningless Verbiage or Misguided Notion?". *Southern California Law Review,* Vol. 67, No. 2, 1994, pp. 287–338.

Gilbert, Lewis D.: *Dividends and Democracy.* American Research Council: 1956, pp. 181–189.

Gillan, S. / Starks L.: "Corporate Governance, Corporate Ownership, and the Role of Institutional Investors: A Global Perspective". *Journal of Applied Finance,* Vol. 13, No. 2, 2003, pp. 4–22.

Gillette, Ann B. / Noe, Thomas H. / Rebello, Michael J.: "Board Structures around the World: An Experimental Investigation". *Review of Finance,* Vol. 12, No. 1, 2008, pp. 93–140.

Gillian, Stuart L. / Starks, Laura T.: "The Evolution of Shareholder Activism in the United States". *Journal of Applied Corporate Finance,* Vol. 19, No. 1, 2007, pp. 55–73.

Gilson R.J.: "Controlling Shareholders and Corporate Governance: Complicating the Comparative Taxonomy". *Harvard Law Review,* Vol. 119, No. 6, 4.2006, pp. 1641–1679.

Gilson, Ronald J. / Gordon, Jeffrey N.: "Controlling Shareholders". *University of Pennsylvania Law Review,* Vol. 152, No. 2, 12.2003, pp. 785–843.

Gilson, Ronald J. / Gordon, Jeffrey N.: "The Agency Costs of Agency Capitalism: Activist Investors and the Revaluation of Governance Rights". *Columbia Law Review,* Vol. 113, No. 4, 5.2013, pp. 863–927.

Gilson, Ronald J. / Kraakman, Reinier: "Reinventing the Outside Director: An Agenda for Institutional Investors". *Stanford Law Review,* Vol. 43, No. 4, 4.1991, pp. 863–906.

Gilson, Ronald J. / Roe, Mark J.: "Understanding the Japanese Keiretsu: Overlaps Between Corporate Governance and Industrial Organization and Industrial Organization". *Yale Law Journal,* Vol. 102, No. 4, 1.1993, pp. 871–906.

Gilson, Ronald J. / Schwartz, Alan: "Constraints on Private Benefits of Control: Ex Ante Control Mechanisms versus Ex Post Transaction Review". *Journal of Institutional and Theoretical Economics,* Vol. 169, No.1, 3.2013, pp. 160–183.

Gilson, Ronald J.: "The Political Ecology of Takeovers: Thoughts on Harmonizing the European Corporate Governance Environment". *Fordham Law Review,* Vol. 61, No. 1, 1992, pp. 161–192.

Gilson, Ronald: "Globalizing corporate governance: convergence of form or function". *The American Journal of Comparative Law*, Vol. 49, No. 2, Spring 2001, pp. 329–357.

Gordon, Jeffrey N.: "Corporations, Markets, and Courts". *Columbia Law Review*, Vol. 91, No. 8, 12.1991, pp. 1931–1988.

Gordon, Jeffrey N.: "Institutions as Relational Investors: A New Look at Cumulative Voting". *Columbia Law Review*, Vol. 94, No. 1, 1.1994.

Gordon, Jeffrey N.: "The Rise of Independent Directors in the United States, 1950–2005: Of Shareholder Value and Stock Market Prices". *Stanford Law Review*, Vol. 59, No. 6, 2007, pp. 1465–1568.

Gordon, Jeffrey N.: *What is Relational Investing and How Cumulative Voting Can Play a Role.* (Columbia University Center for Law & Economic Studies Working Paper No. 97). New York: Center for Law and Economic Studies, Columbia University School of Law, 1993.

Gordon, Lilli A. / Pound, John: "Information, Ownership Structure, and Shareholder Voting: Evidence from Shareholder-Sponsored Corporate Governance Proposals". *The Journal of Finance*, Vol. 48, No. 2, 6.1993, pp. 697–718.

Gow D.: "Germany fears the New "Locusts"", *Guardian*, 4.6.2008.

Gower & Davies: *Principles of modern company law.* Davies, Paul L. / Worthington, Sarah (eds.). Sweet & Maxwell: 9th Edition, London 2012.

Greek Corporate Governance code.

Greenwood, Robin: *The Hedge Fund as Activist.* HBR Working Knowledge: 22.8.2007.

Grossman, Sanford J. / Hart, Oliver D.: "One Share/One Vote and the Market for Corporate Control". *Journal of Financial Economics*, Vol. 20, January-March 1988, pp. 175–202.

Grundfest, Joseph A.: "Subordination of American Capital". *Journal of Finance Economics*, Vol. 27, No. 1, 1990, pp. 89–114.

Grundmann, Stefan / Mülbert, Peter: "Corporate Governance – Europäische Perspektiven". *ZGR*, Vol. 30, No. 2, 2001, pp. 215–223.

Gutiérrez, María / Sáez, Maribel: "Deconstructing Independent Directors". *Journal of Corporate Law Studies*, Vol. 13, No. 1, 4.2013, pp. 63–94.

Haas, Steven M.: "Toward a Controlling Shareholder Safe Harbor". *Virginia Law Review*, Vol. 90, No. 8, 12.2004, pp. 2245–2304.

Haft, Robert J.: "Business Decisions by the New Board: Behavioral Science and Corporate Law". *Michigan Law Review*, Vol. 80, No. 1, 11.1981, pp. 1–67.

Hale K.: "Corporate Law and Stakeholders: Moving Beyond Stakeholder Statutes". *Arizona Law Review*, Vol. 45, No. 3, 2003, pp. 823–856.

Hanks J. Jr.: "Playing With Fire: Nonshareholder Constituency Statues in the 1990s". *Stetson Law Review*, Vol. 21, No. 1, 1991, pp. 97–120.

Hans-Böckler-Stiftung: *Statistiken zur Mitbestimmungslandschaft*, retrieved 10.4.2014, from http://www.boeckler.de/38347.htm.

Hansen, Charles: "The ALI Corporate Governance Project: Of the Duty of Due Care and the Business Judgment Rule, a Commentary". *The Business Lawyer*, Vol. 41, No. 4, 8.1986, pp. 1237–1253.

Hansmann, Henry / Kraakman, Reinier: "The End of History for Corporate Law". *Georgetown Law Review*, Vol. 89, No. 2, 2000, pp. 439–473.

Harris, Milton / Raviv, Artur: "The Theory of Capital Structure". *The Journal of Finance*, Vol. 46, No. 1, 3.1991, pp. 297–355.

Hartmann, Charles J. / Rogers, Pamela Gayle: "The Influence of Smith v. Van Gorkom on Director's and Officer's Liability". *The Journal of Risk and Insurance*, Vol. 58, No. 3, 9.1991, pp. 525–535.

Healy, Paul M. / Palepu, Krishna G.: "Governance and Intermediation Problems in Capital Markets: Evidence from the Fall of Enron". *Journal of Economic Perspectives*, Vol. 17, No. 2, Spring 2003.

Heidrick, Struggles: *European Corporate Governance Report 2011: Challenging Board Performance.* p. 42.

Henn, Harry G. / Alexander, John R.: *Laws of Corporations and Other Business Enterprises.* West Publish Corporation: 3rd Edition, 1983.

Hermalin, Benjamin E. / Weisbach, Michael S.: "Boards of Directors as an Endogenously Determined Institution: A Survey of the Economic Literature, Federal Reserve Bank of New York". *Economic Policy Review* 4.2003, pp. 7–26.

Hill, Charles W. L. / Snell, Scott A.: "External Control, Corporate Strategy, and Board Performance in Research Intensive Industries". *Strategic Management Journal*, Vol. 9, No. 6, 1988, pp. 577–590.

Hillman, Amy J. / Dalziel, Thomas: "Beyond "Independent" Directors: A Functional Approach to Board Independence". *Harvard Law Review*, Vol. 119, No. 5, 3.2006, pp. 1553–1575.

Holderness, Clifford G.: "The Myth of Diffuse Ownership in the United States". *The Review of Financial Studies*, Vol. 22, No. 4, 2009, pp. 1377–1409.

Holmen, Martin / Högfeldt, Peter: "Pyramidal Discounts: Tunneling or Overinvestment?". *International Review of Finance*, Vol. 9, No. 1&2, 2009, pp. 133–175.

Hopt Klaus J. / Markus Roth: *Aktiengesetz: Grosskommentar.* de Gruyter Recht: 4th Edition, 2011.

Hopt, Klaus J. / Wymeersch, Eddy / Kanda, Hideki / Baum, Harald: *Corporate Governance in Context: Corporations, States, and Markets in Europe, Japan, and the US.* Oxford University Press: 2005.

Hopt, Klaus J.: "Comparative Corporate Governance: The State of the Art and International Regulation". *American Journal of Comparative Law*, Vol. 59, No. 1, 2011, pp. 1–83.

Hopt, Klaus J.: "Conflict of Interest, Secrecy and Insider Information of Directors, A Comparative Analysis". *European Company and Financial Law Review*, 2013, pp. 167–193.

Hopt, Klaus J.: "Labor Representation on Corporate Boards: Impacts and Problems for Corporate Governance and Economic Integration in Europe". *International Review of Law and Economics*, Vol. 14, No. 2, 6.1994, pp. 203–214.

Hopt, Klaus J.: "New Ways in Corporate Governance: European Experiments with Labor Representation on Corporate Boards". *Michigan Law Review*, Vol. 82, No. 5/6, Festschrift in Honor of Eric Stein (April – May, 1984), pp. 1338–1363.

Hopt, Klaus J.: „Aktienrecht unter amerikanischem Einfluss". In: *Festschrift für Claus-Wilhelm Canaris*. Beck: Munich, 2007, vol. 2, p. 105.

Hopt, Klaus J.: „Gemeinsame Grundsätze der Corporate Governance in Europa?". *Zeitschrift für Unternehmens- und Gesellschaftsrecht*, Vol. 29, No. 6, 2000, pp. 798–809.

Hopt, Klaus J.: „Interessenwahrung und Interessenkonflikte im Aktien-, Bank- und Berufsrecht – Zur Dogmatik des modernen Geschäftsbesorgungsrechts". *Zeitschrift für Unternehmens- und Gesellschaftsrecht*, Vol. 3, No. 1, 2.2004, pp. 1–184.

Hopt, Klaus J.: „Unternehmensführung, Unternehmenskontrolle, Modernisierung des Aktienrechts – Zum Bericht der Regierungskommission Corporate Governance". In: Hommelhoff, Peter / Lutter, Marcus / Schmidt, Karsten / Schön, Wolfgang / Ulmer, Peter (eds.): Corporate Governance – Gemeinschaftssymposium der Zeitschriften ZHR/ZGR. Heidelberg: Verlag Recht und Wirtschaft, 2002, supplement to ZHR no. 71.

Hu H. / Black B.: "Hedge Funds, Insiders, and the Decoupling of Economic and Voting Ownership: Empty Voting and Hidden (Morphable) Ownership". *Journal of Corporate Finance*, Vol. 13, No. 2–3, 2007, pp. 343–367.

Huang Hui: "Lvlun Gongsi Fa Yitihua: Zhongguo Shijiao ji Qishi" [General Analysis of Converge of Corporate Law: in the Perspective of China]. *Journal of Comparative Law*, Vol. 5, 2013, pp. 61–76.

Huang Jintao: "Wei Gu Gai Gong Si Jiang Bei Cha Yi Hua, Zhang Die Fu Xian Zhi Jiang Bei Xian Zhi Wei Bai Fen Zhi Wu" [If Nor Completing Share Reform, Companies Will Need To Face Additional Restriction in Trading, Including Price Trading Range Will Be Set To 5% Each Day]. *Shang hai zheng quan bao* [Shanghai Securities News] 25.12.2006, retrieved 14.3.2013, from http://news.xinhuanet.com / stock/2006-12/25/content_5527569.htm.

Imai, Ken: *Explaining the Persistence of State-Ownership in China*. Inst. of Developing Economies: Discussion Paper No. 64, 2006, retrieved 15.1.2013, from http://ir.ide.go.jp/dspace/bitstream/2344/130/3/ARRIDE_Discussion_No.064_ imai.pdf, p. 4.

Investment Company Institute: *Investment Company Fact Book – A Review of Trends and Activity in the U.S. Investment Company Industry*. 52nd Edition, 2012.

Ireland, Paddy: “Shareholder Primacy and the Distribution of Wealth”. *The Modern Law Review*, Vol. 68, No. 1, 2005, pp. 49–81.

IRRC: *Controlled Companies in the Standard & Poor's 1500: A Ten Year Performance and Risk Review*, 10.2012, pp. 9–10.

Jacobs, Jack B.: “Patient Capital: Can Delaware Corporate Law Help Revive It?”. *Washington and Lee Law Review*, Vol. 68, No. 4, 2011, pp. 1645–1664.

Jacoby, Sanford M.: “Corporate Governance in Comparative Perspective: Prospects for Convergence”. *Comparative Labor Law and Policy Journal*, Vol. 22, No. 1, 2000, pp. 5–32.

Janssen E.: “The Stakeholder Model: The Influence of the Ownership and Governance Structures”. *Journal of Business Ethics*, Vol. 56, No. 4, 2005, pp. 1–13.

Jarrell, Gregg A. / Brickley, James A. / Netter, Jeffry M.: “The Market for Corporate Control: The Empirical Evidence Since 1980”. *Journal of Economic Perspectives*, Vol. 2, No. 1, 1988, pp. 49–68.

Jensen M.C. / Mecklin W.H.: “Theory of the firm: Managerial behavior, agency costs and ownership structure”. *Journal of Financial Economics*, Vol. 3, No. 4, 1976, pp. 305–360.

Jensen, M.C.: “Agency Costs of Free Cash Flow, Corporate Finance and Takeovers”. *American Economic Review*, Vol. 76, No. 2, 1986, pp. 323–329.

Jensen, Michael C. / Meckling, William: “Theory of the Firm: Managerial Behavior, Agency Costs and Ownership Structure”. *Journal of Law and Economics*, Vol. 3, No. 4, 10.1976, pp. 305–360.

Jensen, Michael C.: “Takeovers: Their Causes and Consequences”. *The Journal of Economic Perspectives*, Vol. 2, No. 1, Winter 1988, pp. 21–48.

Jiang Daxing: “Duli Dongshi: zai Chuangtong Kuangjia zhong Xingdong (Xia)?” [Independent Directors: perform in the traditional System?]. *Law Review*, No. 3, 2003.

Jiang Ping / Wang Weiguo / Zhao Xudong: *Duli Dongshi Sanren Tan* [Discussions on Independent Directors by Three Scholars], retrieved 20.2.2014, from http:// article. chinalawinfo.com/Article_Detail.asp?ArticleId=28364.

Jiangyu Wang: “The Strange Role of Independent Directors in a Two-Tier Board Structure of China's Listed Companies”. *Compliance and Regulatory Journal*, Vol. 3, No. 3, 2008, pp. 47–55.

Jie, Chen / Zhongke, Zhonglian: „Yingzao Dudong Zhize de “Duli” Fenwei“. *Board*, Vol. 1, 2014.

Johnson J.L. / Daily, C.M. / Ellstrand, A.E.: “Board of directors: A review and research agenda”. *Journal of Management*, Vol. 22, No. 3, 1996, pp. 409–438.

Johnson, Jennifer J. / Siegel, Mary: “Corporate Mergers: Redefining the Role of Target Directors”. *University of Pennsylvania Law Review*, Vol. 136, No. 2, 12.1987, pp. 315–416.

Johnson, Lyman P.Q.: "Corporate Officers and the Business Judgment Rule". *The Business Lawyer*, Vol. 60, No. 2, 2.2005, pp. 439–469.

Johnson, Lyman: "After Enron: Remembering Loyalty Discourse in Corporate Law". *Delaware Journal of Corporate Law*, Vol. 28, No. 1, 2003, pp. 27–73.

Johnson, Lyman: "The Modest Business Judgment Rule". *The Business Lawyer*, Vol. 55, No. 2, 2.2000, pp. 625–652.

Kamar, Ehud: "Beyond Competition for Incorporations". *Georgetown Law Journal*, Vol. 94, No. 6, 2006, pp. 1725–1772.

Kaufman, Allen / Englander, Ernie: "A team production model of corporate governance". *Academy of Management Executive*, Vol. 19, No. 3, 2005, pp. 9–22.

Keay A.: "Ascertaining the Corporate Objective: An Entity Maximization and Sustainability Model". *Modern Law Review*, Vol. 71, No. 5, 9.2008, pp. 663–698.

Keay, Andrew R.: "Moving Towards Stakeholderism? Constituency Statutes, Enlightened Shareholder Value and All That: Much A do about Little?" *Business Law Review*, Vol. 22, No. 1, 2011, pp. 1–49.

Keay, Andrew: "Shareholder Primacy in Corporate Law: Can it Survive? Should it Survive?". *European Company and Financial Law Review*, Vol. 7, No. 3, 2010, pp. 369–413.

Kelly G. / Parkinson J.: "The Conceptual Foundations of the Corporation: a Pluralist Approach". In: Parkinson J. / Gamble A. / Kelly G. (eds.): *The Political Economy of the Corporation*. Hart Publishing: 2000.

Kirchner C. / Painter R.W.: "Takeover Defenses under Delaware Law, the Proposed Thirteenth EU Directive and the New German Takeover Law: Comparison and Recommendations for Reform". *The American Journal of Comparative Law*, Vol. 50, No. 3, Summer 2002, pp. 451–476.

Kister, Sandra P.: "China's Share-Structure Reform: An Opportunity to Move Beyond Practical Solutions to Practical Problems". *Columbia Journal of Transnational Law*, Vol. 45, No. 1, 2006, pp. 312–363.

Klein, April: "Firm Performance and Board Committee Structure". *Journal of Law and Economics*, Vol. 41, No. 1, 4.1998, pp. 275–304.

Koppes, Richard H. / Ganske, Lyle G. / Haag, Charles T.: "Corporate Governance out of Focus: The Debate over Classified Boards". *Business Lawyer*, Vol. 54, No. 3, 5.1999, pp. 1023–1055.

Kort, Michael: *Vorstandshandeln im Spannungsverhältnis zwischen Unternehmensinteresse und Aktionärsinteressen*. AG 2012, pp. 605–610.

Kraakman, Reinier / Armour, John / Davies, Paul / Enriques, Luca / Hansmann, Henry B. / Hertig, Gérard / Hopt, Klaus J. / Kanda, Hideki / Rock, Edward B.: *The anatomy of corporate law – A Comparative and Functional Approach*. Oxford University Press: 2nd Edition, 2009.

Kuang, Duan: *Gongsi Zhili Moshi Lun* [Discussions on the Model of Corporate Governance]. Law Press China: 2007.

La Porta, Rafael / Lopez-de-Silanes, Florencio / Shleifer, Anderei: "Corporate Ownership Around the World". *Journal of Finance* Vol. 54, No. 2, 1999, pp. 471–517.

La Porta, Rafael / Lopez-de-Silanes, Florencio / Shleifer, Anderei / Vishny, Robert W.: "Investor Protection and Corporate Valuation". *Journal of Finance,* Vol. 57, No. 3, 2002, pp. 1147–1170.

Langevoort, Donald C.: "The Human Nature of Corporate Boards: Law, Norms, and the Unintended Consequences of Independence and Accountability". *Georgetown Law Journal,* Vol. 89 No. 4, 2000, pp. 797–832.

Laske, Stephan: „Unternehmensinteresse und Mitbestimmung". *ZGR,* Vol. 8, No. 2, 1.1979, pp. 173–200.

Lay Hong Tan / Jiangyu Wang: "Modelling an Effective Corporate Governance System for China's Listed State-Owned Enterprises: Issues and Challenges in a Transitional Economy". *Journal of Corporate Law Studies,* Vol. 7, No. 1, 2007, pp. 143–183.

Lee, Keun / Mathews, John / Wade, Robert: "Rethinking development policy: A new consensus". *Financial Times,* 19.10.2007.

Leech, Nuyes E. / Mundheim, Robert H.: "The Outside Director of the Publicly held Corporation". *The Business Lawyer,* Vol. 31, No. 4, 7.1976, pp. 1799–1838.

Letza, Steve / Sun, Xiuping / Kirkbride, James: "Shareholding Versus Stakeholding: a critical review of corporate governance". *Corporate Governance: An International Review,* Vol. 12, No. 3, 2004, pp. 242–263.

Li Dongping: "Sanda Wenti Kunrao Dudong Zhidu Shijian" [Three Problems Puzzled the Practice of the Independent Director System]. *Zhengquan Shibao* [Securities Times], 23.3.2003.

Li Jianwei: "Lun Woguo Duli Dongshi Chansheng Jigou de Chongjian" [Discussions on the Reconstruction of the Election of Independent Directors]. *Law Science* (Journal of Northwest University of Politics and Law), No. 2, 2004, pp. 67–74.

Li Jianwei: *Duli Dongshi Zhidu Yanjiu – Cong Faxue he Guanlixue de Shuangchong Jiaodu* [Study on Independent Directors – From the Perspective of Law and Management]. China Renmin University Press: 2004.

Li Jianwei: *Gongsi Zhidu, Gongsi Zhili yu Gongsi Guanli* [Corporate System, Corporate Governance and Management]. The People's Court Press: 2005.

Li Yanbing: "Gufen Youxian Gongsi Jianshihui Zhidu zhi Bijiao Yanjiu" [A Comparative Study on the Supervisory Board System of the Stock Corporation]. In: Shen Sibao (ed.): *International Business Law Review,* 2000.

Lin, Chien-Chung: "The Chinese Independent Director Mechanism under Changing Macro Political-Economic Settings: A Review of Its First Decade and Two Possible

Models for the Future". *American University Business Law Review*, Vol. 1, No. 2, 2012, pp. 263–336.

Lin, Laura: "The Effectiveness of Outside Directors as a Corporate Governance Mechanism: Theories and Evidence". *Northwestern University Law Review*, Vol. 90, No. 3, 1996, pp. 898–976.

Lin, Thomas W.: "Corporate Governance in China: Recent Developments, Key Problems, and Solutions". *Journal of Accounting and Corporate Governance*, Vol. 1, No. 1, 6.2004, pp. 1–23.

Lipton, Martin / Rosenblum, Steven A.: "A New System of Corporate Governance: The Quinquennial Election of Directors". *The University of Chicago Law Review*, Vol. 58, No. 1, Winter 1991, pp. 187–253.

Lipton, Martin / Rowe, Paul K.: "Pills, Polls and Professors: A Reply to Professor Gilson". *The Delaware Journal of Corporate Law*, Vol. 27, No. 1, 2002, pp. 1–55.

Lipton, Martin / Wachtell / Lipton / Rosen & Katz: "The Proposed "Shareholder Bill of Rights Act of 2009"". *Wall Street Journal*, Tue. 12.5.2009, retrieved 15.5.2014, from http://blogs.law.harvard.edu/corpgov/2009/05/12/the-proposed-"shareholder-bill-of-rights-act-of-2009"/.

Lipton, Martin: "Corporate Governance in the Age of Finance Corporatism". *University of Pennsylvania Law Review*, Vol. 136, No. 1, 1987, pp. 1–72.

Lipton, Martin: "Takeover Bids in the Target's Boardroom". *Business Lawyer*, Vol. 34, No.1, 1979, pp. 101–134.

Liu Heping: "Shangshi Gongsi Duli Dongshi yu Jianshihui Gaunxi Lun – Jianlun Duli Dongshi Gongneng Dingwei" [Discussions on the Relationship between Independent directors and Supervisory Board – the Role of Independent Directors]. In: Wang Baoshu (ed.): *Essays of Business Law.* Law Press China: Vol. 6, 2000.

Liu Qing: "Duli Dongshi Zhidu Shishi zhong de Wenti yu Duice" [Problems and Countermeasures in the Practice of the Independent Director System]. *Zhengquan Shichang Daobao* [Security Market Herald], 10.12. 2003.

Liufang, Fang: "Duli Dongshi zai Zhongguo: Jiashe he Xianshi" [Independent Directors in China: Hypothesis and Reality], *Tribune of Political Science and Law*, Vol. 26, No. 5, 2008, pp. 110–115.

Loderer C. / Roth L. / Waelchli U. / Joerg P.: "Shareholder Value: Principles, Declarations, and Actions". *Financial Management*, Vol. 39, No. 1, Spring 2010, pp. 5–32.

LoPucki L.: "The Myth of the Residual Owner: An Empirical Study". *Washington University Law Quarterly*, Vol. 82, No. 4, 2004, pp. 1341–1378.

Lu Tong / Yu Baoliang: "GELI DIANQI zhongxiao gudong heyishengchu – jiaqiang jitou touzizhe canyu gongsi zhili de yiyuan he nengli" [How can the medium and small shareholders GELI DIANQI win the election – Enhancement of the motivation and capacity of institutional investors for participation in corporate governance]. *Corporate Governance*, Vol. 7, 2012, pp. 116–119.

Lu Tong: “Corporate Governance in medium and small private PLCs: Characters and Problem”. *Enterprise Business*, Vol. 4, 2013, pp. 5–15.

Ma Gengxin: “Wanshan Woguo Shangshi Gongsi Duli Dongshi Zhidu Jianshe de Sikao” [Some Thoughts on Perfecting the Construction of the Independent Director System in China’s Listed Companies]. *Zheng-Fa Luntan* [Political-Legal Forum], Vol. 20, No. 6, 2002.

Macavoy, Paul W. / Millstein, Iram: *The Recurrent Crisis in Corporate Governance*. Stanford University Press: 2003.

Macey, Jonathan R. / Boot, Arnoud W. A.: “Monitoring Corporate Performance: The Role of Objectivity, Proximity and Adaptability in Corporate Governance”. *Cornell Law Review*, Vol. 89, No. 2, 2004, pp. 356–393.

Macey, Jonathan R. / Miller, Geoffrey: “Corporate Governance and Commercial Banking: A Comparative Examination of Germany, Japan, and the United States”. *Stanford Law Review*, Vol. 48, No. 1, 11.1995, pp. 73–112.

MacIntosh, Jeffrey G.: “Designing an Efficient Fiduciary Law”. *The University of Toronto Law Journal*, Vol. 43, No. 3, Special Issue on Corporate Stakeholder Debate: The Classical Theory and Its Critics, Summer 1993, pp. 425–473.

Mähönen, Jukka T.: “Finland – Corporate Governance: Nordic Tradition with American Spices”. In: Fleckner, Andreas M. / Hopt, Klaus J. (eds.): *Comparative Corporate Governance: A Functional and International Analysis*. Cambridge University Press: 2013, pp. 393–443.

Mahoney J.M. / Mahoney J.T.: “An empirical investigation of the effect of corporate charter antitakeover amendments on stockholder wealth”. *Strategic Management Journal*, Vol. 14, No. 1, 1993, pp. 17–31.

Mahoney J.M. / Murthy, C. Sundara / Mahoney J.T.: “The differential impact on stockholder wealth of various antitakeover provisions”. *Managerial and Decision Economics*, Vol. 17, No. 6, 1996, pp. 531–549.

Mallette, Paul / Fowler, Karen L.: “Effects of Board Composition and Stock Ownership on the Adoption of “Poison Pills””. *The Academy of Management Journal*, Vol. 35, No. 5, 12.1992, pp. 1010–1035.

Manne, Henry G.: “Mergers and the Market for Corporate Control”. *The Journal of Political Economy*, Vol. 73, No. 2, 4.1965, pp. 110–120.

Manning, Bayless: “Reflections and Practical Tips on Life in the Boardroom After Van Gorkom”. *The Business Lawyer*, Vol. 41, No. 1, 11.1985, pp. 1–14.

Marcoux, Alexei M.: “A Fiduciary Argument against Stakeholder Theory”. *Business Ethics Quarterly*, Vol. 13, No. 1, 1.2003, pp. 1–24, 15.

Marens, Richard / Wicks, Andrew: “Getting Real: Stakeholder Theory, Managerial Practice and the General Irrelevance of Fiduciary Duties Owed to Shareholders”. *Business Ethics Quarterly*, Vol. 9, No. 2, 4.1999, pp. 273–293.

Martynova M. / Renneboog L.: “Evidence on the international evolution and convergence of corporate governance regulations”. *Journal of Corporate Finance*, Vol. 17, No. 5, 2011, pp. 1531–1557.

Masouros, Pavlos E.: *Corporate Law and Economic Stagnation: How Shareholder Value and Short-Termism Contribute to the Decline of the Western Economies*. Eleven International Publishing: 28.1.2013.

Matheson, John H. / Norberg, Jon: “Hostile Share Acquisitions and Corporate Governance: A Framework for Evaluating Antitakeover Activities”. *University of Pittsburgh Law Review*, Vol. 47, 1986, pp. 407–491.

Mattes, Hans A.: “The Burden of the Corporate Director Elected Noncumulatively”. *California Law Review*, Vol. 63, No. 2, March, 1975, pp. 463–470.

McCahery, Joseph A. / Vermeulen, Erik P.M. / Hisatake, Masato: “The Present and Future of Corporate Governance: Re-examining the Role of the Board of Directors and Investor Relations in Listed Companies”. *European Company and Financial Law Review*, 2013, pp. 117–163.

McDonnell, Breit H.: “Professor Bainbridge and the Arrowian Moment: A Review of the New Corporate Governance in Theory and Practice”. *Delaware Journal of Corporate Law*, Vol. 34, No. 1, 2009, pp. 139–190.

Medill, Joseph: “The floor speech”. *Columbia Law Review*, Vol. 94, No.1, 1.1994.

Merkt, Hanno: “Germany – Internal and External Corporate Governance”. In: Fleckner, Andreas M. / Hopt, Klaus J. (eds.): *Comparative Corporate Governance: A Functional and International Analysis*. Cambridge University Press: 2013.

Milhaupt, Curtis J. / Pistor, Katharina: *Law and Capitalism: What Corporate Crises Reveal about Legal Systems and Economic Development around the World*. University of Chicago Press: 2008.

Milhaupt, Curtis J.: “The Market for Innovation in the United States and Japan: Venture Capital and the Comparative Corporate Governance Debate”. *Northwestern University Law Review*, Vol. 91, No. 3, 1997, pp. 865–898.

Miller R.: “Ethical Challenges in Corporate-Shareholder and Investor Relations: Using the Value Exchange Model to Analyze and Respond”. *Journal of Business Ethics*, Vol. 7, No. 1–2, 1988, pp. 117–132.

Millon, David: “Theories of the Corporation”. *Duke Law Journal*, Vol. 1990, No. 2, 1995, pp. 201–262.

Millstein, Ira M. / MacAvoy, Paul W.: “The Active Board of Directors and Performance of the Large Publicly Traded Corporation”. *Columbia Law Review*, Vol. 98, No. 5, 1998, pp. 1283–1322.

Minow, Nell: “Shareholders, Stakeholders, and Boards of Directors”. *Stetson Law Review*, Vol. 21, No. 1, 1991, pp. 197–244.

Mitbestimmungsgesetz, 1976.

Mitchell M.L. / Mulherin J.H. / Netter J.M., Poulsen A.B.: "Shark Repellents and Managerial Myopia: An Empirical Test". *The Journal of Political Economy*, Vol. 98, No. 5, 10.1990, pp. 1108–1117.

Mitchell R.K. / Agle B.R. / Wood D.J.: "Toward a theory of stakeholder identification and salience Defining the principle of who and what really counts". *Academy of Management Review*, Vol. 22, No. 4, 1997, pp. 853–886.

Mitchell, Lawrence E.: "A Theoretical and Practical Framework for Enforcing Corporate Constituency Statutes". *Texas Law Review*, Vol. 70, No. 3, 1992, pp. 579–643.

Mitchell, Mark L. / Mulherin, J. Harold: "The Impact of Industry Shocks on Takeover and Restructuring Activity". *Journal of Financial Economics*, Vol. 41, No. 2, 6.1996, pp. 193–229.

Model Business Corporation Act, 3rd Edition, Revised through 2002, adopted by the Committee on Corporate Laws of the Section of Business Law with support of the American Bar Foundation.

Moeller, Sara B. / Schlingemann, Frederik P. / Stulz, Rene M.: "Do Shareholders of Acquiring Firms Gain from Acquisitions?". *National Bureau of Economic Research*, Working Paper 9523, 2.2003, retrieved 12.4.2013, from http://www.nber.org / papers/w9523.

Monks, Robert A.G. / Minow, Nell: *Corporate Governance*. Blackwell Publishing: 2004.

Morgan, Angela / Poulsen, Annette B. / Wolf, Jack G. / Yang, Tina: "Mutual Funds as Monitors: Evidence from Mutual Fund Voting". *Journal of Corporate Finance*, Vol. 17, No. 4, 9.2011, pp. 914–928.

Mülbert, Peter O.: „Shareholder Value aus rechtlicher Sicht". *Zeitschrift für Unternehmens- und Gesellschaftsrecht*, 1997, Vol. 26, No. 2, pp. 129–172.

Murphy, Michael E.: "The Nominating Process for Corporate Boards of Directors – A Decision-Making Analysis". *Berkeley Business Law Journal*, Vol. 5, No. 2, 2008, pp. 131–193.

NASDAQ Manual Marketplace Rule 4350(c)-(d) (2006), retrieved 27.3.2013, from http://www.sec.gov/rules/other/nasdaqllcf1a4_5/nasdaqllcamendrules4000.pdf.

New York Stock Exchange Listed Company Manual 303A.02 Independence Tests, retrieved 17.2.2013, from http://nysemanual.nyse.com/LCMTools/Platform Viewer.asp ?selectednode=chp_1_4_3_3&manual=%2Flcm%2Fsections%2Flcm-sections%2F.

Ni Shoubin: "Zhongguo Shangshi Gongsi Dongshihui Zhili yu Zhidu Wanshan" [Improvement of the Governance and Institution of the Board in Listed Companies of China]. *Hebei Law Science*, Vol. 24, No. 9, 2006, pp. 22–27.

Nolan, Peter H.: "China at the crossroads". *Polity Press*, 1st Edition, 2004.

O'Connor, Marleen A.: "The Human Capital Era: Re-conceptualizing Corporate Law to Facilitate Labor-Management Cooperation". *Cornell Law Review*, Vol. 78, No. 5, 1993, pp. 899–965.

O'Sullivan M.: "The innovative enterprise and corporate governance". *Cambridge Journal of Economics*, Vol. 24, No, 4, 2000, pp. 393–416.

OECD: *OECD principles of corporate governance*, 2004.

OECD: *Related Party Transactions and Minority Shareholder Rights*, 2012.

On Kit Tam: "Ethical Issues in the Evolution of Corporate Governance in China". *Journal of Business Ethics*, May 2002, Vol. 37, No. 3, pp. 303–320.

Orts E.: "Beyond Shareholders: Interpreting Corporate Constituency Statutes". *George Washington Law Review*, Vol. 61, No. 1, 1993, pp. 14–135.

Palmiter, Alan R.: "Reshaping the Corporate Fiduciary Model: A Director's Duty of Independence". *Texas Law Review*, Vol. 67, No. 7, 1989, pp. 1351–1464.

Parkinson J.E.: *Corporate Power and Responsibility*. Oxford University Press: 1993.

Parrino, Robert / Richard W. Sias / Laura T. Starks: "Voting with Their Feet: Institutional Ownership Changes around Forced CEO Turnover". *Journal of Financial Economics*, Vol. 68, No. 1, 2003, pp. 3–46.

Partnoy F.: "Financial Innovation in Corporate Law". *Iowa Journal of Corporation Law*, Vol. 31, 2006, pp. 799–828.

Pease, Donald E.: "Outside Directors: Their Importance to the Corporation and Protection from Liability". *Delaware Journal of Corporate Law*, Vol. 12, No. 1, 1987, pp. 25–106.

Peerenboom R.: *China Modernizes: Threat to the West or Model for the* Rest. Oxford University Press: 2008, pp. 36–43.

Peng M.W.: "Outside directors and firm performance during institutional transitions". *Strategic Management Journal*, Vol. 25, No. 5, 2004, pp. 453–471.

Personick, Martin E.: *IRRC Corporate Governance Service 2005 Background Report F: Voting Issues: Confidential and Cumulative Voting*. Investor Responsibility Research Center, 2.2005.

Pinto, Arthur R.: "Globalization and the Study of Comparative Corporate Governance". *Wisconsin International Law Journal*, Vol. 23, No. 477, 2005, pp. 477–511.

Pizzo, Michele: "Related party transactions under a contingency perspective". *Journal of Management and Governance*, Vol. 17, No. 2, 2013, pp. 309–330.

Plessis J.J. Du / Großfeld B. / Luttermann C. / Saenger I. / Sandrock O.: *German Corporate Governance in International and European Context*. Springer: 2nd Edition, 2012.

Porter, Michael E.: "Capital Choices: Changing the Way America Invests in Industry". *Journal of Applied Corporate Finance*, Vol. 5, No. 2, Summer 1992, pp. 4–16.

Pound J.: "Beyond takeovers: Politics comes to corporate control". *Harvard Business Review*, Vol. 70, No. 2, 1992, pp. 83–93.

Pozen, Robert C.: *Insitutional Perspective on Shareholder Nomination of Corporate Directors.* Harvard Law School – John M. Olin Center for Law, Economics and Business: Discussion Paper Series No. 429, 8.2003.

Pozen, Robert C.: *Institutional Perspective on Shareholder Nomination of Corporate Directors.* Harvard Law School, John M. Olin Center for Law: Economics and Business Discussion Paper Series No. 429, 8.2003.

Principles of Corporate Governance: Analysis and Recommendations, Tentative Draft No. 4, 1985, Note on Proposed Revisions in Part III of Tentative Draft No. 2.

Research Center of Corporate Governance of China: *Report of Corporate Governance Index and Evaluation in 2012*, retrieved 12.5.2013, from http://www.022net.com/2012/11-25/471843353297915.html.

Research Team of "Guidelines for Performance of Independent Directors in Listed Companies" in the China Association for Public Companies: "The Great Possibility of Enhancing the Role of Independent Directors – Abstract of the Report on the Performance of Independent Directors". *China Securities Journal*, A14, 16.1.2014.

Ribstein, Larry E.: "Market vs. Regulatory Responses to Corporate Fraud: A Critique of the Sarbanes-Oxley Act of 2002". *Journal of Corporation Law*, Vol. 28, No. 1, Fall 2002, pp. 1–74.

Robertson D.: "Shell cuts jobs as profits plunge 70%". *The Times*, 30.7.2009.

Roe, Mark J.: "Political preconditions to separating ownership from corporate control". *Stanford Law Review*, Vol. 53, No. 3, 2000, pp. 539–606.

Rolf, Skog / Sjöman, Erik: "Corporate boards in Sweden". In: Davies, Paul / Hopt, Klaus / Nowak, Richard / van Solinge, Gerard (eds.): *Corporate Boards in Law and Practice.* Oxford University Press: 2013, pp. 617–652.

Romano, Roberta: "A Cautionary Note on Drawing Lessons From Comparative Corporate Law". *Yale Law Journal*, Vol. 102, 1993, pp. 2021–2037.

Romano, Roberta: "Public Pension Fund Activism in Corporate Governance Reconsidered". *Columbia Law Review*, Vol. 93, No. 4, 1993, pp. 795–853.

Rongqing, Ding / Hongzhen, Zhang: "Cong Guoji Bijiao Kan Woguo Guquan Jizhongdu" [Discussions on Corporate Concentrated Ownership of China from International View], *Shichang Zhoukan Caijing Luntan* [Market Weekly Economics], Vol. 11, 2004, pp. 23–24.

Rosenstein, Stuart / Wyatt, Jeffrey G.: "Outside Directors, Board Independence, and Shareholder Wealth". *Journal of Financial Economics*, Vol. 26, No. 2, 8.1990, pp. 175–191.

Rossi, Stefano / Volpin, Paolo: "Cross-Country Determinants of Mergers and Acquisitions". *Journal of Financial Economics*, Vol. 74, No. 2, 2004, pp. 277–304.

Roth, Markus: *Private Altersvorsorge: Betriebsrentenrecht und individuelle Vorsorge: Eine rechtsvergleichende Gesamtschau.* Mohr Siebeck: 1st Edition, 2009, pp. 209–210.

S. Chatterjee / J. Harrison / D. Bergh: "Failed hostile takeover attempts, corporate governance and refocusing". *Strategic Management Journal*, Vol. 24, No. 1, 2003, pp. 87–96.

Salancik G.R. / Pfeffer J.: "Effects of ownership and performance on executive tenure in U.S. corporations". *Academy of Management Journal*, Vol. 23, No. 4, 1980, pp. 653–664.

Sarbanes-Oxley Act, Public Law 107–204, 116 State 745, enacted on July 30th, 2002.

Scharfstein, David: "The Disciplinary Role of Takeovers". *The Review of Economic Studies*, Vol. 55, No. 2, 4.1988, pp. 185–199.

Schipani, Cindy A. / Liu, Junhai: "Corporate Governance in China: Then and Now". *Columbia Business Law Review*, Vol. 2002, No. 1, 2002, pp. 1–69.

Schmidt, Reinhard H. / Maßmann, Jens: *Drei Mißverständnisse zum Thema "Shareholder Value"*. (Working Paper Series: Finance and Accounting 31) Goethe University Frankfurt am Main, Department of Finance: 2.1999.

Schneider, Uwe H. / Strenger, Christian: „Corporate Governance -Grundsätze" (German Panel on Corporate Governance). *Die Aktiengesellschaft: AG*; Zeitschrift für das gesamte Aktienwesen, für deutsches, europäisches und internationales Unternehmens- und Kapitalmarktrecht, Vol. 45, No. 3, 2000, p. 106–113.

Schneper, William D. / Guillén, Mauro F.: "Stakeholder Rights and Corporate Governance: A Cross-National Study of Hostile Takeovers". *Administrative Science Quarterly*, Vol. 49, No. 2, 2004, pp. 263–295.

Securities and Exchange Commission: *Facilitating Shareholder Director Nominations*, 17 CFR PARTS 200, 232, 240 and 249, 16.9.2010.

Shan, Yuan G. / Taylor, Dennis W.: "Related-party disclosures in the two-tier board system in China: Influences of ownership structure and board composition". *Corporate Board: Role, Duties and Composition*, Vol. 4, No. 1, 2008, pp. 37–49.

Shanghai Association of Listed Companies' Board of Director Secretaries & Jinxin Institute of Securities: "Duli Dongshi Zenmoyang le?" [How Are the Independent Directors?]. *Zhengquan Shibao* [Securities Times], 7.8.2003.

Shanghai Research Center of Security Markets, Chinese Corporate Governance Report: *Independence and Effectiveness of Board*. Fudan University Press: 2004.

Shanghai Shang Bao [Shanghai Commercial Daily], 11.1.2013, retrieved 14.3.2013, from http://www.shbiz.com.cn/Item/198957.aspx.

Shanghai Stock Exchange: *The Results and Analysis of the Questionnaire Survey on Corporate Governance of Listed Companies*. Shangshi Gongsi [Listed Companies], 12.2000, pp. 11–25.

Sheehy, Benedict: "The Importance of Corporate Models, Economic and Jurisprudential Values and the Future of Corporate Law". *De Paul Business and Commercial Law Journal*, Vol. 2, No. 3, 2004, pp. 463–513.

Shenzhen Stock Exchange: *Guidelines for Investor Rights Protection in Small and Medium Board of Enterprise*, 13.1.2006.

Shenzhen Stock Exchange: *Guidelines of the Shenzhen Stock Exchange for Standardized Operation of Companies Listed on the Small and Medium-Sized Enterprise Board*, 28.7.2010.

Shenzhen Stock Exchange: *Listing Rules of Growth Enterprise Market (GEM) in Shenzhen Stock Exchange*, 2012.

Shleifer, Andrei / Summers, Lawrence H.: "Breach of Trust in Hostile Takeovers". In: Auerbach, Alan J (ed.): *Corporate Takeovers: Causes and Consequences*. NBER book: 8.1987, pp. 33–68.

Shleifer, Andrei / Vishny, Robert W.: "A Survey of Corporate Governance". *Journal of Finance*, Vol. 52, No. 2, 1997, pp. 737–783.

Shnell, James H.: "A Procedural Treatment of Derivative Suit Dismissals by Minority Directors". *California Law Review*, Vol. 69, No. 3, 1981, pp. 885–910.

Siems, Mathias M.: *Convergence in Shareholder Law (International Corporate Law and Financial Market Regulation)*. Cambridge University Press: 2008, pp. 367–368.

Simpson, Scott V.: "The Emerging Role of the Special Committee – Ensuring Business Judgment Rule Protection". *Business Lawyer*, Vol. 43, No. 2, 1988, pp. 665–690.

Singh A. / Weisse B.: "Corporate governance, competition, the new international financial architecture and large corporations in emerging markets". *Center for Business Research Working: Paper No. 250*. University of Cambridge: 2002.

Sjafjell, Beate: *Towards a Sustainable European Company Law – A Normative Analysis of the Objectives of EU Law, with the Takeover Directive as a Test Case*. (European company law series, Vol. 3). Kluwer Law International: 2009.

Smith M.P.: "Shareholder activism by institutional investors: Evidence from CalPERS". *Journal of Finance*, Vol. 51, No. 1, 1996, pp. 227–252.

Smith, D. Gordon: "The Shareholder Primacy Norm". *Journal of Corporation Law*, Vol. 23, No. 2, Winter 1998, pp. 277–323, 323.

Smith, Thomas A.: "The Efficient Norm for Corporate Law: A Neo-traditional Interpretation of Fiduciary Duty". *Michigan Law Review*, Vol. 98, No.1, 1999, pp. 214–269.

Social Security Fund Council: *Weekly on Stocks*, 18.1.2012, retrieved 3.7.2013, from http://news.ihongpan.com/12/0118/seocs083550.html.

Spanish Corporate Governance Code, Special Working Group, 2006.

Springer J.: "Corporate Constituency Statutes: Hollow Hopes and False Fears" *Annual Survey of American Law*, Vol. 1999, No. 1, 1999, pp. 85–128.

Stapledon, Geof P.: *Institutional Shareholders and Corporate Governance*. Clarendon Press: 1995.

State Council: "Several Opinions on Promoting Reform and Opening-up and Stable Development of Capital Market". *Guofa [2004] No. 3.*

Storetrax.com. Inc. v. Gurland, 915 A 2d 991 (2007).

Stout, Lynn A.: "In Praise of Procedure: An Economic and Behavioral Defense of Smith v. Van Gorkom and the Business Judgment Rule". *Northwestern University Law Review*, Vol. 96, No. 2, 2002, pp. 675–693.

Strine, Leo E. Jr.: "Can We Do Better by Ordinary Investors? A Pragmatic Reaction to the Dueling Ideological Mythologists of Corporate Law". *Columbia Law Review*, Vol. 114, No. 2, 3.2014, pp. 449–502.

Strine, Leo E. Jr.: "One Fundamental Corporate Governance Question We Face: Can Corporations Be Managed for the Long Term Unless Their Powerful Electorates Also Act and Think Long Term?". *Business Lawyer*, Vol. 66, No. 1, 11.2010, pp. 1–32.

Strine, Leo E. Jr.: "Response, Toward a True Corporate Republic: A Traditionalist Response to Bebchuk's Solution for Improving Corporate America". *Harvard Law Review*, Vol. 119, 2006, pp. 1759–1783.

Stulz R.M.: "Managerial Control of Voting Rights: Financing Policies and the Market for Corporate Control". *Journal of Financial Economics*, Vol. 20, 1988, pp. 25–54.

Sturdy, Herbert L.: "Mandatory Cumulative Voting: An Anachronism". *Business Lawyer* Vol. 16, No. 3, 4.1961, pp. 550–576.

Thamm, Christian: "Minority shareholder monitoring and German corporate governance: empirical evidence and value effects". In: Schiereck, Dirk (ed.): *Corporate Finance and Governance*, Band 13, 2013.

The Economist: *Together they stand.* 16.7.2005, p. 14.

The former Reflection Group on the Future of EU Company Law: "Response to the European Commission's Action Plan on Company Law and Corporate Governance". *European Company and Financial Law Review*, 2013, pp. 304–327.

Tobin, James M.: "The Squeeze on Directors-Inside Is Out". *Business Lawyer*, Vol. 49, No.4, 1994, pp. 1707–1760.

Tonello, Matteo / Rabimov, Stephan: "The 2010 Institutional Investment Report: Trends in Asset Allocation and Portfolio Composition". The Conference Bd., Inc., 2010, p. 22 table 10, retrieved 22.2.2013, from http://ssrn.com/abstract=1707512 (on file with the Columbia Law Review).

Tong, Lu: "Corporate Governance in medium and small private PLCs: Characters and Problem". *Enterprise Business*, Vol. 4, 2013, pp. 5–15, 7.

Tosi H.L. / Gomez-Mejia L.R.: "The decoupling of C.E.O. pay and performance: An agency theory perspective". *Administrative Science Quarterly*, Vol. 39, No. 2, 1989, pp. 169–189.

Tung F.: "The New Death of Contract: Creeping Corporate Fiduciary Duties for Creditors". *Emory Law Journal*, Vol. 57, 2008, pp. 809–871.

Tuschke A. / Luber M.: "Corporate Governance in Germany: Converging Towards Shareholder Value-Orientation or Not So Much?". In: Rasheed A. / Yoshikawa, T. (eds.): *The convergence of corporate governance: promise and prospects.* Palgrave Macmillan: 2012, pp. 75–92.

UK Corporate Update: *European related party transaction rules: the impact on listed companies,* 11.9.2014.

Van Bekkum, Jaron / Hijink, Steven / Micheal C. / Schouten, Jaap W.: "Netherlands-Corporate governance in the Netherlands". In: Fleckner, Andreas M. / Hopt, Klaus J. (eds.): *Comparative Corporate Governance: A Functional and International Analysis.* Cambridge University Press: Winter, 2013, pp. 648–701.

van der Weide M.: "Against Fiduciary Duties to Corporate Stakeholders". *Delaware Journal of Corporate Law,* Vol. 21, No. 1, 1996, pp. 27–86.

VBL: *Die Vermögensanlage der VBL,* retrieved 5.5.2014, from http://www.vbl.de /de/wir_ueber_uns/vermoegensanlage/.

Veasey, E. Norman / Di Guglielmo, Christine T.: "How Many Masters Can a Director Serve? A Look at the Tensions Facing Constituency Directors". *The Business Lawyer,* Vol. 63, No. 3, 5.2008, pp. 761–775.

Veasey, E. Norman: "Policy and Legal Overview of Best Corporate Governance Principles". *SMU Law Review,* Vol. 56, No. 4, 2003, pp. 2135–2150.

Veasey, E. Norman: "Seeking a Safe Harbor from Judicial Scrutiny of Directors' Business Decisions – An Analytical Framework for Litigation Strategy and Counseling Directors". *The Business Lawyer,* Vol. 37, No. 3, April 1982, pp. 1247–1274.

Veasey, E. Norman: "The Defining Tension in Corporate Governance in America". *The Business Lawyer,* Vol. 52, No. 2, 2.1997, pp. 393–406.

Veasey, E. Norman: "The New Incarnation of the Business Judgment Rule in Takeover Defenses". *Delaware Journal of Corporate Law,* Vol. 11, No. 2, 1986, pp. 503–512.

Velasco, Julian: "The Fundamental Rights of the Shareholder". *UC Davis Law Review,* Vol. 40, No. 2, 2006, pp. 407–467.

Ventoruzzo, Marco: "Empowering Shareholders in Directors' Elections: A Revolution in the Making". *European Company and Financial Law Review,* Vol. 8, No. 2, 6.2011, pp. 105–144.

Von Hein J.: *Die Rezeption US-amerikanischen Gesellschaftsrechts in Deutschland.* Mohr Siebeck: Tübingen, 2008.

Von Werder, Axel: „Ökonomische Grundfragen der Corporate Governance". In: Hommelhoff, Peter / Hopt, Klaus J. / Von Werder, Axel (eds.): *Handbuch Corporate Governance.* Otto Schmidt Vertrag: 2nd Edition, Köln 2009.

Wade, Cheryl L.: "What Independent Directors Should Expect from Inside Directors: Smith v. Van Gorkom as a Guide to Intra-Firm Governance". *Washburn Law Journal,* Vol. 45, No. 6, 2006, pp. 367–387.

Wallman S.: "The Proper Interpretation of Corporate Constituency Statutes and Formulation of Director Duties". *Stetson Law Review*, Vol. 21, No. 1, 1991, pp. 163–196.

Wang, Wallace Wen-Yeu / Chen, Jian-Lin: "Bargaining for Compensation in the Shadow of Regulatory Giving: The Case of Stock Trading Rights Reform in China". *Columbia Journal of Asian Law*, Vol. 20, No. 298, 2006, pp. 298–356.

Watson, Towers: *Global Pension Assets Study*, retrieved 12.7.2014, from http://www.towerswatson.com/en/Insights/IC-Types/Survey-Research-Results/2013/01/Global-Pensions-Asset-Study-2013.

Weisbach, Michael S.: "Outside Directors and CEO Turnover". *Journal of Financial Economics*, Vol. 20, 1988, pp. 431–460.

Weng, Charlie Xiaochuan: "Chinese Shareholder Protection and the Influence of the US Law: The Idiosyncratic Economic Realities and Mismatched Agency Problem Solutions". *Securities Regulation Law Journal*, 11.4.2012, pp. 1–36.

Wenjia, Yan: "Cumulative Voting: In the US (Declining), in China (Rising) and the EU (Not-Adopted)". *ECFR*, Vol. 12, No. 1, 4.2015, pp. 79–109.

Werner, Walter: "Corporation Law in Search of Its Future". *Columbia Law Review*, Vol. 81, No. 1981, 1611–1666.

Wertpapier-Übernahme-Gesetz (Act on Take-overs), 20.12. 2001.

Wiedemann: „Grundfragen der Unternehmensverfassung". *ZGR*, Vol. 4, No. 4, 1.1975, pp. 385–432.

Woolf, Terence: "The Venture Capitalist's Corporate Opportunity Problem". *Columbia Business Law Review*, Vol. 2001, No. 2, pp. 473–508.

Wu Xiaoping: "Huiqian Goutong: Duli Dongshi Zhize bentuhua Tanyi" [Discussions before the Board's Meeting: Study on the Localization of Independent Directors' Functions], *Law Research*, Vol. 4, 2014, pp. 97–104.

Xi, Chao: "Institutional Shareholder Activism in China: Law and Practice". *International Company and Commercial Law Review*, Vol. 17, 2006.

Xu Qing: "Woguo Shangshi Gongsi Leiji Toupiao Zhidu Cunzai Quexian" [Loopholes Exist in the Cumulative Voting System of Chinese Listed Companies], *Shanghai Zhengquan Bao* [Shanghai Securities News], 16.9.2004.

Xu Xiaosong: "Gongsi Zhili: "Jiegou" yihuo "Wenti"" [Corporate Governance: "Structure" or "Problem"]. *Zhengfa Luntan* [Tribune of Political Science and Law], Vol. 31, No. 6, 11.2013, pp. 61–68.

Yan Xuefeng / Zhu Linchu: "Fahui Zhuanchang Zuohao Dongshi" [Be a Good Director Based on Professional Knowledge]. *Board*, Vol. 10, 2013.

Yang Hua: *Gonsi Zaizao: Zhongguo Shangshi Gongsi Zhili Jiegou de Xinlujing* [Restructure of Corporations: New Path for the Listed Corporations of China], Zhongxin Press: 2011.

Yi Rentao / Lv Xinzhi: "Duli Dongshi Zhidu Qushe Lun" [On The Transplantation Of Independent Director], *Law Science Magazine*, No. 8, 2011, pp. 121–123.

Yun, Gu Gong / Luo, Pei Xin: "Lun Wo guo Jian li Du li Dong shi Zhi du de Ji ge Fa lu Wen ti" [On Several Legal Issues of the Establishment of Independent Director in China]. *China Legal Science*, June, 2001.

Zhao Xiaohui / Tao Junjie: "Duli Dongshi Zhidu yi Jiji Kewei" [Independent Directors betweenthebeetleandtheblock], *ChinaBusinessTimes*, 9.10.2010, Front Page.

Zhong, Gan Pei: "Lun Wan shan Wo guo Shang shi Gong si Zhi li Jie gou zhong de Jian shi Zhi du" [Comment on Improving Supervisors Mechanism in the Governance Structure in Chinese Listed Companies]. *China Legal Science*, 5.2001.

Zhu Ciyun / Lin Kai: "Gongsi Zhidu Qutong Lilun Jianshi Xia de Zhonguo Gongsi Zhili Pingxi" [Analysis of Chinese Corporate Governance under the Theory of Converge of Corporate Governance], *Law Research*, Vol. 5, 2013, pp. 24–41.

Zhu Ciyun / Zhongguo Yinru: "Duli Dongshi Zhidu Yingzhuyi de Ruogan Wenti" [Several Issues about the Adoption of Independent Directors]. In: *Gongsi Zhili yu Ziben Shichang Jianguan-Bijiao yu Jiejian* [Corporate Governance and Regulation of Security Market-Comparison and Reference]. Beijing University Press: 2003.

Zhu Ciyun: "Xinde Linian yu Xinde Shijiao-Ping Dalu "Gongsifa" de Xiugai" [New Ideas and Perspectives-Discussions on the amendment of "Company Law"]. *Study on Yue Dan Civil and Business Law*, Vol. 10. Qinghua University Press: 2006.

Zhu Ciyun: *Gongsifa Yuanlun* [Theories of Corporate Law]. Qinghua University Press: 2011.

Zingales L.: "In Search of New Foundations". *Journal of Finance*, Vol. 55, No. 4, 2000, pp. 1623–1653.

Zou, Hong / Adams, Mike B.: "Corporate ownership, equity risk and returns in the People's Republic of China". *Journal of International Business Studies*, Vol. 39, No. 7, 10/11. 2008, pp. 1149–1168, 1151.

Cases

Aronson v. Lewis, 473 A.2d 805 (Del. 1984).

Auerbach v. Bennett, 47 N.Y.2d 619, 393 N.E.2d 994, 419 N.Y.S.2d 920 (1979).

Baumgardner v. Stockley, 13 N.E. 279 (Ohio 1887).

Bennett v. Propp, 187 A.2d 405 (Del. 1962).

Blasius Indus., v. Atlas Corp., 564 A.2d 651 (Del. Ch. 1988).

Bligh v Brent, 2 Y & C Ex 268 (1837).

Bodell v. General Gas & Electric Corp., 140 A. 264 (Del. 1927).

Brehm v. Eisner, 746 A.2d 244 (Del. 2000).

CA, Inc. v. Afscme Employees Pension Plan, 953 A.2d 227 (Del. 2008).

Cede & Co. v. Technicolor, Inc., 634 A.2d 345 (Del. 1993).

Central Iowa Power Co-op. v. Consumers Energy, 741 NW 2d 822 (2007).

Citron v. Fairchild Camera & Instrument Corp., 569 A.2d 53, 64 (Del. 1989).

Credit Lyonnais Bank Nederland NV v. Pathe Communications Corp., 1991 WL 277 (Del. Ch. 1991).

Dodge v. Ford Motor Co., 170 N.W 668 (Mich. 1919).

Dynamics Corp. of Am. v. CTS Corp., 794 F.2d 250 (7th Cir. 1986), rev'd on other grounds, 107 S. Ct. 1637 (1987).

eBay Domestic Holdings, Inc. v. Newmark, 16 A.3d 1, 33 (Del. Ch. 2010).

Enterra Corp. v. SGS Associates, 600 F. Supp. 678 (E.D. Pa. 1985).

Galef v. Alexander, 615 F. 2d 51 (US Court of Appeals, 2d Cir. 1980).

Guth v. Loft, Inc., 5 A.2d 503, 510 (Del. 1939).

Hanson Trust PLC v. ML SCM Acquisition, Inc., 781 F.2d 264, 276 (2d Cir. 1986).

Hilton Hotels Corp. v. ITT Corp., 978 E Supp. 1342 (D. Nev. 1997).

Humphrys v. Winous Co., 133 N.E.2d 780 (Ohio 1956).

In re: Aquila Inc. Shareholders Litigation, 2002 WL 27815 (Del. Ch. Jan. 3, 2002).

In re MAXXAM, Inc., 659 A.2d 760 (Del. Ch. 1995).

In re Pure Resources Inc., Shareholders Litigation, 808 A.2d 421 (Del. Ch. 2002).

In re RJR Nabisco, Inc. Shareholders Litig., 1989 WL 7036 (Del. Ch. 1989).

In re Siliconix Inc. Shareholders Litigation, 2001 WL 716787 (Del. Ch. June, 2001).

In re Trados Inc. S'holder Litig., 73 A.3d 17 (Del. Ch. 2013).

Ivanhoe Partners v. Newmont Mining Corp., Nos. 9281 (Del. Ch. Oct. 15, 1987).

Jones v. H. F. Ahmanson & Co., 1 Cal. 3d 93, 460 P.2d 464, 81 Cal. Rptr. 592 (1969).

Joy v. North, 692 E2d 880 (2d Cir. 1982), cert denied, 460 U.S. 1051 (1983).

Jungein FS v. Caemmerer, 1978, 547 ff.

Kahn v. Lynch Communications Systems, Inc., 638 A. 2d 1113.

Kahn v. Lynch Communications Systems, Inc., 669 A. 2d 79.

Kahn v. Tremont Corp., 694 A.2d 422 (Del. 1997).

Kahn v. United States Sugar Corp., Court of Chancery of the State of Delaware, New Castle, December 10, 1985, 11 Del. J. Corp. L. 908 (Del. Ch. Dec. 10, 1985).

Kamen v. Kemper Fin. Servs., Inc., 908 E2d 1338, 1343 (7th Cir. 1990), rev'd on other grounds, 500 U.S. 90 (1991).

Kumpf v. Steinhaus, 779 E2d 1323 (7th Cir. 1985).

Lewis v. Anderson, 6I5 F.2d 778 (9th Cir. 1980).

Malone v. Brincat, 722 A.2d 5 (Del. 1998).

Marciano v. Nakash, 535 A.2d 400 (Del. 1987).

Martin Marietta Corp. v. Bendix Corp, 549 F. Supp. 623 (D. Md. 1982).
Mills Acquisition Co. v. MacMillan, Inc., 559 A.2d 1261 (Del. 1988), appeal dismissed, 548 A.2d 498 (1988).
Moran v. Household Int'l, Inc., 500 A.2d 1346 (Del. 1985).
N. Am. Catholic Educ. Programming Found., Inc. v. Gheewalla, 930 A.2d 92 (Del. 2007).
Panter v. Marshall Field & Co., 646 F.2d 271 (7th Cir.) cert. denied, 454 US 1092 (1981).
Paramount Communications, Inc. v. Time Inc., 571 A.2d 1140 (Del. 1989).
Polk v. Good, 507 A.2d 531 (Del. 1986).
Puma v. Marriott, 283 A.2d 693 (Del. Ch. 1971).
Revlon, Inc. v. MacAndrews & Forbes Holdings, Inc., 506 A.2d 173 (Del. 1985).
Robert M. Bass Group, Inc. v. Evans, 552 A.2d 1227 (Del. Ch. 1988).
Rome v. Archer, 197 A.2d 49 (Del. 1964).
Rosenblatt v. Getty Oil Co., 493 A.2d 929 (Del. 1985).
Samjens Partners I v. Burlington Indus., Inc., 663 F. Supp. 614, 625 (S.D.N.Y. 1987).
Selheimer v. Manganese Corp. of Am., 423 Pa. 563, 224 A. 2d 634 (Pa. Super. Ct. 1966).
Seminaris v. Landa, 662 A.2d 1350 (Del. 1995).
Sinclair Oil Corp. v. Levien, 280 A.2d 717 (Del. 1971).
Smith v. Brown-Borhek Co., 414 Pa. 325. 488 A.2d 858 (Del. 1985).
Smith v. Van Gorkom, 488 A.2d 858 (Del. 1985).
Solomon v. Pathe Communications Corp., 672 A.2d 35 (Del. 1996).
Storetrax.com. Inc. v. Gurland, 915 A 2d 991 (2007).
Warshaw v. Calhoun, 221 A.2d 487 (Del. 1966).
Weinberger v. UOP, Inc., 457 A.2d 701 (Del. 1983).
Unitrin, Inc. v. American Gen. Corp., 651 A.2d 1361 (Del. 1995).
Unocal Corp. v. Mesa Petroleum Co, 493 A.2d 946 (Del. 1985).
Zapata Corp. v. Maldonado, 430 A.2d 779 (Del. 1981).

Introduction

Issues of corporate governance are currently found on most countries' political agendas, including those of the most important Economy giants around the world, such as Europe, China and the US. In the current company law debate, corporate governance doubtlessly tends to be overshadowed by the prevailing Anglo-American law, whose corporate governance systems have significant global influence.[1] According to United States scholars writing on the subject with little dissent, the agreement is that the convergence will center upon a set of governance parameters closely resembling the American model of corporate governance.[2] At the end of the last century, Professor D. Gordon Smith asserted in a very well-regarded piece that the shareholder primary theory "was one of the most overrated doctrines in corporate law."[3] In terms of considering the corporation's objective, shareholder primacy is often the only theory set out in most finance and economics texts, as well as many law texts. Undoubtedly, there is substance in what Professor Stephen Bottomley states, adopting the view that the theory "exercises a powerful grip on the mind-set of corporate managers and officers."[4] In their article *The End of History for Corporate Law,* Professors Hansmann and Kraakman conclude that the other primary models of managerial power, including labor influence or state control, have failed and that the US model of shareholder primacy – which encourages the related depth of the capital markets – can inevitably reduce the cost of capital for corporations and will continue to prevail.[5] They recognize that even with a convergence towards shareholder primacy, different countries may approach larger societal

1 See Sjafjell, Beate: *Towards a Sustainable European Company Law – A Normative Analysis of the Objectives of EU Law, with the Takeover Directive as a Test Case.* (European company law series, Vol. 3). Kluwer Law International: 2009.

2 See Bratton, William W. / McCahery, Joseph A.: "Comparative Corporate Governance and the Theory of the Firm: The Case Against Global Cross Reference". *Columbia Journal of Transnational Law,* Vol. 38, No. 2, 1999, pp. 213–298; Romano, Roberta: "A Cautionary Note on Drawing Lessons From Comparative Corporate Law". *Yale Law Journal,* Vol. 102, 1993, pp. 2021–2037, 2036; Coffee, John C.: "The Future as History: The Prospects for Global Convergence in Corporate Governance and Its Implications". *Northwest University Law Review,* Vol. 93, No. 3, 1999, pp. 641–785, 679–680; Hansmann, Henry / Kraakman, Reinier: "The End of History for Corporate Law". *Georgetown Law Review,* Vol. 89, No. 2, 2000, pp. 439–473.

3 See Smith, D. Gordon: "The Shareholder Primacy Norm". *Journal of Corporation Law,* Vol. 23, No. 2, Winter 1998 , pp. 277–323, 323.

4 See Bottomley, Stephen: *The Constitutional Corporation.* Ashgate Publishing, Ltd.: 1.1.2007, p. 8.

5 See Hansmann, Henry / Kraakman, Reinier: "The End of History for Corporate Law". *Georgetown Law Review,* Vol. 89, No. 2, 2000, pp. 439–473, 443.

issues differently, although they believe that interests are better protected outside the parameters of corporate governance.[6]

Due to the strong influence of the shareholder-centered model, both China and the EU have taken stronger measures to protect minority shareholders. In this respect, representation of minority shareholders on the board – in particular, the system of cumulative voting that was originally designed by the US to protect minority shareholders from the prejudice of a majority who could form rings to control absolutely[7] as well as abuse and plunder the property of the minorities[8] – has become a frequently-discussed problem in China and the EU, where the core agency costs are triggered by controlling shareholders.

However, in the US, the cumulative voting has declined while the number of independent directors who helped lock in shareholder value as the guide for management behavior have risen. Mandatory cumulative voting fell into strong disfavor in the 1990s, leaving only five remaining adherents, namely Arizona, Nebraska, North Dakota, South Dakota and West Virginia, none of which is a major commercial state.[9] Accordingly, companies incorporated in these states account for less than 1% of all companies in the Investor Responsibility Research Center Institute's (IRRC) core research universe.[10] Deregulation has meant a steady decline regarding the use of cumulative voting.[11]

As an emerging and growth-leading economy, China has placed strong emphasis on establishing a corporate governance system and is a good example to illustrate this trend: on one side, it is under the pressure of promoting corporations to expand its scale and boost the growth of security markets as well as to increase its international competitiveness; and on the other side, corporations with concentrated ownership still predominate and small shareholders are inactive in the company oversight, based upon the Company Law – strongly influenced by German corporate law – that was first enacted in December 1993 and came into effect in mid-1994 . On October 27,

---

6 See Branson, Douglas M.: "The Very Uncertain Prospect of "Global" Convergence in Corporate Governance". *Cornell International Law Journal*, Vol. 34, No. 2, 2001, p. 321–362, 350–352.

7 See Editors, Law Review: "Cumulative Voting: Removal, Reduction and Classification of Corporate Boards". The University of Chicago Law Review: Vol. 22, No. 3, Spring 1955, pp. 751–759,752.

8 See Ventoruzzo, Marco: "Empowering Shareholders in Directors' Elections: A Revolution in the Making". *European Company and Financial Law Review*, Vol. 8, No. 2, 6.2011, pp. 105–144, 142.

9 See Gordon, Jeffrey N.: "Institutions as Relational Investors: A New Look at Cumulative Voting". *Columbia Law Review*, Vol. 94, No. 1, 1.1994, pp. 124–192, 145–146.

10 See Personick, Martin E.: *IRRC Corporate Governance Service 2005 Background Report F: Voting Issues: Confidential and Cumulative Voting*. Investor Responsibility Research Center, 2.2005.

11 See Gordon, Jeffrey N.: "Institutions as Relational Investors: A New Look at Cumulative Voting". *Columbia Law Review*, Vol. 94, No. 1, 1.1994, pp. 124–192, 145–146.

2005, after one year of preparation and one year and a half of deliberation, the Eighteenth Session of the Standing Committee of the Tenth National People's Congress promulgated a revised Company Law (hereinafter "Company Law of 2005" or "Company Law"), adopting cumulative voting and independent directors. The system of independent representatives of minority shareholders is supposed to protect the interests of minority shareholders through cumulative voting to elect supervisors and directors who can represent them to control and manage the corporation.

On December 28, 2013, the Company Law 2005 was further amended by the sixth Session of the Standing Committee of the Twelfth National People's Congress (hereinafter "Company Law of 2013"). The amendment means the deregulation of the company establishment, including cancelling restrictions on the minimum registered capital,[12] the minimum raised share capital,[13] the proportion of currency capital[14] as well as submitting a certificate of capital verification for the registration of incorporation.[15] However, it brings no changes to the corporate governance systems. Although the provision of cumulative voting and independent directors remains, Article 106 has been changed into Article 105, which stipulates that "When the shareholders' assembly elects directors or supervisors, it may, according to the articles of association or resolution of the shareholders' assembly, adopt a cumulative voting system. The term 'cumulative voting system' as mentioned in this Law refers to a system of voting by shareholders for the election of directors or supervisors at a session of the shareholders' assembly in which the shareholder can multiply his voting rights by the number of candidates and direct them all towards

---

12 Specifically, the minimum amount of the registered capital of a joint stock limited company (RMB 5 million Yuan) in Article 81 para. 2 sentence 2 of the Company Law 2005 and the minimum amount of registered capital of a one-person limited liability company (RMB 100, 000 Yuan) in Article 59 para. 1 of the Company Law 2005 are deleted. Furthermore, Article 7 of the Company Law 2013 cancels the requirement for stating registered capital in the company business license. Instead, it allows the company bylaws to decide the amount of capital contributions subscribed by shareholders. In addition, Article 178 para. 2 sentence 3 of the Company Law 2005, which stipulated "The registered capital of the company after reducing its registered capital shall not be any lower than the minimum amount prescribed for by law", is abolished.

13 The following provisions of the Company Law 2005 are abolished: Article 26 and Article 81 para. 1, which stipulated that "the minimum amount of initial capital contributions to be made by all initiators shall be not less than 20% of the total registered capital, and the remaining amount shall be paid off by the initiators within 2 years as of the day when the company is established, while for an investment company, the remaining amount may be paid off within 5 years."

14 Article 27 para. 3 of the Company Law 2005 – which provided that "the amount of the capital contributions in currency paid by all the shareholders shall be not less than 30% of the registered capital of the limited liability company" – is also abolished.

15 The capital verification – as a requirement for applying incorporation registration – provided by Article 29, Article 30 and Article 84 para. 2 sentence 3 of the Company Law 2005 is cancelled.

one candidate, director or supervisor." Furthermore, Article 123 has become Article 124, providing that "A listed corporation shall have independent directors and the concrete measures shall be formulated by the State Council."

Generally speaking, US law and legal practices have had an important influence on European law: the reforms in continental European corporate governance over the last two decades highlight the efforts in terms of enacting corporate governance systems that may help protect minority shareholders of listed corporations by strengthening the shareholders' voices in corporate governance, such as the power to authorize or ratify some transactions and resolutions in potential conflicts of interest.[16] Many of the issues such as independent directors, compensation, auditing, accounting rules, voting, takeovers and stock market regulation seem to suggest that the shareholder primacy agenda and investors' protection are gaining attention.

The adoption of independent directors according to the Commission Recommendation of 15 February 2005 on the role of non-executive or supervisory directors of listed companies and on the committees of the (supervisory) board (2005/162/EC) (hereinafter "Commission Recommendation") – which shows the shareholder primacy view's strong influence on European company law[17] – aims to eliminate and prevent conflicts of interest[18] and particularly stresses the non-executive or supervisory directors' role in overseeing executive or managing directors and dealing with situations involving conflicts of interests to restore confidence in financial markets.[19] It has triggered the issue that Green Paper: The EU Corporate Governance Framework in 2011 (hereinafter "EU Green Paper of 2011") proposed in question (21) by asking "Do you think that minority shareholders need additional rights to represent their interests effectively in companies with controlling or dominating shareholders?"[20] A positive answer would justify the recourse to the multiple-winner

---

16 See Hopt, Klaus J.: „Aktienrecht unter amerikanischem Einfluss". In: *Festschrift für Claus-Wilhelm Canaris*. Beck: Munich, 2007, vol. 2, p. 105; Enriques, Luca / Volpin, Paolo: "Corporate Governance Reforms in Continental Europe". *Journal of Economic Perspectives*, Vol. 21, No. 1, 2007, pp. 117–140, 128–131.

17 See Sjafjell, Beate: *Towards a Sustainable European Company Law – A Normative Analysis of the Objectives of EU Law, with the Takeover Directive as a Test Case.* (European company law series, Vol. 3). Kluwer Law International: 2009, p. 53.

18 See Commission Recommendation, (2).

19 See Commission Recommendation, (3).

20 EU Green Paper of 2011, p. 17. It is a combination of legislation and soft law, namely national corporate governance codes applied on a "comply or explain" basis, which gives companies and their shareholders an important degree of flexibility. To identify the issues most relevant to good corporate governance in the EU and prepare the Green Paper, the Commission conducted interviews with a sample of listed companies from different Member States and different economic sectors, with different levels of capitalization and different shareholding structures. It also held meetings with corporate governance experts as well as representatives of the investor community and civil society.

voting systems,[21] such as cumulative voting. However, as reported in the Feedback Statement Summary of Responses to the Commission Green Paper on the EU Corporate Governance Framework (hereinafter "Feedback Statement"), the vast majority of respondents – sharing the view that minority shareholders are already sufficiently protected[22] – are opposed to the board representation of minority shareholders, arguing that additional rights are merely likely to increase the potential for abuse and that granting them would be contrary to shareholder equality.[23] Therefore, the EU Action Plan of European Company Law and Corporate Governance – a modern legal framework for more engaged shareholders and sustainable companies (hereinafter "EU Action Plan") – does not mention this system.

Thus, as a powerful measure to elect representatives of minority shareholders, cumulative voting has been replaced by independent directors in the US and was not adopted in the EU, which instead introduced independent directors. However, it is accepted in China, which emphasizes more its role in electing independent directors. This dissertation attempts to analyze the reasons for the declining trend of cumulative voting. In my mind, one reason is that the role of an independent director in controlling related-party transactions (RPTs) serves as an important alternative for cumulative voting, while the other reason is that cumulative voting has conflicts with the long governance established as the core corporate governance value by the US, the EU and China. Accordingly, rather than supporting one approach over another in the fundamental debate on corporate governance – i.e. the shareholder value vs. stakeholder value debate – it aspires to represent an intermediate "third way".[24] Based upon the different attitudes among the three economic giants for cumulative voting – which is a small but non-negligible system designed for minority

---

21 See Davies, Paul L. / Hopt, Klaus J.: "Corporate Boards in Europe – Accountability and Convergence". *American Journal Comparative Law*, Vol. 61, No. 2, 2013, pp. 301–375, 338.

22 "Many respondents advanced two arguments in particular: one being that additional rights are only likely to increase the potential for abuse by minority shareholders and are contrary to shareholders equality; the other that minority shareholders do not form a homogenous group." See Feedback Statement, p. 22.

23 See Feedback Statement, p. 16. Cumulative voting has been criticized as, in fact, allowing greater power to directors who are either shareholders themselves or hold the proxies of smaller shareholders. See Gordon, Jeffrey N.: "Institutions as Relational Investors: A New Look at Cumulative Voting". *Columbia Law Review*, Vol. 94, No. 1, 1.1994, pp. 124–192, 142–160; More obviously, cumulative voting cannot help the typical public shareholder in a listed company, who holds far less than the minimum proportion – one divided by the total number of directors – required to elect a single director. Clarke, Donald C.: "Nothing but Wind? The Past and Future of Comparative Corporate Governance". *American Journal of Comparative Law*, Vol. 59, No. 1, 2011, pp. 75–110, 89.

24 See Masouros, Pavlos E.: *Corporate Law and Economic Stagnation: How Shareholder Value and Short-Termism Contribute to the Decline of the Western Economies.* Eleven International Publishing: 28.1.2013, p. 271.

shareholders' protection in public listed companies (PLCs) – this dissertation attempts to show that despite the converge of corporate governance value among the US and EU as well as China, a persistence of diversity in corporate governance remains and it is unclear whether convergence is either desirable or inevitable.

The dissertation encompasses five chapters. The first chapter tries to provide a background of the adoption of cumulative voting and independent directors by generalizing the increasing of shareholders' protection in China and the EU as well as putting the emphasis on the fundamental reasons for the increasing of shareholders' protection, namely the reason for adopting cumulative voting and independent directors in China and EU – the global influence of US shareholder-centered model, which represents itself by the dispersed corporate ownership and the pressure of developing capital market. In the second chapter, it expounds the negative attitudes of the US and the EU towards cumulative voting and proposes that cumulative voting has been replaced by the independent directors. The subsequent chapter introduces the new form of cumulative voting in China and the justifications for its adoption, as well as its problems in practice. Although China's legislation encourages the use of cumulative voting in the listed corporations, the role of independent directors is much more strongly emphasized. In the fourth chapter, the dissertation focuses on the primary reason for the declining trend of cumulative voting, namely the role of independent directors and shareholders' meeting in controlling RPTs. The fifth chapter discusses the other important reason – conflicts between cumulative voting and long governance – which means that the interests of different stakeholders should be subject to the whole benefit of corporations and thus warrant a reasonable balance among them.

First Chapter: Increasing Minority Shareholders' Protection in China and the EU

Due to the agency problem caused by controlling shareholders, the globalization of capital markets and the rise of institutional investors as well as greater shareholder activism, it is clear that the shareholder primacy theory – which became preeminent in corporation law in Anglo-American jurisdictions – is now the global dominant theory. Professor Stephen Bainbridge has helpfully divided the theory into two limbs, namely the objective of the corporation should be to maximize shareholder wealth and shareholders should have ultimate control of the corporation.[25] The theory has been developed to the point where it now provides that directors are to manage the corporation in such a way that ensures the wealth of shareholders being maximized to the fullest. Put simply, this means that the directors will endeavor to make as much money as they can for the shareholders. Effectively, this can be seen as involving the directors in protecting and enhancing the investment of shareholders in the corporation.[26] Both China and the EU have introduced several systems for protecting shareholders. This part focuses on the influence of such model, which constitutes the main reason for adopting cumulative voting in China and the discussion of minority representatives in the EU.

A. Concentrated Corporate Ownership and Rising Institutional Investors

The influence of the shareholder-centered model first represents itself by the dispersed corporate ownership. The corporate governance stream in finance research has long established that a firm's ownership structure – describing the relationships among the stakeholders – is the most significant factor influencing the system of corporate governance and performance.[27] According to the German Stock Corporations

25 See Bainbridge, Stephen M.: "Director Primacy: The Means and Ends of Corporate Governance". *Northwestern University Law Review*, Vol. 97, No. 2, Winter 2003, pp. 547–618, 573.

26 Friedman M.: "The Social Responsibility of Business is to Increase its Profits". *New York Times Magazine*, 13.9.1970, Section 6, p. 33.

27 See Shleifer, Andrei / Vishny, Robert W.: "A Survey of Corporate Governance". *Journal of Finance*, Vol. 52, No. 2, 1997, pp. 737–783, 738; Demsetz, Harold / Lehn, Kenneth: "The Structure of Corporate Ownership: Causes and Consequences". *Journal of Political Economy*, Vol. 93, No. 6, 1985, pp. 1155–1177, 1155; Cubbin, John / Leech, Dennis: "The Effect of Shareholding Dispersion on the Degree of Control in British Companies: Theory and Measurement". *Economic Journal*, Vol. 93, No. 370, 1983, pp. 351–369, 353; Fama, E.F. / Jensen M.C.: "The separation of ownership and control". *Journal of Law and Economics*, Vol. 26, No. 2, 1983, pp. 301–328, 301; Jensen M.C. /

Act (Aktiengesellschaftsrecht, hereinafter "AktG"), a majority stake of less than 75% allows wide control over the management of the corporation but is subject to a blocking minority, which is constituted by a minority stake greater than 25% and may be able to prevent issues of new shares or the dismissal of members of the supervisory board. For example, Article 182 (1) rules that a resolution to increase the share capital against contributions shall require a majority of not less than three-quarters of the share capital represented at the passing of the resolution. Furthermore, Article 202 (1) and (2) provide that the articles may authorize the management board – for a period not exceeding five years after registration of the company – to increase the share capital up to a specified par value (authorized capital) by issuing new shares against contributions. Such authorization may also be granted by amendment of the articles for a period not exceeding five years as from the date or registration of such amendment of the articles. The resolution of the shareholders' meeting shall require a majority of not less than three-quarters of the share capital represented at the passing of the resolution. In addition, Article103 (1) stipulates that members of the supervisory board who have been elected by the shareholders' meeting without being bound by nominations may be removed pursuant to the resolution of the shareholders' meeting prior to the expiration of their term of office. Such a resolution shall require a majority of not less than three-quarters of the votes cast. Moreover, the blockholdings of smaller than 5 percent are classified as being widely held. For example, Article 327a(1) rules that upon request of a shareholder holding 95 percent of the share capital (principal shareholder), the shareholders meeting of a stock corporation or partnership limited by shares may resolve the transfer of the other shareholders' (minority shareholders') shares to the principal shareholder against the payment of adequate cash compensation. A common measure of ownership concentration is whether one shareholder owns at least 20 percent of a company's voting rights, whereby such a shareholder is called a "controlling shareholder."[28]

The controlling shareholder could control the development of companies[29] because their large holdings justify an investment in monitoring[30] and help them

---

Mecklin W.H.: "Theory of the firm Managerial behavior, agency costs and ownership structure". *Journal of Financial Economics*, Vol. 3, No. 4, 1976, pp. 305–360, 310; La Porta, Rafael / Lopez-de-Silanes, Florencio / Shleifer, Anderei: "Corporate Ownership Around the World". *Journal of Finance* Vol. 54, No. 2, 1999, pp. 471–517, 471.

28 See Enriques, Luca / Volpin, Paolo: "Corporate Governance Reforms in Continental Europe". *Journal of Economic Perspectives*, Vol. 21, No. 1, 2007, pp. 117–140, 118.

29 See Lu Tong: "Corporate Governance in medium and small private PLCs: Characters and Problem". *Enterprise Business*, Vol. 4, 2013, pp. 5–15, 7.

30 See Bainbridge, Stephen M.: "The Politics of Corporate Governance: Roe's Strong Managers, Weak Owners". *Harvard Journal of Law & Public Policy*, Vol. 18, No. 1–10, 1995, pp. 671–737, 692; Unitrin, Inc. v. American Gen. Corp., 651 A.2d 1361, 1383 n. 33 (Del. 1995) (stating that the fact "[t]hat institutions held a high percentage of Unitrin's stock is not as significant as the fact that the relatively concentrated percentage of stockholdings would facilitate a bidder's ability to communicate the

overcome the collective action problem as well as have an incentive to exercise their voice through activism, which is primarily a matter of campaigning and voting at shareholder meetings,[31] while the concentrated ownership introduces secondary agency relations because large investors have the possibility – as well as an incentive – to expropriate minority shareholders by benefiting themselves from a disproportionately large share of the firm's revenues.[32] The structure combines the agency problem of the firm being controlled by an insider who owns a fraction of the equity with the agency problem of the firm being controlled by an insider who is insulated from the influence of other shareholders and the market of corporate control.[33] The fundamental problem is that the large investors might try to treat themselves preferentially at the expense of other investors and employees. Their ability to do so is particularly strong if their control rights are significantly in excess of their cash flow rights.[34] Bebchuk, Kraakman and Triantis show that such structures have the potential to create very large agency costs that are an order of magnitude larger than those associated with controlling shareholders who hold a majority of the cash flow rights

---

merits of its position"); Minow, Nell: "Shareholders, Stakeholders, and Boards of Directors". *Stetson Law Review*, Vol. 21, No. 1, 1991, pp. 197–244, 227 (arguing that "large institutional investors... are just too big to sell out of a company every time they disagree with management"); Tobin, James M.: "The Squeeze on Directors-Inside Is Out". *Business Lawyer*, Vol. 49, No.4, 1994, pp. 1707–1760, 1731 (stating that selling a large stake of a firm would depress the price of the stock).

31 See Pound J.: "Beyond takeovers: Politics comes to corporate control". *Harvard Business Review*, Vol. 70, No. 2, 1992, pp. 83–93, 84; Smith M.P.: "Shareholder activism by institutional investors: Evidence from CalPERS". *Journal of Finance*, Vol. 51, No. 1, 1996, pp. 227–252, 227.

32 See Shleifer, Andrei / Vishny, Robert W.: "A Survey of Corporate Governance". *Journal of Finance*, Vol. 52, No. 2, 1997, pp. 737–783, 739.

33 See Jensen, M.C.: "Agency Costs of Free Cash Flow, Corporate Finance and Takeovers". *American Economic Review*, Vol. 76, No. 2, 1986, pp. 323–329; Stulz R.M.: "Managerial Control of Voting Rights: Financing Policies and the Market for Corporate Control". *Journal of Financial Economics*, Vol. 20, 1988, pp. 25–54; Cronqvist, Henrik / Nilsson, Mattias: "Agency Costs of Controlling Minority Shareholders". *The Journal of Financial and Quantitative Analysis*, Vol. 38, No. 4, 12.2003, pp. 695–719, 699.

34 See Grossman, Sanford J. / Hart, Oliver D.: "One Share/One Vote and the Market for Corporate Control". *Journal of Financial Economics*, Vol. 20, January-March 1988, pp. 175–202; Harris, Milton / Raviv, Artur: "The Theory of Capital Structure". *The Journal of Finance*, Vol. 46, No. 1, 3.1991, pp. 297–355; "This cost of concentrated ownership becomes particularly important when others – such as minority investors – have their own firm-specific investments to make, which are distorted because of possible expropriation by the large investors." Shleifer, Andrei / Vishny, Robert W.: "A Survey of Corporate Governance". *Journal of Finance*, Vol. 52, No. 2, 1997, pp. 737–783, 758; Bebchuk, Lucian A. / Weisbach, Michael S.: "The State of Corporate Governance Research". *The Review of Financial Studies*, Vol. 23, No. 3, Corporate Governance, 3.2010, pp. 939–961, 948.

in their companies.[35] Such abuse of power may be carried out in various ways, including the extraction of direct private benefits through excessive pay and bonuses for employed family members and associates, inappropriate related party transactions, systematic bias in business decisions and changes in the capital structure through special issuance of shares favoring the controlling shareholder.[36] Financial scandals in companies with concentrated ownership, like Parmalat, in which – unlike Enron – the family-controlled management and advisors structured the group's various financial arrangements to enrich members of the Tanzi family at the expense of the shareholders and creditors.[37] As the Article III A 2 of the OECD Principles rules, minority shareholders should be protected from abusive actions by – or in the interest of – controlling shareholders acting either directly or indirectly and should have effective means of redress.[38]

I. China

It took just three decades for China to transform itself into the world's second largest economy. The achievement of China's economic results from its market-oriented economic reform, which started in 1978. During the economic reform, a major task was to transform the planned economy – which was previously dominated by state-owned enterprises (SOEs) – into a market-oriented one, whereby privately

---

35 See Bebchuk, Lucian A. / Kraakman, Reinier / Triantis, George: "Stock Pyramids, Cross-Ownership and Dual Class Equity: The Mechanisms and Agency Costs of Separating Control from Cash-Flow Rights". In: Morck R. (ed.): *Concentrated Corporate Ownership.* NBER: 2000, pp. 445–460; Bebchuk, Lucian A.: "A Rent-Protection Theory of Corporate Ownership and Control". In: National Bureau of Economic Research: *Working Paper 7203*, 1999, retrieved 12.3.2013, from http://www.nber.org/papers/w7203.

36 See *OECD Principles*, pp. 41–42. "Inefficient controlling shareholders have given rise to a huge variety of sophisticated techniques to tunnel assets, profits, and corporate opportunities."

37 See Coffee, John C.: "A Theory of Corporate Scandals: Why the US and Europe Differ". *Oxford Rev of Economic Policy*, Vol. 21, No.2, 2005, pp. 198–211, 200; Ferrarini G. / Giudici P.: "Financial Scandals and the Role of Private Enforcement: The Parmalat Case". In: Armour, John / McCahery, Joseph (eds.): *After Enron: Improving Corporate Law and Modernising Securities Regulation in Europe and the US*". Oxford University Press, 2006, pp. 159–213, p. 159; La Porta, Rafael / Lopez-de-Silanes, Florencio / Shleifer, Anderei: "Corporate Ownership Around the World". *Journal of Finance* Vol. 54, No. 2, 1999, pp. 471–517; Bertrand, Marianne / Mehta, Paras / Mullainathan, Sendhil: "Ferreting Out Tunneling: An Application to Indian Business Groups". *The Quarterly Journal of Economics*, Vol. 117, No. 1, 2.2002, pp. 121–148; Holmen, Martin / Högfeldt, Peter: "Pyramidal Discounts: Tunneling or Overinvestment?". *International Review of Finance*, Vol. 9, No. 1&2, 2009, pp. 133–175; Friedman E. / Johnson S. / Mitton T.: "Propping and Tunneling". *Journal of Comparative Economics*, Vol. 31, No. 4, 12.2003, pp. 732–750.

38 See *OECD Principles*, p. 20.

owned corporations and many novel governance structures and corporate law concepts have accompanied the shift from a closed, centralized system to a market-oriented economy.[39] Through transforming SOEs into different kinds of limited liability companies or shareholding companies, both central and local governments would delegate more freedom to managers and continue to enhance productivity, helping the state to retain control through its status as the largest shareholder while shielding the state from the survival or loss of the enterprise.[40] Today, the aggregate number of PLCs in China has reached more than 3,000. Moreover, as disclosed by the supervision and management meeting of the State-owned Assets Supervision and Administration Commission of the State Council (SASAC) on January 10, 2013, there were 953 SOEs being PLCs in 2012, accounting for 38.5% of all A-share PLCs. Their market value reached 13.71 trillion RMB, accounting for 51.4% of total market capitalization of A-share PLCs.[41] Therefore, after the reform, the SOEs still possess a dominant position within China's economy.

The Chinese stock market can be classified into two broad categories according to their tradability on secondary markets before 2005. Non-tradable stocks include state shares, legal person shares and employee shares, while the tradable counterpart is held by diffuse shareholders. With respect to the official definition of the non-tradable part, state shares are held by government agencies or state-authorized organizations at either the central or local level, whereas legal person shares are those owned by domestic institutions and enterprises with a legal person status. This split-share system – which was a unique product from the very early stage of the Chinese stock market – was the result of a compromise between the need to privatize SOEs and the healthy, gradual development of the stock market by its nature.[42] "What the split-share system created was basically a lock-in system which prohibited most shares from being traded but allowed a portion of ownership to be

39 See Lin, Chien-Chung: "The Chinese Independent Director Mechanism under Changing Macro Political-Economic Settings: A Review of Its First Decade and Two Possible Models for the Future". *American University Business Law Review*, Vol. 1, No. 2, 2012, pp. 263–336, 265.

40 See Lin, Chien-Chung: "The Chinese Independent Director Mechanism under Changing Macro Political-Economic Settings: A Review of Its First Decade and Two Possible Models for the Future". *American University Business Law Review*, Vol. 1, No. 2, 2012, pp. 263–336, 265.

41 See *Shanghai Shang Bao* [Shanghai Commercial Daily], 11.1.2013, retrieved 14.3.2013, from http://www.shbiz.com.cn/Item/198957.aspx .

42 See Wang, Wallace Wen-Yeu / Chen, Jian-Lin: "Bargaining for Compensation in the Shadow of Regulatory Giving: The Case of Stock Trading Rights Reform in China". *Columbia Journal of Asian Law*, Vol. 20, No. 298, 2006, pp. 298–356, 312–318; Kister, Sandra P.: "China's Share-Structure Reform: An Opportunity to Move Beyond Practical Solutions to Practical Problems". *Columbia Journal of Transnational Law*, Vol. 45, No. 1, 2006, pp. 312–363, 313.

freely-transferable."[43] In the early stage of SOEs reform, the idea of this design was to set up a modern stock market with an appropriate amount of equity in the market, attract both domestic and foreign investors to invest and help transform SOEs into partially private companies.[44] However, the distinction between tradable and non-tradable shares also created several serious issues. Limiting the tradability of shares controlled by the state meant that the state was locked into many enterprises. "The State still was responsible for their management and financial performance but could not enjoy the fruit of a company's better performance."[45] From the viewpoint of private investors, the split-share structure led to their minority position always being subject to the majority's mistreatment and prevented them from obtaining larger control to further influence their company.

As a result, in 2005, Chinese security authorities started an initiative to repeal the split-share system.[46] This was achieved through a private negotiation among non-tradable shareholders and tradable share owners.[47] Through providing certain forms of compensation to tradable share owners by non-transferable shareholders, both of them can reach an agreement based upon which securities authorities may lift the non-trading restriction of the non-tradable shares and allow those shares to be traded on the stock exchange.[48] On December 25, 2006, more than 94% of listed companies on the Shanghai and Shenzhen stock exchanges had completed their negotiation and successfully repealed the non-trading restriction of non-tradable shares, while 74 companies were in the process of doing so.[49]

---

43 Kister, Sandra P.: "China's Share-Structure Reform: An Opportunity to Move Beyond Practical Solutions to Practical Problems". *Columbia Journal of Transnational Law*, Vol. 45, No. 1, 2006, pp. 312–363, 314.

44 See Kister, Sandra P.: "China's Share-Structure Reform: An Opportunity to Move Beyond Practical Solutions to Practical Problems". *Columbia Journal of Transnational Law*, Vol. 45, No. 1, 2006, pp. 312–363, 314.

45 See Wang, Wallace Wen-Yeu / Chen, Jian-Lin: "Bargaining for Compensation in the Shadow of Regulatory Giving: The Case of Stock Trading Rights Reform in China". *Columbia Journal of Asian Law*, Vol. 20, No. 298, 2006, pp. 298–356, 306.

46 See Wang, Wallace Wen-Yeu / Chen, Jian-Lin: "Bargaining for Compensation in the Shadow of Regulatory Giving: The Case of Stock Trading Rights Reform in China". *Columbia Journal of Asian Law*, Vol. 20, No. 298, 2006, pp. 298–356, 309–312.

47 See Wang, Wallace Wen-Yeu / Chen, Jian-Lin: "Bargaining for Compensation in the Shadow of Regulatory Giving: The Case of Stock Trading Rights Reform in China". *Columbia Journal of Asian Law*, Vol. 20, No. 298, 2006, pp. 298–356, 332.

48 See Wang, Wallace Wen-Yeu / Chen, Jian-Lin: "Bargaining for Compensation in the Shadow of Regulatory Giving: The Case of Stock Trading Rights Reform in China". *Columbia Journal of Asian Law*, Vol. 20, No. 298, 2006, pp. 298–356, 339.

49 See Huang Jintao: "Wei Gu Gai Gong Si Jiang Bei Cha Yi Hua, Zhang Die Fu Xian Zhi Jiang Bei Xian Zhi Wei Bai Fen Zhi Wu" [If Nor Completing Share Reform, Companies Will Need To Face Additional Restriction in Trading, Including Price Trading Range Will Be Set To 5% Each Day]. *Shang hai zheng quan bao* [Shanghai Securities News] 25.12.2006, retrieved 14.3.2013, from http://news.xinhuanet.com/

Although the legal restriction of non-trading was repealed and the situation has been gradually improving through private investor participation and business competition development, the capital structure of many of the publicly traded Chinese companies is still concentrated in the hands of the state, local governments and rising wealthy entrepreneurs.[50] According to the "Evaluation of Corporate Governance in Top 100 PLCs of China in 2012", as the most important indicator judging ownership concentration, the average number of shareholdings of the largest shareholders remained to be more than 40%, despite having declined between 2010 and 2012, while the maximum shareholding ratio occupied by the top five shareholders reached 90% and the average number of shareholdings even hit 59%.[51] In 2012, there were 84 listed corporations whose largest shareholder was the state, which was not only the second largest shareholder of 49 corporations, but also the third largest stockholder of 39 corporations, while only 13 corporations found their largest shareholders in private enterprises.[52] Therefore, the remaining state capital power and its impact on corporate law and the economic development of China continue to be extensive.

State ownership of corporations leads to the phenomenon of "absent ownership" (suoyouzhe quewei): it is not the collective action problems, but rather the internal and organizational problems of the state as a shareholder, which in China is often represented by various government agencies, that prevent effective shareholder monitoring. "Specifically speaking, while the ultimate ownership of state-held shares rests with the central/local government, control and monitoring responsibilities are delegated to various government departments or agencies which normally hold voting rights but no cash flow rights, and as bureaucrats, they are unlikely to have sufficient incentives to closely monitor the operation of state-owned corporations under their control."[53] Consequently, the listed corporations are mainly controlled by top management and directors who can easily manipulate the board

---

stock/2006-12/25/content_5527569.htm; For a complete list of companies that have finished transformation, see China Securities Regulatory Commission: List of Companies, List of Trading Reform, retrieved 14.3.2013, from http://www.csrc.gov.en/pub/newsite/flb/lfzl/jnlfssyzn/xzzf/200612/t20061230_77097.htm.

50 See Imai, Ken: *Explaining the Persistence of State-Ownership in China.* Inst. of Developing Economies: Discussion Paper No. 64, 2006, retrieved 15.1.2013, from http://ir.ide.go.jp/dspace/bitstream/2344/130/3/ARRIDE_Discussion_No.064_imai.pdf, p. 4.

51 See *Evaluation of Corporate Governance in Top 100 PLCs of China in 2012*, retrieved 15.1.2013, from http://wenku.baidu.com/view/74f36a20a5e9856a561260d6.html., p. 16.

52 See *Evaluation of Corporate Governance in Top 100 PLCs of China in 2012*, retrieved 15.1.2013, from http://wenku.baidu.com/view/74f36a20a5e9856a561260d6.html., p. 16.

53 Zou, Hong / Adams, Mike B.: "Corporate ownership, equity risk and returns in the People's Republic of China". *Journal of International Business Studies*, Vol. 39, No. 7, 10/11. 2008, pp. 1149–1168, 1151.

and plunder the assets of the corporation.[54] Such a prominent complaint regarding the current regime governing the powers and responsibilities of enterprise managers is “insider control” (neibu ren kongzhi).

Private PLCs account for 90.2% in GEM (growth enterprise market) and occupy 77.59% in medium-sized and small PLCs, while they only take up 29.44% on the main boards of PLCs. In terms of the ownership structure, by the end of 2011 the average shareholding percentage of the largest shareholders – which always represent families or natural persons in the listed companies of GEM – reached 33.55%, rising to 37.10% in medium-sized and small PLCs.[55] The presence of a controlling shareholder can reduce an agency problem by introducing closer monitoring of the management due to their larger stakes in a firm.[56] With a controlling shareholder, the fundamental governance problem is not opportunism by executives and directors at the expense of public shareholders at large, but rather opportunism by the controlling shareholder at the expense of the minority shareholders.[57]

The current agency problem in PLCs in China is more complicated. Some public companies remain in the hands of the state, whereby the agency problem exists between management and minority shareholders with incidental and sporadic stewardship intervention by state controlling shareholders. Moreover, the growing number of private parties acquiring control of public companies also necessitates regulations addressing the controlling agency problem.[58] Both controlling shareholders and managers may engage in self-beneficial trades, advancing personal, familial and political agendas that hamper corporate performance, “expropriating” the profits of lower-tier companies in a pyramid business group.[59] In this respect, Chinese scholars and policy-makers have been concerned to search for new mechanisms of corporate governance – such as cumulative voting and independent directors – to protect minority shareholders. According to Article 1 para.2 of Independent Directors Opinion, pursuant to the requirements of the relevant laws and regulations, these Guiding Opinions and the company’s articles of association, an independent director should conscientiously perform his duties and responsibilities, safeguard

54 Shanghai Research Center of Security Markets, Chinese Corporate Governance Report: *Independence and Effectiveness of Board.* Fudan University Press: 2004, p. 35.
55 Tong, Lu: “Corporate Governance in medium and small private PLCs: Characters and Problem”. *Enterprise Business*, Vol. 4, 2013, pp. 5–15, 7.
56 *OECD Principles*, pp. 41–42.
57 Bebchuk, Lucian A. / Weisbach, Michael S.: “The State of Corporate Governance Research”. *The Review of Financial Studies*, Vol. 23, No. 3, Corporate Governance, 3.2010, pp. 939–961, 948.
58 See Weng, Charlie Xiaochuan: “Chinese Shareholder Protection and the Influence of the US Law: The Idiosyncratic Economic Realities and Mismatched Agency Problem Solutions”. *Securities Regulation Law Journal*, 11.4.2012, pp. 1–36, 19.
59 See Claessens, S. / Djankov, S. / Lang L.H.P.: “The separation of ownership and control in East Asian corporations”. *Journal of Financial Economics*, Vol. 58, No. 1–2, 2000, pp. 81–112.

the company's overall interests and, in particular, pay attention to ensure that the lawful rights and interests of small and medium shareholders are not prejudiced.

II. European Union

In close similarity with China, the corporations of many European continental countries have traditionally been seen as having more concentrated ownership, with groups of shareholders such as families, corporate groups or financial institutions owning significant percentages of shares.[60] As the EU Green Paper of 2011 states, "Minority shareholder engagement is difficult in companies with controlling shareholders, which remain the predominant governance model in European companies."[61] For example, the German corporate ownership was traditionally known for its concentrated ownership and extensive cross holdings by banks, insurance companies and industrial conglomerates and is characterized by coalitions of active majority shareholders, which are primarily families and other companies,[62] while the publicly traded shareholdings are also dispersed and often in the minority.[63]

Due to the globalization of the economy and the development of a European capital market, similar to China, the rise of institutional shareholdings,[64] primarily insurance companies, pension funds and collective investment schemes as well as hedge funds reflects a significant development. Non-national shareholders hold some 44% of the shares in EU listed companies. Most of these investors are institutional investors and asset managers. It was reported that the first signs of shareholder activism were detected in 2010 when Hermes – an activist investor domiciled in the UK – tried to block the re-election of Claus Wucherer as chairperson of the management board of Infineon Technologies AG. Although only 27.5% of shareholders voted against his reappointment, it was seen as significant among public companies.[65] Institutional shareholding is prevalent in some European countries,

---

60 See Marco Becht, Ailsa Röell, Blockholdings in Europe: An International Comparison, European Economic Review, Vol. 43, No. 4–6, 1999, pp. 1049–1056, 1049.

61 EU Green Paper of 2011, p. 3.

62 See Sjafjell, Beate: *Towards a Sustainable European Company Law – A Normative Analysis of the Objectives of EU Law, with the Takeover Directive as a Test Case.* (European company law series, Vol. 3). Kluwer Law International: 2009, p. 75; Becht, Marco / Röell, Ailsa: "Blockholdings in Europe: An International Comparison". *European Economic Review*, Vol. 43, No. 4–6, 1999, pp. 1049–1056, 1049.

63 See Pinto, Arthur R.: "Globalization and the Study of Comparative Corporate Governance". *Wisconsin International Law Journal*, Vol. 23, No. 477, 2005, pp. 477–511, 482.

64 See La Porta, Rafael / Lopez-de-Silanes, Florencio / Shleifer, Anderei: "Corporate Ownership Around the World". *Journal of Finance* Vol. 54, No. 2, 1999, pp. 471–517; Faccio M. / Lang L.H.P.: "The Ultimate Ownership of Western European Corporations". *Journal of Financial Economics*, Vol. 65, No. 3, 2001, pp. 365–395.

65 See Altman, Ken: *Current Corporate Governance Trends in Germany*, 14.5.2010, retrieved 12.7.14, from http://blogs.law.harvard.edu/corpgov/2010/05/14/current-corporate-governance-trends-in-germany/.

such as Sweden with 85% of the total shareholding in listed companies, in France with 40% of the CAC 40 companies, and similarly for the top-tier Swiss listed companies. In other European countries, institutional investment still lags behind owing to special factors: in Italy due to prevailing blockholder control and in Germany, where a lack of significant pension assets corresponds with a lack of deep capital markets, particularly given the labor's dependence on the state old age retirement and pension system rather than on their own saving and investing. Pension assets in the United Kingdom, Switzerland and the Netherlands exceed their gross domestic product (GDP),[66] while German pension assets only account for 498 billion Euro, significantly less than half of the total market capitalization of German equity.[67] For example, the largest German public pension fund is the "Versorgungsanstalt des Bundes und der Länder"(hereinafter "VBL"), which provides occupational pensions for public employees at the federal and state levels and has over 16 billion Euro under management,[68] compared to CalPERS with 257 billion Dollars.[69]

Despite domestic institutional investors playing a minor role in Germany, foreign institutional investors are assumed to hold the majority of shares in most German blue chips (DAX-30 companies),[70] where foreign shareholding – in particular foreign institutional shareholding – is very considerable; an example is the Deutsche Börse AG, where the large private German banks sold out their shareholdings some years ago under a changed tax system. According to data from the Deutsche Bundesbank, considerably more than 40% of shares – in terms of market value – are in the hands of foreign investors.[71] More generally, the Rhineland capitalism model with its close

66 Watson, Towers: *Global Pension Assets Study*, retrieved 12.7.2014, from http://www.towerswatson. com/en/Insights/IC-Types/Survey-Research-Results/2013/01/Global-Pensions-Asset-Study-2013, p. 7.

67 "About 170 billion euro of occupational pension assets is invested in DAX 30-companies, which invest about 30% in equity." See Watson, Towers: *Global Pension Assets Study*, retrieved 12.7.2014, from http://www.towerswatson.com/en/Insights/IC-Types/Survey-Research-Results/2013/01/Global-Pensions-Asset-Study-2013, p. 13.

68 VBL: *Die Vermögensanlage der VBL*, retrieved 5.5.2014, from http://www.vbl.de/de/wir_ueber_uns/ vermoegensanlage/.

69 CalPERS: *CalPERS Investments* 5.5.2014, retrieved 12.7.2014, from http://www.calpers.ca.gov/index.jsp? bc=/investments/home.xml.

70 Ernst & Young: *Wem gehört der DAX? Analyse der Aktienärsstruktur der DAX-Unternehmen*, 27.4.2012, retrieved 15.7.2014, from http://www.handelsblatt. com/finanzen/boerse-maerkte/boerse-inside/boersenindex-wem-der-dax-gehoert/8187798.html.

71 Deutsche Bundesbank Eurosystem: *Statistic Über Wertpapierinvestments*, 2012, retrieved 15.7.2014, from http://www.bundesbank.de/Redaktion/DE/Downloads/Service/Meldewesen/Bankenstatistik/Depotstatistik/berichtsschema_statistik_wert papierinvestments.pdf?__blob=publicationFile.

intertwining of German industry and banks has been disappearing over the years[72] and foreign institutions potentially play more of a role in prompting changes in corporate governance practices compared with domestic institutions.[73] With the increase in external funding of occupational pensions – mostly by DAX-30 companies – the employee representatives of the supervisory board can no longer be considered representatives of a "different form of capital".[74]

Generally speaking, the German system of financing, managing and controlling enterprises has experienced profound transform in the past two decades. Globalization of the economy and liberalization of capital markets are drivers of the debate concerning corporate governance, since worldwide operating institutional investors have played an increasingly decisive role in financing German enterprises. If a company wants to acquire capital, it turns to the national and international capital market.[75] The situation in Germany began to change with the increasing internationalization of capital markets that emerged in the mid-1980s. Some of the largest German corporations began to rely more on foreign investors. "It was mainly economic difficulties that attracted public attention in the 1980s when shareholders were rediscovered as investors, resulting in companies satisfying their financial needs by capital increases or the sale of a corporation's common shares to public investors."[76] In recent years, global and European portfolio investors have played an increasing role in financing German enterprises and corporate governance.[77] The ownership structure of the 30 largest public corporations has rapidly evolved towards the Anglo-American model of widely spread ownership in recent years. Between 2001 and 2009, the average proportion of shares held by diverse investors in DAX-Enterprises increased from 64.5% to 82.6%. Among the DAX-Enterprises, majority shareholders only exist in Beiersdorf AG (50.46% in possession of Maxinvest AG) and Volkswagen

72 See Davies, Paul L. / Hopt, Klaus J.: "Corporate Boards in Europe – Accountability and Convergence". *American Journal Comparative Law*, Vol. 61, No. 2, 2013, pp. 301–375, 361.

73 See Gillan, S. / Starks L.: "Corporate Governance, Corporate Ownership, and the Role of Institutional Investors: A Global Perspective". *Journal of Applied Finance*, Vol. 13, No. 2, 2003, pp. 4–22, 14; Ferreira M. / Matos P.: "The Colors of Investors' Money: The Role of Institutional Investors around the World?". *Journal of Financial Economics*, Vol. 88, No. 3, 2008, pp. 499–533, 515.

74 See Roth, Markus: *Private Altersvorsorge: Betriebsrentenrecht und individuelle Vorsorge: Eine rechtsvergleichende Gesamtschau.* Mohr Siebeck: 1st Edition, 2009, pp. 209–210.

75 Plessis J.J. Du / Großfeld B. / Luttermann C. / Saenger I. / Sandrock O.: *German Corporate Governance in International and European Context.* Springer: 2nd Edition, 2012, p. 10.

76 Plessis J.J. Du / Großfeld B. / Luttermann C. / Saenger I. / Sandrock O.: *German Corporate Governance in International and European Context.* Springer: 2nd Edition, 2012, p. 10.

77 See Plessis J.J. Du / Großfeld B. / Luttermann C. / Saenger I. / Sandrock O.: *German Corporate Governance in International and European Context.* Springer: 2nd Edition, 2012, p. 10.

AG (50.74% in possession of Porsche Automobil Holding SE), where not the equity shares, but rather the preferred shares are represented in DAX-Enterprise, which is regarded as 100% shares being held by disperse investors.[78]

Despite the dramatic growth of dispersed ownership of German public corporations, according to the EU Green Paper of 2011, the corporation with controlling shareholders remains the dominant model in the EU and the ownership of companies is not so decentralized as being classified as the wide dispersion of stock ownership.[79] Concentrated corporate ownership gives rise to its own particular agency problems or potential conflicts of interest, namely the agency problem of controlling shareholders taking advantage of the minority shareholders in publicly traded corporations. Furthermore, with increasingly dispersed ownership and the rise of institutional investors in continental European countries, there is clearly a rise of activism among institutional investors who are also concerned about the potential for exploitation, given the likelihood that – as minority owners and largely passive owners – they may be exploited by other more powerful owners with greater access to private information.[80] Institutional investors may choose to communicate their views to other shareholders[81] and provide an effective lobby group to advance the protections for minority shareholders in the jurisdictions with concentrated shareholders by promoting the independence of directors.[82]

B. Pressure of Developing a Capital Market

The influence of the shareholder-centered model represents itself in the pressure of developing a capital market. All large-scale firms share a key common function: "Capital must be gathered, management must be selected and disciplined, and information must be transmitted to core decision-makers. A firm not adopting the best structure would be hurt either in its profits and value or in its ability to raise

78 As the most important German Stock Index, DAX measures the development of 30 largest enterprises with the highest sale volume in German capital market and represents about 80% capital in stock exchange of Germany. Retrieved 20.3.2013, from http://www.bpb.de/nachschlagen/zahlen-und-fakten/globalisierung/52596/aktionaersstruktur-dax.

79 See *EU Green Paper of 2011*, p. 16.

80 See Clark, Gordon L.: "Financial Valuation of the German Model: The Negative Relationship Between Ownership Concentration and Public Market Returns, 1997–2001". *Economic Geography*, Vol. 81, No. 1, 2005, pp. 11–29, 24.

81 See Choi, Stephen: "Proxy Issue Proposals: Impact of the 1992 SEC Proxy Reforms". *Journal of Law, Economics, & Organization*, Vol. 16, No. 1, 4.2000, pp. 233–268, 260.

82 Stapledon, Geof P.: *Institutional Shareholders and Corporate Governance*. Clarendon Press: 1995, p. 4; Gordon, Jeffrey N.: "The Rise of Independent Directors in the United States, 1950–2005: Of Shareholder Value and Stock Market Prices". *Stanford Law Review*, Vol. 59, No. 6, 2007, pp. 1465–1568. The role of institutional investors in improving corporate governance will be discussed in details in the Second Chapter.

new capital. Countries that fail to adopt efficient rules would inflict costs on their corporations, which would then be worth less and would then be less able to raise capital; as a result, firms, factories, and businesses might suffer, or they might migrate away from the country."[83] If there is a prosperous equity market, corporations have more money from investors to expand the scale of their production and operation. As Hansmann and Kraakman hold, shareholders may promote efficiency and the maximization of aggregate wealth for the benefit of society as a whole because social welfare in a competitive environment is served by maximizing corporation value, thereby generally advancing economic efficiency and increasing social wealth.[84] One study concluded that: "Empirical evidence indicates that increasing shareholder value does not conflict with the long-run interests of other stakeholders. Winning corporations seem to create relatively greater values for all stakeholders. Shareholders are the only stakeholders of a corporation who simultaneously maximize everyone's claim in maximizing their own."[85] The emerging consensus flows from the "widespread disenchantment with a privileged role for managers, employees, or the state in corporate affairs" and the growing belief – based upon "logic and experience" – that shareholder-oriented corporations are the best means to achieve the end of "aggregate social welfare".[86] The shareholder value objective is likely to hold greater importance and will drive the conception of the board in competitive

83 Bebchuk, Lucian A. / Roe, Mark J.: "A Theory of Path Dependence in Corporate Ownership and Governance". *Stanford Law Review*, Vol. 52, No. 1, 11.1999, pp. 127–170, 134. See also Easterbrook, Frank H. / Fischel, Daniel R.: *The economic structure of corporate law*. Harvard University Press: 1991, p. 212–218 (arguing that competition induces convergence in state rules); Demsetz, Harold: "The Structure of Ownership and the Theory of the Firm". *Journal of Law and Economics*, Vol. 26, No. 2, Corporations and Private Property: A Conference Sponsored by the Hoover Institution, 6.1983, pp. 375–390 (arguing that there is an ineluctable pressure on corporate structures toward efficiency).

84 See Hansmann, Henry / Kraakman, Reinier: "The End of History for Corporate Law". *Georgetown Law Review*, Vol. 89, No. 2, 2000, pp. 439–473, 443; See also Baums, Theodor / Scott, Kenneth E.: "Taking Shareholder Protection Seriously? Corporate Governance in the United States and Germany". *The American Journal of Comparative Law*, Vol. 53, No. 1, 2005, pp. 31–75, 35; O'Sullivan M.: "The innovative enterprise and corporate governance". *Cambridge Journal of Economics*, Vol. 24, No, 4, 2000, pp. 393–416, 395.

85 See Copeland T. / Koller T. / Murrin J.: *Valuation, Measuring and Managing, McKinsey & Company Inc.* 5th Edition, 26.7.2010, p. 22.

86 See Ireland, Paddy: "Shareholder Primacy and the Distribution of Wealth". *The Modern Law Review*, Vol. 68, No. 1, 2005, pp. 49–81, 73; "Corporate enterprise should be organized and operated to serve the interests of society as a whole, and that the interests of shareholders deserve no greater weight in this social calculus than do the interests of any other members of society. The point is simply that now, as a consequence of both logic and experience, there is a consensus that the best means to this end (that is, the pursuit of aggregate social welfare) is to make corporate managers strongly accountable to shareholder interests and, at least in direct terms,

global capital and product markets.[87] The critical point of convergence is pressure in the case of public companies, the competition for shareholders and international lobbying, as well as the stronger dependence of more firms on international capital markets.[88] Competition for capital under conditions of mobility will drive jurisdictions to adopt more shareholder-friendly rules.[89] Legal constraints on the ability of controlling shareholders to expropriate minority shareholders could reduce the cost of outside equity capital for corporations.[90] As La Porta, Lopez-de-Silanes, Shleifer and Vishny hold, "where laws are protective of outside investors and well enforced, investors are willing to finance corporations, and financial markets are both broader and more valuable."[91] As a result, for the further growth of corporations, the corporate law should adopt measures to attract general public investment, especially through increasing the protection of shareholders and the confidence of investors in the notion that the capital they provide will be protected from misuse or misappropriation by corporate managers, board members or controlling shareholders who may have the opportunity to engage in activities that advance their own interests at the expense of non-controlling shareholders.[92]

This is exactly what is happening: "Equity markets are growing not only in Europe, but throughout the developed world, and with this the economic logic of the market is inevitably asserting itself, subjecting corporations to its inexorable will and compelling convergence on the more efficient shareholder-oriented model."[93] According to William D. Schneper and Mauro F. Guillén:

---

only to those interests."; Hansmann, Henry / Kraakman, Reinier: "The End of History for Corporate Law". *Georgetown Law Review*, Vol. 89, No. 2, 2000, pp. 439–473, 448.

87 See Gordon, Jeffrey N.: "The Rise of Independent Directors in the United States, 1950–2005: Of Shareholder Value and Stock Market Prices". *Stanford Law Review*, Vol. 59, No. 6, 2007, pp. 1465–1568, 1511.

88 See Siems, Mathias M.: *Convergence in Shareholder Law (International Corporate Law and Financial Market Regulation)*. Cambridge University Press: 2008, pp. 367–368.

89 See Hopt, Klaus J. / Wymeersch, Eddy / Kanda, Hideki / Baum, Harald: *Corporate Governance in Context: Corporations, States, and Markets in Europe, Japan, and the US*. Oxford University Press: 2005, p. 324.

90 See Kraakman, Reinier / Armour, John / Davies, Paul / Enriques, Luca / Hansmann, Henry B. / Hertig, Gérard / Hopt, Klaus J. / Kanda, Hideki / Rock, Edward B.: *The anatomy of corporate law – A Comparative and Functional Approach*. Oxford University Press: 2nd Edition, 2009, p. 22.

91 La Porta, Rafael / Lopez-de-Silanes, Florencio / Shleifer, Anderei / Vishny, Robert W.: "Investor Protection and Corporate Valuation". *Journal of Finance*, Vol. 57, No. 3, 2002, pp. 1147–1170, 1147; See also Kamar, Ehud: "Beyond Competition for Incorporations". *Georgetown Law Journal*, Vol. 94, No. 6, 2006, pp. 1725–1772, 1725.

92 *OECD Principles*, p. 40.

93 See Ireland, Paddy: "Shareholder Primacy and the Distribution of Wealth". *The Modern Law Review*, Vol. 68, No. 1, 2005, pp. 49–81, 74.

That is, if all firms exhibit a decreasing orientation to shareholder interests, then a diversified investment strategy can hardly insulate shareholders from the share-price-diminishing effects of a management hat considers the interests of shareholders merely some among many to be considered in determining what to do. Indeed, if stakeholder-oriented management were adopted universally, one would expect a universal collapse of equity markets and the inability of firms to obtain equity capital. Equity markets offer no protection once the damage of stakeholder-oriented management is done.[94]

As Alexei M. Marcoux holds:

Portfolio diversification cannot protect shareholders if stakeholder-oriented management becomes widespread (as stakeholder theorists surely hope). That is, if all firms exhibit a decreasing orientation to shareholder interests, then a diversified investment strategy can hardly insulate shareholders from the share-price-diminishing effects of a management that considers the interests of shareholders merely some among many to be considered in determining what to do. Indeed, if stakeholder-oriented management were adopted universally, one would expect a universal collapse of equity markets and the inability of firms to obtain equity capital (because, as Easterbrook and Fischel note, arrangements of this sort would hardly be palatable to investors). Equity markets offer no protection once the damage of stakeholder-oriented management is done.[95]

Thus, the EU has adopted measures to attract general public investment and increase successful companies' demand for risk capital, as well as to promote the relaxation of obstacles to cross-border investment, especially through increasing the protection of shareholders and the confidence of investors.[96] The Second Company Law Directive on the formation of public limited liability companies and the maintenance and alteration of their capital[97] and the Third and Sixth Company Law Directive

94 Schneper, William D. / Guillén, Mauro F.: "Stakeholder Rights and Corporate Governance: A Cross-National Study of Hostile Takeovers". *Administrative Science Quarterly*, Vol. 49, No. 2, 2004, pp. 263–295, 268; See also Marcoux, Alexei M.: "A Fiduciary Argument against Stakeholder Theory". *Business Ethics Quarterly*, Vol. 13, No. 1, 1.2003, pp. 1–24, 15.

95 Marcoux, Alexei M.: "A Fiduciary Argument against Stakeholder Theory". *Business Ethics Quarterly*, Vol. 13, No. 1, 1.2003, pp. 1–24, 15.

96 See Davies, Paul L. / Hopt, Klaus J.: "Corporate Boards in Europe – Accountability and Convergence". *American Journal Comparative Law*, Vol. 61, No. 2, 2013, pp. 301–375, 325; Enriques L. / Gatti M.: "EC Reforms of Corporate Governance and Capital Markets Law: Do They Tackle Insiders' Opportunism?". *Northwestern Journal of International Law and Business*, Vol. 28, No. 1, 2007, pp. 1–45, 3.

97 See Directive 2012/30/EU of the European Parliament and of the Council of 25 October 2012 on coordination of safeguards, which – for the protection of the interests of members and others – are required by Member States of companies within the meaning of the second paragraph of Article 54 of the Treaty on the Functioning of the European Union, in respect of the formation of public limited liability companies and the maintenance and alteration of their capital with a view to making such safeguards equivalent.

on mergers and divisions have been simplified.[98] Rules on corporate governance statements have been introduced in the Accounting Directive,[99] the Tenth Company Law Directive on cross-border mergers.[100] The promulgation of the Financial Services Action Plan – which contained a significant commitment to the substantive harmonization of the law relating to securities markets – has adopted the capital market legislation such as the Market Abuse Directive,[101] the Prospectus Directive,[102] the Directive on Markets in Financial Instruments[103], and the Transparency Directive.[104] Reforms aimed to make national capital markets more attractive at a time when international competition in equity capital was increasing due to deregulation, globalization and large-scale privatizations.[105] Changes were spurred as part of the European Community's efforts to institute a common regulatory framework for European financial markets, especially concerning disclosure issues.[106]

In particular, the Directive 2004/25/EC of the European Parliament and of the Council of April 21, 2004 on takeover bids (hereinafter "Takeover Directive") – which

---

98 See Directive 2007/63/EC of the European Parliament and of the Council of 13 November 2007 amending Council Directives 78/855/EEC and 82/891/EEC as regards the requirement of an independent expert's report on the occasion of merger or division of public limited liability companies; Directive 2009/109/EC of the European Parliament and of the Council of 16 September 2009 amending Council Directives 77/91/EEC, 78/855/EEC and 82/891/EEC, and Directive 2005/56/EC as regards reporting and documentation requirements in case of mergers and divisions.

99 See Directive 2013/34/EU of the European Parliament and of the Council of 26 June 2013 on the annual financial statements, consolidated financial statements and related reports of certain types of undertakings, amending Directive 2006/43/EC of the European Parliament and of the Council and repealing Council Directives 78/660/EEC and 83/349/EEC.

100 See Directive 2005/56/EC of the European Parliament and of the Council of 26 October 2005 on cross-border mergers of limited liability companies.

101 See Directive 2003/6/EC of the European Parliament and of the Council of 28 January 2003 on insider dealing and market manipulation (market abuse).

102 See Directive 2003/71/EC of the European Parliament and of the Council of 4 November 2003 on the prospectus to be published when securities are offered to the public or admitted to trading and amending Directive 2001/34/EC.

103 See Directive 2004/39/EC of the European Parliament and of the Council of 21 April 2004 on markets in financial instruments amending Council Directives 85/611/EEC and 93/6/EEC and Directive 2000/12/EC of the European Parliament and of the Council and repealing Council Directive 93/22/EEC.

104 See Directive 2004/109/EC of the European Parliament and of the Council of 15 December 2004 on the harmonization of transparency requirements in relation to information about issuers whose securities are admitted to trading on a regulated market and amending Directive 2001/34/EC.

105 See Kamar, Ehud: "Beyond Competition for Incorporations". *Georgetown Law Journal*, Vol. 94, No. 6, 2006, pp. 1725–1772, 1765.

106 See Ferran, Eilis: *Building an EU Securities Market.* Cambridge University Press: 2004, p. 58.

lays out rules governing corporate control transactions and tender offers for EU listed companies – aimed to promote the integration of the national economies constituting the "single market" and enhance the competitiveness of European industry as against non-European rivals by facilitating takeover bids, especially cross-border ones.[107] In the minds of EU policy-makers, the harmonization efforts were supposed to achieve the two-fold goal of providing market players with a common regulatory platform for takeover bids and creating a playing field in pan-European corporate control contests, whereby no Member State regulation would have granted companies any particular benefit or penalization *vis-à-vis* other EU peers.[108] As the EU Commission put it in its 2002 proposal:

> *The Lisbon European Council placed this directive, which forms part of the Financial Services Action Plan, among the priorities as regards the integration of European financial markets by 2005. [...] Under the circumstances, the Commission considers it essential to provide a European framework for cross-border takeover bids as part of the Financial Services Action Plan. Such transactions can contribute to the development and reorganization of European firms, a key condition for withstanding international competition and developing a single capital market.*[109]

In terms of China, the major concern is that the public may lose faith in corporate stock as an investment, raising the cost of capital throughout the economy because shareholders can enlarge the pool of capital available for productive investment and essential for the large-scale enterprises to obtain economies of scope and scale.[110] China has realized the importance of developing a capital market for the growth of the economy in the "Several Opinions on Promoting Reform and Opening-up and Stable Development of Capital Market" drafted by the State Council in 2004:

> *Developing capital markets is a task of strategic importance linked to the fulfilling of the strategic goal of quadrupling China's GDP within the first two decades of this century. First, it will facilitate the improvement of the socialist market economy, bring into fuller play the role of capital markets in optimizing resources allocation, and effectively turn social capital into long-term investment. Second, it will facilitate the restructuring and*

107 See Davies P. / Schuster, Edmund – Philipp / Van de Walle de Ghelcke, Emilie : "The Takeover Directive as a Protectionist Tool?". In: Bernitz, Ulf / Ringe, Wolf-Georg (eds.): *Company Law and Economic Protectionism: New Challenges to European Integration.* Oxford University Press: 2010, p. 105–157, 105.

108 See Enriques L. / Gatti M.: "Is There a Uniform EU Securities Law After the Financial Services Action Plan?" *Stanford Journal of Law, Business & Finance,* Vol. 14, No. 1, 2008, pp. 43–81, 64.

109 European Commission: *Proposal for a Directive of the European Parliament and of the Council on Takeover Bids,* 10.2002, p. 3.

110 See Baums, Theodor / Scott, Kenneth E.: "Taking Shareholder Protection Seriously? Corporate Governance in the United States and Germany". *The American Journal of Comparative Law,* Vol. 53, No. 1, 2005, pp. 31–75, 34.

strategic transformation of the state-owned sector of the economy and accelerate the development of the non-state-owned sectors. Third, it will facilitate the increase of the ratio of direct financing, improve the structure and efficiency of the financial market, and maintain financial security.[111]

Focusing on the further improving the corporate governance of listed companies and promoting the standardized operation of listed companies, Article 5 of this document proposes that "we should regulate the acts of controlling shareholders and prosecute those committing acts to damage the interests of listed companies or those of small and medium-sized shareholders." Companies need risk capital to take advantage of new opportunities and capture economies of scale and scope. Public investors who can diversify their shareholdings are the cheapest risk bearers. Eugene Fama and Michael Jensen made the point explicitly: "Common stock allows residual risk to be spread across many residual claimants who individually choose the extent to which they bear risk and who can diversify across organizations offering such claims."[112] In this respect, Chinese scholars and policy-makers were concerned to search for new mechanisms of corporate governance to protect minority shareholders from the prejudice of dominating shareholders and management to develop the Chinese capital market.[113] Jeffrey Gordon has shown that the capital markets' evolving informational efficiency facilitated the vastly expanded role of independent directors in corporate governance.[114] Independent directors provide a buffer between corporate management and the capital markets, which allows courts to rely on the directors' assessments of how best to create value rather than the courts having to make such assessments themselves.[115] On January 31, 2004, the State Council of China issued "Several Opinions on Promoting the Reform and Opening-up and Stable Development of Capital Market", which underscores the importance of independent directors in the reform and development of China's capital

---

111 China State Council: "Several Opinions on Promoting Reform and Opening-up and Stable Development of Capital Market". *Guofa [2004] No. 3.*

112 Fama, Eugene F. / Jensen, Michael C.: "Agency Problems and Residual Claims". *Journal of Law & Economics*, Vol. 26, No. 2, 6.1983, pp. 327–349, 329.

113 See Lee, Keun / Mathews, John / Wade, Robert: "Rethinking development policy: A new consensus". *Financial Times*, 19.10.2007; Bolton, Patrick / Becht, Marco / Röell, Alisa: "Corporate governance and control". In: Constantinides G.M. / Harris M. / Stulz R. M. (eds.): *Handbook of the Economics of Finance*. Elsevier: 1st Edition, Vol. 1, chapter 1, 2003, pp. 1–109, 7.

114 See Gordon, Jeffrey N.: "The Rise of Independent Directors in the United States, 1950–2005: Of Shareholder Value and Stock Market Prices". *Stanford Law Review*, Vol. 59, No. 6, 2007, pp. 1465–1568, 1541–1561.

115 See Gordon, Jeffrey N.: "The Rise of Independent Directors in the United States, 1950–2005: Of Shareholder Value and Stock Market Prices". *Stanford Law Review*, Vol. 59, No. 6, 2007, pp. 1465–1568, 1523–1526.

market.[116] The Preface of the Code of Corporate Governance for Listed Companies in China (hereinafter "the Code") provides:

> *"In accordance with the basic principles of the Company Law, the Securities Law and other relevant laws and regulations, as well as the commonly accepted standards in international corporate governance, the Code of Corporate Governance for Listed Companies is formulated to promote the establishment and improvement of modern enterprise system by listed companies, to standardize the operation of listed companies and to bring forward the healthy development of the securities market of our country."*

C. Increasing Minority Shareholders' Protection in China and the EU

The view that the Anglo-American-inspired corporate governance system is the best solution for all economies also seems to have influenced the requirements that central global development actors such as the World Bank and the OECD have imposed – expressly or implicitly – upon developing countries,[117] without always giving sufficient consideration to the differences among situations in developing countries (which is needed to build up their financial infrastructures and the competitiveness of their businesses), and that have been set in the rich, developed countries over centuries.[118] The OECD principles of corporate governance (hereinafter "OECD Principles") – which are recognized as an influential, objective set of corporate governance principles and represent the first initiative by an inter-governmental organization to develop the core elements of a good corporate governance regime[119]-

116 See China State Council: *Some Opinions of the State Council on Promoting the Reform, Opening and Steady Growth of Capital Markets*, 31.1.2004.

117 See Singh A. / Weisse B.: "Corporate governance, competition, the new international financial architecture and large corporations in emerging markets". *Center for Business Research Working: Paper No. 250.* University of Cambridge: 2002, pp. 5–8.

118 See Lee, Keun / Mathews, John / Wade, Robert: "Rethinking development policy: A new consensus". *Financial Times*, 19.10.2007; Bolton, Patrick / Becht, Marco / Röell, Alisa: "Corporate governance and control". In: Constantinides G.M. / Harris M. / Stulz R. M. (eds.): *Handbook of the Economics of Finance.* Elsevier: 1st Edition, Vol. 1, chapter 1, 2003, pp. 1–109, 7.

119 "OECD determines the way companies are managed and controlled. An effective corporate governance framework is of crucial importance because well-run companies are likely to be more competitive and more sustainable in the long term. In the formulation of the Organization for Economic Cooperation and Development, an international organization of developed countries that accept the principles of representative democracy and a free market economy: Corporate governance is the system by which business corporations are directed and controlled. The corporate governance structure specifies the distribution of rights and responsibilities among different participants in the corporation, such as the board, managers,

make it clear that the corporate governance framework should protect and facilitate the exercise of shareholders' rights and ensure the equitable treatment of all shareholders, including minority and foreign shareholders.[120] Both China and the EU seem to at least accept the importance of improving their corporate governance rules with a shareholder-focused model.

I. China

As an emerging and growth-leading economy, China has also placed strong emphasis on establishing a corporate governance system. Based upon the Company Law – which was first enacted in December of 1993 and came into effect in mid-1994 and was strongly influenced by German corporate law – on October 27, 2005, after one year of preparation and one year and a half of deliberation, the Eighteenth Session of the Standing Committee of the Tenth National People's Congress promulgated a revised Company Law, which adopted cumulative voting and independent directors. On December 28, 2013, the Company Law 2005 was further amended by the sixth Session of the Standing Committee of the Twelfth National People's Congress. The amendment means the deregulations of the company establishment, including cancelling restrictions on the minimum registered capital,[121] the minimum raised

---

shareholders and other stakeholders, and spells out the rules and procedures for making decisions on corporate affairs. By doing this, it also provides the structure through which the company objectives are set, and the means of attaining those objectives and monitoring performance." Feinerman, James V.: "New Hope for Corporate Governance in China?". *The China Quarterly*, No. 191, 9.2007, pp. 590–612, 592.

120 *OECD Principles*, p. 20. OECD comprises five themes: protection of shareholders' rights; equitable treatment of all shareholders, including minority and foreign shareholders; recognition of the rights of stakeholders as established by law; ensuring timely and accurate disclosure of all material matters regarding the corporation; and effective monitoring of management by the board, with board account ability to the company and the shareholders.

121 More specifically, the minimum amount of the registered capital of a joint stock limited company (RMB 5 million Yuan) in Article 81 para. 2 sentence 2 of the Company Law 2005 and the minimum amount of registered capital of a one-person limited liability company (RMB 100, 000 Yuan) in Article 59 para. 1 of the Company Law 2005 is deleted. Furthermore, Article 7 of the Company Law 2013 cancels the requirement for stating registered capital in the company business license. Instead, it allows the company bylaws to decide the amount of capital contributions subscribed by shareholders. In addition, Article 178 para. 2 sentence 3 of the Company Law 2005, which stipulated "The registered capital of the company after reducing its registered capital shall not be any lower than the minimum amount prescribed for by law", is abolished.

share capital,[122] the proportion of currency capital[123] as well as the submission of a certificate of capital verification for the registration of incorporation,[124] although it brings no changes in the corporate governance systems.

Furthermore, in 2002 the China Securities Regulatory Commission (CSRC)[125] and the State Economic and Trade Commission (SETC)[126] drafted the Code, which is applicable to all listed companies within the boundary of the People's Republic of China.[127] It establishes the basic principles for the corporate governance of listed companies, the means for the protection of investors' interests and rights, the basic behavior rules and moral standards for directors, supervisors, managers and other senior management members based upon the basic principles of the Company Law, the Securities Law and other relevant laws and regulations, as well as the commonly accepted standards in international corporate governance to promote the

122 The following provisions of the Company Law 2005 are abolished: Article 26 and Article 81 para. 1, which stipulated that "the minimum amount of initial capital contributions to be made by all initiators shall be not less than 20% of the total registered capital, and the remaining amount shall be paid off by the initiators within 2 years as of the day when the company is established, while for an investment company, the remaining amount may be paid off within 5 years."

123 Article 27 para. 3 of the Company Law 2005 – which provided that "the amount of the capital contributions in currency paid by all the shareholders shall be not less than 30% of the registered capital of the limited liability company" – is also abolished.

124 The capital verification – as a requirement for applying incorporation registration, provided by Article 29, Article 30 and Article 84 para. 2 sentence 3 of the Company Law 2005 – is cancelled.

125 "CSRC, a ministerial-level public institution directly under the State Council, performs a unified regulatory function, according to the relevant laws and regulations, and with the authority by the State Council, over the securities and futures market of China, maintains an orderly securities and futures market order, and ensure a legal operation of the capital market." More information about CSRC is retrieved on 23.1.2015, from http://www.csrc.gov.cn/pub/csrc_en/about/intro/200811/t20081130_67718.html, 30.11.2008.

126 SETC – a ministerial-level public institution directly under the State Council, which closed in 2003 – was responsible for the macro-economy regulation and control. Subsequently, it was replaced by the Department of Commerce, which plays a central role in regulating national and international trade and international economy cooperation today.

127 "The Code Listed companies shall act in the spirit of the Code in their efforts to improve corporate governance. Requirements of the Code shall be embodied when listed companies formulate or amend their articles of association or rules of governance. The Code is the major measuring standard for evaluating whether a listed company has a good corporate governance structure, and if major problems exist with the corporate governance structure of a listed company, the securities supervision and regulation authorities may instruct the company to make corrections in accordance with the Code." CSRC, SETC, Code of Corporate Governance for Listed Companies in China, 7.1. 2001, Preface.

establishment and improvement of modern enterprise system by listed companies, standardize the operation of listed companies and bring forward the development of the securities market.[128] Article 1 provides that as the owner of a company, the shareholders shall enjoy the legal rights stipulated by laws, administrative regulations and the company's articles of association. A listed company shall establish a corporate governance structure sufficient for ensuring the full exercise of shareholders' rights. Article 2 provides that the corporate governance structure of a company shall ensure fair treatment toward all shareholders, especially minority shareholders. All shareholders are to enjoy equal rights and bear the corresponding duties based upon the shares that they hold. Article 19 provides: "The controlling shareholders owe a duty of good faith toward the listed company and other shareholders. The controlling shareholders of a listed company shall strictly comply with laws and regulations while exercising their rights as investors, and shall be prevented from damaging the listed company's or other shareholders' legal rights and interests, through means such as assets restructuring, or from taking advantage of their privileged position to gain additional benefit."

The Company Law and the Code provide some important rights, through which shareholders can directly participate and monitor the management of corporations. First of all, Article 33 provides that the shareholder shall be entitled to consult and copy the articles of association, records of the shareholders' meetings, resolutions of the meetings of the board of directors, resolutions of the meetings of the board of supervisors as well as financial reports. The shareholders may request to consult the accounting books of the company. Where a shareholder requests to consult the accounting books of the company, he or she shall submit to the company a written request stating the motives. If the company – pursuant to any justifiable reason – considers that the shareholder's request to consult the accounting books for any improper purpose which may damage the legitimate interests of the company, it may reject the request of the shareholder by providing a written reply including an explanation within 15 days after the shareholder submits a written request. If the company rejects the request of any shareholder to consult the accounting books, the shareholder may plead the people's court to demand the company to approve consultation. Article 97 rules that the shareholders shall be entitled to refer to the articles of association, register of the shareholders, counterfoil of corporate bonds, records of the shareholders' assemblies, records of the meetings of the board of directors, records of the meetings of the board of supervisors and financial reports and may bring forward proposals or raise questions about the business operation of the company.

Second, Article 102 stipulates that for a shareholders' assembly to be held, a notice shall be given to every shareholder 20 days in advance, stating the time and place of the assembly as well as the matters to be deliberated. In terms of a temporary shareholders' assembly, a notice shall be given to every shareholder 15 days in advance. Regarding the issuance of unregistered shares, the time and

---

128 *The Code*, Preface.

place of the assembly as well as the matters to be deliberated at the assembly shall be announced 30 days in advance. The shareholders separately or aggregately holding 3% or more of the shares of the company may put forward a written temporary proposal to the board of directors 10 days before a shareholders' assembly is held. The board of directors may notify other shareholders within 2 days and submit the temporary proposal to the shareholders' assembly for deliberation. The contents of a temporary proposal shall fall within the scope to be decided by the shareholders' assembly and the temporary proposal shall have a clear topic for discussion and matters to be decided. The shareholders' assembly shall not make any decision on any matter not listed in the notice as mentioned in the preceding two paragraphs. If the holders of unregistered shares attend the shareholders' assembly, they shall have their shares preserved in the company during the period from 5 days before the assembly is held to the day when the shareholders' assembly is closed.

Third, Article 150 provides that if the shareholders' meeting or assembly demands a director, supervisor or senior manager to attend the meeting as a non-voting delegate, he/she shall do so and answer the shareholders' inquiries. The directors and senior managers shall faithfully offer relevant information and materials to the board of supervisors or the supervisor of the limited liability company with no board of supervisors, and none of them may obstruct the board of supervisors or supervisor from exercising their authorities.

Fourth, Articles 40 and 101 stipulate that if the board of directors or the executive director and the board of supervisors or supervisor does not convene or preside over such meetings, the shareholders representing 10% or more of the voting rights may convene and preside over such meetings on their own initiative. Article 42 rules that every shareholder shall be notified 15 days before a shareholders' meeting is held, unless otherwise prescribed by the articles of association or contracted by all the shareholders. A shareholders' meeting shall make records of the decisions on the matters discussed at the meeting, whereby the shareholders who attend the meeting shall affix their signatures to the records. Article 100(3) provides that an annual session of the shareholders' assembly shall be held each year. Under any of the following circumstances, a temporary shareholders' assembly shall be held within two months at the request of the shareholders separately or aggregately holding 10% or more of the company's shares. Article 106 provides that a shareholder may entrust an agent to attend a shareholders' assembly. The agent shall present a power of attorney issued by the shareholder to the company and shall exercise his/her voting rights within the authorised scope.

Furthermore, Article 22 provides that a resolution of the shareholders' meeting, shareholders' assembly or board of directors of the company that violates any law or administrative regulation shall be null and void. Where the procedures for convoking and the voting form of a shareholders' meeting or shareholders' assembly or meeting of the board of directors violate any law, administrative regulation or the articles of association or the resolution is in violation of the articles of association of the company, the shareholders may request the people's court to revoke it within 60 days after the resolution is made. If the shareholders initiate a lawsuit, according to the preceding paragraph, the people's court shall – in light of the company's request – demand the shareholders to provide a corresponding guarantee.

Finally, Article 151 provides shareholders with the right to file a lawsuit against directors or senior managers. First, when a director or senior manager is under the circumstance as stated in Article 149 of this Law, the shareholders separately or aggregately holding 1% or more of the total shares of the company may require the board of supervisors or the supervisor of the limited liability company with no board of supervisors to file in writing a lawsuit in the people's court. Second, if the supervisor is under the circumstance as stated in Article 149 of this Law, the aforementioned shareholders may require the board of directors or the executive director of the limited liability company with no board of directors to file in writing a lawsuit in the people's court. Third, if the board of supervisors or the board of directors refuses to file a lawsuit after it receives a written request as mentioned in the preceding paragraph, or fails to file a lawsuit within 30 days after receiving the request, or – in an emergency – if the failure to file a lawsuit immediately will cause unrecoverable damages to the interests of the company, the shareholders as listed in the preceding paragraph may directly file a lawsuit in the people's court on their own behalf. Fourth, in case the legitimate rights and interests of a company are impaired and losses are caused to the company, the shareholders as mentioned in the preceding paragraph may initiate a lawsuit in the people's court in light of the provisions of the preceding two paragraphs. In the Code, Article 4 stipulates that shareholders shall have the right to protect their interests and rights through civil litigation or other legal means in accordance with the laws and administrative regulations. In the event that the resolutions of shareholders' meetings or the resolutions of the board of directors are in breach of laws and administrative regulations or infringe upon the shareholders' legal interests and rights, the shareholders shall have the right to initiate litigation to stop such a breach or infringement. The directors, supervisors and managers of the company shall bear the liability of compensation in cases where they violate laws, administrative regulations or articles of association and cause damage to the company during the performance of their duties. Shareholders shall have the right to request the company to sue for such compensation in accordance with law.

II. European Union

On the other hand, the reforms in continental European corporate governance over the last two decades highlight the efforts in terms of enacting corporate governance systems that may help to protect minority shareholders of listed corporations by strengthening the shareholders' voices in corporate governance such as the power to authorize or ratify some transactions and resolutions in potential conflicts of interest.[129] Many of the issues such as independent directors, compensation, auditing,

129 See Enriques, Luca / Volpin, Paolo: "Corporate Governance Reforms in Continental Europe". *Journal of Economic Perspectives*, Vol. 21, No. 1, 2007, pp. 117–140, 128–131.

accounting rules, voting, takeovers and stock market regulation seem to suggest that the shareholder primacy agenda and investors' protection gain increased attention. According to the Commission Recommendation (7):

> *The presence of independent representatives on the board, capable of challenging the decisions of management, is widely considered as a means of protecting the interests of shareholders and other stakeholders. In companies with a dispersed ownership, the primary concern is how to make managers accountable to weak shareholders. In companies with controlling shareholders, the focus is more on how to make sure that the company will be run in a way that sufficiently takes into account the interests of minority shareholders. Ensuring adequate protection for third parties is relevant in both cases. Whatever the formal board structure of a company, the management function should therefore be subject to an effective and sufficiently independent supervisory function. Independence should be understood as the absence of any material conflict of interest; in this context, proper attention should be paid namely to any threats which might arise from the fact that a representative on the board has close ties with a competitor of the company.*

The EU Action Plan was revealed in the 2003 Communication from the Commission on Modernizing Company Law and Enhancing Corporate Governance in the European Union,[130] which was prepared based upon a report by the High Level Group of company law experts appointed by Commissioner Bolkestein and chaired by Jaap Winter. There are two main pillars for corporate governance reform, one of which is modernizing the board of directors. First, in terms of board composition, non-executive or supervisory directors who – in the majority – are independent should take decisions in key areas where executive directors have conflicts of interest, such as remuneration and supervision of audit of company accounts. Second, the directors' remuneration regime should require disclosure of remuneration policy and details of individual directors in the annual accounts, prior approval by the shareholder meeting of share and share option schemes in which directors participate and proper recognition in the annual accounts of the costs of such schemes for the company. Third, the collective responsibility of all board members for key financial and non-financial statements should be clearly recognized under national legal systems. The proposals relative to board composition found detailed specification in the Commission Recommendation, which shows that the shareholder primacy views strongly influence European company law[131] and aim to eliminate and prevent conflicts of interest.[132] In particular, they stress the non-executive or supervisory directors' role

---

130 Commission of the European Communities: *Communication from the Commission to the Council and the European Parliament, Modernizing Company Law and Enhancing Corporate Governance in the European Union – A Plan to Move Forward*, 21.5.2003.

131 See Sjafjell, Beate: *Towards a Sustainable European Company Law – A Normative Analysis of the Objectives of EU Law, with the Takeover Directive as a Test Case.* (European company law series, Vol. 3). Kluwer Law International: 2009, p. 53.

132 See *Commission Recommendation*, (2).

in overseeing executive or managing directors and dealing with situations involving conflicts of interests to restore confidence in financial markets,[133] the proposals relative to directors' remuneration found specification in the Commission to directors' remuneration of December 14, 2004 fostering an appropriate regime for the remuneration of directors of listed companies and those on collective responsibility were translated into Articles 50b and 50c of Directive 78/660/EEC on the annual accounts of certain types of companies.

The other pillar involved strengthening shareholders' rights in terms of electronic access to information and procedural rights (to ask questions, table resolution, vote in absentia and participate in general meetings via electronic means). The Commission proposed that the facilities relevant to the exercise of similar rights should be offered to shareholders throughout the EU, while specific problems related to cross-border voting should be urgently resolved. This led to the adoption of the Directive 2007/36/EC of the European Parliament and of the Council of 11 July 2007 on the exercise of certain rights of shareholders in listed companies (hereinafter "Shareholders Rights Directive").

The Shareholder Rights Directive stipulates equal treatment of shareholders as a principle[134]. Shareholders have the right to receive information prior to the general meeting,[135] the right to put items on the agenda of the general meeting and table draft resolutions,[136] the right to facilitate participation in the general meeting by electronic means,[137] the right to ask questions,[138] proxy voting rights[139]. The removal of certain impediments to the effective exercise of voting rights[140] is also stipulated. These measures mainly focus on enhancing the shareholders' engagement rights in general meeting and voting rights, because shareholders have the right to influence the decision-making process of corporations and play a crucial role in promoting better governance of companies through participating in shareholders' meetings and voting for important corporate issues. Accordingly, they act on both the interest of the company and their own interests.

However, the case for enhancing shareholder activism in Europe through regulatory harmonization is rather weak. Their success in terms of the voting results is limited across Europe, irrespective of the issue that proposals are on the rise as a result of the financial crisis or the adoption of the EU Shareholder Rights Directive.[141] First,

---

133 See *Commission Recommendation*, (3).
134 See *Shareholders Rights Directive*, Article 4.
135 See *Shareholders Rights Directive*, Article 5.
136 See *Shareholders Rights Directive*, Article 6.
137 See *Shareholders Rights Directive*, Article 8.
138 See *Shareholders Rights Directive*, Article 9.
139 See *Shareholders Rights Directive*, Article 10.
140 See *Shareholders Rights Directive*, Article 13.
141 Belcredi, Massimo / Bozzi, Stefano / Di Noia, Carmine: "Board elections and shareholder activism: the Italian experiment, Boards and Shareholders in European Listed Companies: Facts, Context and Post-crisis Reforms". In: Belcredi, Massimo / Ferrarini,

safeguarding the engagement rights of shareholders is fundamentally dependent on the their own initiatives, which will proceed based upon a cost-benefit analysis (aside from cases in which their incentives are clearly distorted). Second, in order to become active, investors' incentives crucially depend on the characteristics of the firm, such as its ownership structure. In controlled companies, minority shareholders may rationally choose to remain passive, knowing that they can only weakly influence corporate decisions.[142] Third, the diversity of institutional contexts in the EU – for instance, the divergence of national rules dealing with the distribution of powers between boards and shareholders – undermines regulatory harmonization, which would have different impacts across countries.

Thus, as the fruit of the 2012 public consultation of various discussions with many stakeholders and of the European Commission's own analysis, the "EU Action Plan" – which outlines the initiatives that the Commission intends to take to modernize the company law and corporate governance framework – announces a number of initiatives including a potential revision of the Shareholder Rights Directive. It identifies enhancing transparency and engaging shareholders as main lines of action and suggests: "Companies need to provide better information about their corporate governance to their investors and society at large. At the same time companies should be allowed to know who their shareholders are and institutional investors should be more transparent about their voting policies so that a more fruitful dialogue on corporate governance matters can take place."[143] Shareholders should be encouraged to engage more in corporate governance. They should be offered more possibilities to oversee remuneration policy and related party transactions, whereby shareholder cooperation should be made easier. In addition, a limited number of obligations will need to be imposed on institutional investors, asset managers and proxy advisors to bring about effective engagement.[144] Consequently, the Proposal for a Directive of the European Parliament and of the Council amending Directive 2007/36/EC regarding the encouragement of long-term shareholder engagement and Directive 2013/34/EU regarding certain elements of the corporate governance statement (hereinafter "the proposal") having taken the measures of improving the engagement of institutional investors and asset managers, strengthening the link between pay and performance of directors, improving shareholder oversight

Guido (eds.): *International Corporate Law and Financial Market Regulation.* Cambridge University Press: 2.2014, pp. 1–66, 46.

142 "Shareholders thus traditionally proved to be rationally apathetic. For the average shareholder, the necessary investment of time and effort in making informed voting decisions simply was not worthwhile. Instead, shareholders traditionally adopted the aforementioned Wall Street Rule; namely, it's easier to switch than fight." See Bainbridge, Stephen M.: *The New Corporate Governance in Theory and Practice.* Oxford University Press: 7.2008, p. 203.

143 *EU Action Plan*, p. 4.

144 *EU Action Plan*, p. 4.

on related party transactions, enhancing the transparency of proxy advisors and facilitating the exercise of rights flowing from securities for investors.

Furthermore, the influence of banks is declining and regulatory initiatives in Germany have created transparency for investors. The weak shareholder rights view–with small investors not participating in corporate governance–is outdated.[145] The Foreword of the German Corporate Governance Code (hereinafter "GCGC") Sentences 2 and 3 provide that: "The Code aims at making the German Corporate Governance system transparent and understandable. Its purpose is to promote the trust of international and national investors, customers, employees and the general public in the management and supervision of listed German stock corporations."[146] Germany has enacted significant corporate law reforms to strengthen the mechanisms of internal governance, empower shareholders, enhance disclosure requirements and toughen public enforcement. Special emphasis has been placed upon empowering minority shareholders and disclosure, which are the most effective tools for countering abuses by dominant shareholders.[147] Germany banned multiple-voting shares in 1998 and prohibited banks from acting as a client's proxy if they own more than 5 percent of the shares. More generally, the rules on bank voting of clients' shares were revised to discourage the clients' tendency to let banks decide freely on how to vote and hence – as a rule – support management.[148] Recent legal reforms appear to embrace these changes by allocating more powers to shareholders to fend for their own rights, even at the cost of breaching social harmony, the objective that has long been used to fend off demands for stronger legal rights.[149] The case of an activist shareholder, Cevian Capital, who acquired a 10.07% stake in

145 Thamm, Christian: "Minority shareholder monitoring and German corporate governance: empirical evidence and value effects". In: Schiereck, Dirk (ed.): *Corporate Finance and Governance*, Band 13, 2013, p. 94.

146 In its introduction, the German Code states that: "The Code aims at making the German Corporate Governance system transparent and understandable. Its purpose is to promote the trust of the international and national investors, customers, employees and the general public in the management and supervision of listed German stock corporations." *The German Corporate Governance Code* (hereinafter "GCGC"), 26.5.2010; Davies, Paul L. / Hopt, Klaus J.: "Corporate Boards in Europe – Accountability and Convergence". *American Journal Comparative Law*, Vol. 61, No. 2, 2013, pp. 301–375, 325; Enriques L. / Gatti M.: "EC Reforms of Corporate Governance and Capital Markets Law: Do They Tackle Insiders' Opportunism?". *Northwestern Journal of International Law and Business*, Vol. 28, No. 1, 2007, pp. 1–45, 3.

147 See Enriques, Luca / Volpin, Paolo: "Corporate Governance Reforms in Continental Europe". *Journal of Economic Perspectives*, Vol. 21, No. 1, 2007, pp. 117–140, 137.

148 See Enriques, Luca / Volpin, Paolo: "Corporate Governance Reforms in Continental Europe". *Journal of Economic Perspectives*, Vol. 21, No. 1, 2007, pp. 117–140, 132–133.

149 See Milhaupt C.J. / Pistor K.: *Law and Capitalism: What Corporate Crises Reveal about Legal Systems and Economic Development Around the World.* The University of Chicago Press: 2008, p. 86.

the German stock corporation Demag Cranes in May 2010, followed by the acquisition of Demag Crane by the US competitor Terex Corporation, presented some evidence for the strong shareholder rights perspective. There are three key takeaways from the case of Demag Cranes: (i) minority shareholder rights in Germany appear to be strong; (ii) minority shareholders have the possibility to secure board representation; and (iii) minority shareholder activism can have an impact on a firm's corporate governance.[150] A study called "Minority shareholder monitoring and German corporate governance: empirical evidence and value effects" examines the monitoring activities of activist minority shareholders in Germany between January 1999 and May 2011.[151] The evidence presented in this study further includes an overview of cases of supervisory board representation by small investors and the empirical evidence supports the strong shareholder rights perspective in Germany, with small investors actively participating in corporate governance.[152]

150 See Thamm, Christian: "Minority shareholder monitoring and German corporate governance: empirical evidence and value effects". In: Schiereck, Dirk (ed.): *Corporate Finance and Governance*, Band 13, 2013, p. 94.

151 See Thamm, Christian: "Minority shareholder monitoring and German corporate governance: empirical evidence and value effects". In: Schiereck, Dirk (ed.): *Corporate Finance and Governance*, Band 13, 2013, p. 25.

152 See Thamm, Christian: "Minority shareholder monitoring and German corporate governance: empirical evidence and value effects". In: Schiereck, Dirk (ed.): *Corporate Finance and Governance*, Band 13, 2013, p. 94.

Second Chapter: Negative Attitudes towards Cumulative Voting in the US and the EU

The voting right of shareholders to select supervisors and directors is the most important type of shareholder rights and perhaps the only fundamental way for shareholders to exercise control in corporate affairs.[153] Having originally been drafted as a way to protect minority shareholders from the "overreaching" of a majority who could form rings to control absolutely and abuse and plunder the property of the minorities by allowing a shareholder to multiply the number of votes that he/she has, as determined by the number of shares he holds, by the number of directors to be elected and cast all his/her votes for any one candidate or distribute his/her votes among the candidates in any way he/she chooses,[154] cumulative voting has been deregulated in the US and is not adopted in the EU.

A. Importance of Voting Right

In essence, cumulative voting is a method of voting. Prior to discussing it, we should demonstrate the importance of shareholders' voting rights. A well-known, often-quoted Delaware opinion in Blasius Industries v. Atlas Corporation states that "the shareholder franchise is the ideological underpinning upon which the legitimacy of directorial power rests"[155]. As the court explains, voting rights are "critical to the theory that legitimates the exercise of power by some (directors and officers) over vast aggregations of property that they do not own"[156]. Robert Monks and Nell Minow perceive the governance structure of stock corporations in analogy to representative democracy, arguing that US legislators sought to strengthen this form in the 1930s, when they enacted the securities laws that required disclosure of information to the market:

> *Lawmakers tried to set up a process of corporate accountability – an impartial set of rules preserving the widest possible latitude for shareholders to protect their financial interests. In searching for a reliable and familiar model, they turned to America's own traditions of political accountability.*

153 See Easterbrook, Frank / Fischel, Daniel: "Voting in Corporate Law". *Journal of Law and Economics*, Vol. 26, No. 2, 1983, pp. 395–427, 395.

154 Henn, Harry G. / Alexander, John R.: *Laws of Corporations and Other Business Enterprises*. West Publish Corporation: 3rd Edition, 1983, p. 495.

155 Blasius Indus. v. Atlas Corp., 564 A.2d 651,659 (Del. Ch. 1988).

156 Blasius Indus. v. Atlas Corp., 564 A.2d 651,659 (Del. Ch. 1988).

> *Shareholders were seen as voters, boards of directors as elected representatives, proxy solicitations as election campaigns, corporate charters and by-laws as constitutions and amendments. Just as political democracy acted to guarantee the legitimacy of governmental or public power, the theory went, so corporate democracy would control – and therefore legitimate – the otherwise uncontrollable growth of power in the hands of private individuals. Underpinning that corporate democracy, as universal franchise underpinned its political counterpart, was the principle of one share, one vote.*[157]

In terms of cumulative voting, the major public proponents of cumulative voting ever since the 1950s have been the Gilbert brothers, who annually presented such shareholder proposals at some firms, arguing that minority representation was an essential feature of shareholder democracy.[158] Lucian Bebchuk also claims that meaningful democratic voice in the governance system is necessary to confer legitimacy on corporate directors.[159] Moreover, logic suggests that large shareholders rarely have an interest in interfering with the smooth functioning of the board. When a large shareholder attempts to interfere, it is often a sign of some pathology. Cumulative voting is an incomplete cure for the pathology, although it is better than the alternative of a unified board stolidly supporting management as the company slides toward disaster.[160] A more diverse board could not only better represent different shareholders, but also reduce corporate conflicts and the need to use litigation as a protection for minority shareholders.[161]

This view can obtain support from an economic perspective, given that a corporation is simply a name for a great web of contractual arrangements,[162] whereby the

157 Monks, Robert A.G. / Minow, Nell: *Corporate Governance.* Blackwell Publishing: 2004, p. 126.

158 See Gilbert, Lewis D.: *Dividends and Democracy.* American Research Council: 1956, pp. 181–189.

159 See Bebchuk, Lucian A.: "The Myth of the Shareholder Franchise". *Virginia Law Review,* Vol. 93, No. 675, 2007, pp. 675–732, 676; Bebchuk, Lucian A.: "The Case for Increasing Shareholder Power". *Harvard Law Review,* Vol. 118, No. 835, 2005, pp. 833–914, 837.

160 See Gordon, Jeffrey N.: "Institutions as Relational Investors: A New Look at Cumulative Voting". *Columbia Law Review,* Vol. 94, No. 1, 1.1994, pp. 124–192, 170–174 (describing the value of cumulative voting in overcoming the rational apathy of institutional investors).

161 See Ventoruzzo, Marco: "Empowering Shareholders in Directors' Elections: A Revolution in the Making". *European Company and Financial Law Review,* Vol. 8, No. 2, 6.2011, pp. 105–144, 143.

162 See Jensen M.C. / Mecklin W.H.: "Theory of the firm: Managerial behavior, agency costs and ownership structure". *Journal of Financial Economics,* Vol. 3, No. 4, 1976, pp. 305–360, 305; Alchian, Armen / Demsetz, Harold: "Production, Information Costs, and Economic Organization". *American Economic Review,* Vol. 62, No. 5, 12.1972, pp. 777–795, 778; Fama, Eugene: "Agency Problems and the Theory of the Firm". *The Journal of Political Economy,* Vol. 88, No. 2, 1980, pp. 288–307, 288.

voting right is the right that is universally held by shareholders to make all decisions not otherwise provided by contract because someone must have the residual power to act (or delegate) when contracts are not complete. The code of corporate law is a standard form contract for issues of corporate structure. On many occasions, the legal rules will not be sufficiently detailed.[163] The structural rules and the fiduciary principle together cover only the outline of the relations among corporate actors, whereas something must fill in the details: voting serves this function.[164] The voting right acts as a channel that connects the shareholder – who bears the risk of the company's success or failure (referred to as the "residual claimant") – and the managers, who have the power to steer the company on the desired course.[165] Shareholders are called "residual claimants" because – in contrast to employees and creditors – their compensation is not specified by a contract and if the company were to be liquidated they would only receive their investment back after all the other claimants are paid. As Judge Frank H. Easterbrook and Professor Daniel R. Fischel – the principle exponents of this theory – explain:

> *Shareholders are the residual claimants to the firm's income. Creditors have fixed claims and employees generally negotiate compensation schedules in advance of performance. The gains and losses from abnormally good or bad performance are the lot of shareholders, whose claims stand last in line. As the residual claimants, shareholders have the appropriate incentives (collective choice problems notwithstanding) to make discretionary decisions ... [M]anagers' knowledge that they are being monitored by those have the right incentives ... leads managers to act in shareholders' interests in order to advance their own careers and to avoid being ousted.*[166]

In economic theory, voting rights are instrumental, not essential, but they serve to attain a pre-conceived goal (e.g. maximizing profits), and to make it accountable to the shareholders. Voting legitimized management power by making management accountable to the will of the shareholders.[167] Shareholder voting offers the potential to serve as a mediated market constraint on managerial power, mediated in the sense that it enables shareholders collectively to exercise control in a more moderated fashion than by selling their stock, either to a hostile bidder or into the

---

163 See Easterbrook, Frank H. / Fischel, Daniel R.: "Corporate Control Transactions". *Yale Law Journal*, Vol. 91, No. 4, 1982, pp. 698–737, 698.

164 See Easterbrook, Frank H. / Fischel, Daniel R.: "The Proper Role of a Target's Management in Responding to a Tender Offer". *Harvard Law Review*, Vol. 94, No. 6, 1981, pp. 1161–1204, 1170–1171.

165 See Easterbrook, Frank H. / Fischel, Daniel R.: *The economic structure of corporate law*. Harvard University Press: 1991, p. 67.

166 Easterbrook, Frank H. / Fischel, Daniel R.: *The economic structure of corporate law*. Harvard University Press: 1991, p. 67.

167 See Cahn, Andreas / Donald, David C.: *Comparative Company Law: Text and Cases on the Laws Governing Corporations in Germany, the UK and the USA*. Cambridge: July 2010, p. 473.

open market. For shareholders who believe that a corporation's strategic direction is misguided, a shift in board representation may carry this message. For shareholders who believe that management is overly entrenched, governance changes such as increasing shareholder nomination power or dismantling takeover defenses may be appropriate. Moreover, improving corporate governance through proxy contests is far less costly than a hostile takeover, thus making it potentially viable in large public companies.[168]

Professor Lilli A. Gordon and John Pound perceive the anti-takeover devices that governments tend to adopt as proof that takeovers are inferior to controlling management through voting.[169] Properly understood, shareholder voting is not an integral aspect of the corporate decision-making structure, but rather an accountability device of last resort to be used sparingly. Indeed, as Robert Clark observes, the proper way in which shareholder voting rights are used to hold corporate directors and officers accountable is not through the exercise of individual voting decisions but rather collectively in the context of a takeover.[170] Because shares are freely transferable, a bidder who believes that the firm is being run poorly can profit by offering to buy a controlling block of stock at a premium over the market and subsequently displacing the incumbent managers, which presumably will result in an increase in firm value exceeding the premium paid by the bidder for control. Hence, shareholder voting only properly comes into play as an accountability "when management performance is sufficiently degraded from expectations" to make a takeover fight worth waging.[171] Voters may elect directors and give them discretionary powers over things that voters could otherwise control.[172] In particular, the most significant matter subject to the vote and approval of the shareholders is the election of directors, because the main source of corporate control for a shareholder lies in his/her ability to elect representatives on the board of directors who are responsible for running the corporations.[173]

---

168 See Fisch, Jill E.: "The Overstated Promise of Corporate Governance – Corporate Governance: Promises Kept, Promises Broken by Jonathan Macey". *The University of Chicago Law Review*, Vol. 77, No. 2, Spring 2010, pp. 923–958, 935.

169 See Gordon, Lilli A. / Pound, John: "Information, Ownership Structure, and Shareholder Voting: Evidence from Shareholder-Sponsored Corporate Governance Proposals". *The Journal of Finance*, Vol. 48, No. 2, 6.1993, pp. 697–718.

170 See Clark, Robert Charles: *Corporate Law*. New York: Aspen Publishers, 1986, p. 95.

171 See Bainbridge, Stephen M.: *The New Corporate Governance in Theory and Practice*. Oxford University Press: 7.2008, p. 236.

172 See Easterbrook, Frank H. / Fischel, Daniel R.: "The Proper Role of a Target's Management in Responding to a Tender Offer". *Harvard Law Review*, Vol. 94, No. 6, 1981, pp. 1161–1204, 1170–1171.

173 See Velasco, Julian: "The Fundamental Rights of the Shareholder". *UC Davis Law Review*, Vol. 40, No. 2, 2006, pp. 407–467, 411.

B. Decline of Cumulative Voting and the Rise of Independent Directors in the US

In the US, cumulative voting spread relatively rapidly throughout the late-19th century, whereby seven states had adopted mandatory cumulative voting provisions by 1880 and this number had increased to eighteen by 1900. Later on, some states began to enact permissive cumulative voting statutes.[174] The use of cumulative voting peaked in the 1940s, when 22 states mandated it and 15 specifically permitted it. Forty percent of 2,900 major corporations surveyed then allowed cumulative voting for the election of directors.[175] However, several important states adopted permissive provisions, including New York (1892), New Jersey (1900), and then – as part of its move to corporate preeminence – Delaware (1917).[176] In particular, Delaware law definitely did not require minority stockholders to have board representation.[177]

However, mandatory cumulative voting fell into great disfavor in the 1990s, leaving only five remaining adherents – Arizona, Nebraska, North Dakota, South Dakota and West Virginia – none of which is a major commercial state.[178] Accordingly, companies incorporated in these states account for less than 1% of all companies in IRRC's core research universe.[179] The Model Business Corporate Act (MBCA) adopted mandatory cumulative voting in the 1950s and subsequently shifted to the allowance of choosing permissive cumulative voting in 1955, before finally abolished the opt-out form and provided the opt-in model only in 1984.[180]

Deregulation has meant a steady decline regarding the use of cumulative voting.[181] As the adherents to mandatory cumulative voting argued, if cumulative voting were desirable, it "should not be at the will of incorporators who may compose the majority group, nor should a majority be afforded the opportunity to withdraw

174 See Baumgardner v. Stockley, 13 N.E. 279, 280 (Ohio 1887); Bowes, Harlowe E. / De Bow, Ledlie A.: "Cumulative Voting at Elections of Directors of Corporations". *Minnesota Law Review,* Vol. 21, No. 4, 1937, pp. 351–370, 355.

175 See Gordon, Jeffrey N.: "Institutions as Relational Investors: A New Look at Cumulative Voting". *Columbia Law Review,* Vol. 94, No. 1, 1.1994, pp. 124–192, 145.

176 See Gordon, Jeffrey N.: "Institutions as Relational Investors: A New Look at Cumulative Voting". *Columbia Law Review,* Vol. 94, No. 1, 1.1994, pp. 124–192, 145.

177 See 8 Del. C. 1953, § 214; 56 Del. Laws, c. 50; 57 Del. Laws, c. 148, § 37; 57 Del. Laws, c. 421, § 5; 71 Del. Laws, c. 339, § 32.

178 See Gordon, Jeffrey N.: "Institutions as Relational Investors: A New Look at Cumulative Voting". *Columbia Law Review,* Vol. 94, No. 1, 1.1994, pp. 124–192, 145–146.

179 See Personick, Martin E.: *IRRC Corporate Governance Service 2005 Background Report F: Voting Issues: Confidential and Cumulative Voting.* Investor Responsibility Research Center, 2.2005.

180 Article 7.28(b) of MBCA stipulates that "Shareholders do not have a right to cumulate their votes for directors unless the articles of incorporation so provide."

181 See Gordon, Jeffrey N.: "Institutions as Relational Investors: A New Look at Cumulative Voting". *Columbia Law Review,* Vol. 94, No. 1, 1.1994, pp. 124–192, 145–146.

any such grant at its pleasure by amending the corporate charter or by-laws."[182] Thus, cumulative voting has all but vanished among publicly traded firms.[183] Of the 1,500 major US corporations tracked by IRRC, 14.4% allowed cumulative voting in 1996 and the percentage gradually decreased to 8.3% by 2004.[184] According to the IRRC Corporate Governance Service 2005 Background Report F, cumulative voting has declined and fewer than 10% of American corporations now practice it.[185] The protection of minority shareholders under U.S. law today is principally transaction- rather than governance-based. The historical concern that American law showed for the rights of minority shareholders in structuring corporate governance rules – a concern suggested by the widespread requirement of mandatory cumulative voting at the beginning of the twentieth century – is now long past.[186]

I. Weakening of the Market for Corporate Control

In fact, the decline of cumulative voting – which followed the weakening of the market for corporate control, which was active in the 1970s and 1980s – can be attributed to misuse in hostile takeovers, which became a fearful threat and almost one-quarter of the major US corporations received an unwanted bid[187] and presented a sustained challenge to managerial control. Although both theory and evidence support the idea that hostile takeovers may solve governance problems and concur to reduce agency

---

182 See Bowes, Harlowe E. / De Bow, Ledlie A.: "Cumulative Voting at Elections of Directors of Corporations". *Minnesota Law Review,* Vol. 21, No. 4, 1937, pp. 351–370, 370.

183 See Easterbrook, Frank / Fischel, Daniel: "Voting in Corporate Law". *Journal of Law and Economics,* Vol. 26, No. 2, 1983, pp. 395–427, 395; Corporations and Private Property: "A Conference Sponsored by the Hoover Institution". *Journal of law and economics,* Vol. 26, No. 2, 6.1983, pp. 395–427, 409.

184 See Personick, Martin E.: *IRRC Corporate Governance Service 2005 Background Report F: Voting Issues: Confidential and Cumulative Voting.* Investor Responsibility Research Center, 2.2005.

185 See Personick, Martin E.: *IRRC Corporate Governance Service 2005 Background Report F: Voting Issues: Confidential and Cumulative Voting.* Investor Responsibility Research Center, 2.2005.

186 See Kraakman, Reinier / Armour, John / Davies, Paul / Enriques, Luca / Hansmann, Henry B. / Hertig, Gérard / Hopt, Klaus J. / Kanda, Hideki / Rock, Edward B.: *The anatomy of corporate law – A Comparative and Functional Approach.* Oxford University Press: 2nd Edition, 2009, p. 68.

187 Even very large firms came under attack from financial buyers, whose access to the junk bond market meant that they could engineer a highly leveraged transaction that would ultimately be repaid through the sale of various corporate divisions and other assets (a "bust-up"). See Mitchell, Mark L. / Mulherin, J. Harold: "The Impact of Industry Shocks on Takeover and Restructuring Activity". *Journal of Financial Economics,* Vol. 41, No. 2, 6.1996, pp. 193–229, 195.

costs[188] because takeover targets are often poorly performing firms and their managers are removed once the takeover succeeds, the market for corporate control – which places an unprecedented emphasis upon shareholder value as the ultimate corporate objective – come to be seen as an excessively way of solving the managerial agency problem and some takeovers are economically irrational-funded by cheap debt and leading to excessive leverage, while at the same time hostile takeovers may transfer wealth from stakeholders to shareholders of target firms.[189]

As the dominant law and economics view of the 1980s, Easterbrook and Fischel argued that incumbent management should be precluded from interfering with hostile takeovers owing to the clear benefits of the takeover market. Accordingly, they advocated a policy of management passivity.[190] They also argued that both shareholder monitoring and intra-firm monitors such as independent directors were inadequate to reduce such costs.[191] Thus, they concluded that a hostile bidder was the best monitor because it could surmount the free rider problem, which left individual shareholders without substantial incentives to expend resources on monitoring and enforcement.

Other commentators disagreed, arguing that not all takeovers were efficient. Indeed, they claimed that some takeovers were economically irrational-funded by cheap debt, leading to excessive leverage. These concerns have renewed resonance in today's market. According to takeover critics, some takeovers largely comprise wealth transfers-from one group of shareholders to another, from creditors to shareholders and from employees to shareholders.[192] Some takeovers take advantage of

---

188 For the positive view of the market for corporate control, see generally Manne, Henry G.: "Mergers and the Market for Corporate Control". *The Journal of Political Economy*, Vol. 73, No. 2, 4.1965, pp. 110–120; Jensen, Michael C.: "Takeovers: Their Causes and Consequences". *The Journal of Economic Perspectives*, Vol. 2, No. 1, Winter 1988, pp. 21–48; Scharfstein, David: "The Disciplinary Role of Takeovers". *The Review of Economic Studies*, Vol. 55, No. 2, 4.1988, pp. 185–199; Jarrell, Gregg A. / Brickley, James A. / Netter, Jeffry M.: "The Market for Corporate Control: The Empirical Evidence Since 1980". *Journal of Economic Perspectives*, Vol. 2, No. 1, 1988, pp. 49–68; S. Chatterjee / J. Harrison / D. Bergh: "Failed hostile takeover attempts, corporate governance and refocusing". *Strategic Management Journal*, Vol. 24, No. 1, 2003, pp. 87–96.

189 See Shleifer, Andrei / Summers, Lawrence H.: "Breach of Trust in Hostile Takeovers". In: Auerbach, Alan J (ed.): *Corporate Takeovers: Causes and Consequences.* NBER book: 8.1987, pp. 33–68, 34.

190 See Easterbrook, Frank H. / Fischel, Daniel R.: "The Proper Role of a Target's Management in Responding to a Tender Offer". *Harvard Law Review*, Vol. 94, No. 6, 1981, pp. 1161–1204, 1164.

191 See Easterbrook, Frank H. / Fischel, Daniel R.: "The Proper Role of a Target's Management in Responding to a Tender Offer". *Harvard Law Review*, Vol. 94, No. 6, 1981, pp. 1161–1204, 1173.

192 Perhaps the best-known advocate of management discretion in response to an unsolicited takeover offer is Martin Lipton. See Lipton, Martin / Rowe, Paul K.:

market conditions to buy out shareholders at a temporary premium, reflecting an unfair bargain price. Shareholder collective action problems couple with – in some cases – incomplete disclosure and coercive structures make it difficult for shareholders to identify these situations and distinguish them from truly value-enhancing transactions. In addition, the takeover market is limited in its applicability as a corporate governance mechanism. Takeovers are costly and some companies are simply too large to be bought. The cost of financing requires appropriate credit market conditions. Most importantly, takeovers are only effective if a company's stock price is undervalued. If the stock price is too high, whether owing to a general market bubble or company-specific fraud, the takeover market does not offer a mechanism for correction.[193] To date, the empirical analysis of takeovers has failed to resolve the dispute over their efficiency.

Due to cumulative voting, an insurgent can obtain a significant measure of success merely by obtaining enough votes for board representation, from which the insurgent can plan another campaign or press for new business strategies. Indeed, it was the most convincing anti-cumulative voting argument brought forward in the 1950s:

> *"The 'raider' is pictured as using cumulative voting to elect a minority of the directors either as a first step toward eventually electing a majority of the directors and wresting control from a dedicated and successful management in order to carry out his personal designs; or as a means of pressuring that management, through harassing conduct and threats in and out of directors meetings, into taking the action demanded by the 'raider' at the expense of the majority stockholders. Such action might take the form of acquiring some property in which the 'raider' is interested, declaring unwise dividends or other action to cause a temporary rise in the market price of the stock so that he can take a profit at capital gain rates, or the corporation buying out his shares at an exorbitant price."*[194]

"Pills, Polls and Professors: A Reply to Professor Gilson". *The Delaware Journal of Corporate Law*, Vol. 27, No. 1, 2002, pp. 1–55, 29. (observing that managers may have better information than shareholders about firm value); Lipton, Martin: "Takeover Bids in the Target's Boardroom". *Business Lawyer*, Vol. 34, No.1, 1979, pp. 101–134, 107 (finding that in over half of the failed takeover attempts studied, shareholders were better off than they would have been if the takeover bid had been successful); Moeller, Sara B. / Schlingemann, Frederik P. / Stulz, Rene M.: "Do Shareholders of Acquiring Firms Gain from Acquisitions?". *National Bureau of Economic Research*, Working Paper 9523, 2.2003, retrieved 12.4.2013, from http://www.nber.org /papers/w9523.

193 See Fisch, Jill E.: "The Overstated Promise of Corporate Governance – Corporate Governance: Promises Kept, Promises Broken by Jonathan Macey". *The University of Chicago Law Review*, Vol. 77, No. 2, Spring 2010, pp. 923–958, 942.

194 Sturdy, Herbert L.: "Mandatory Cumulative Voting: An Anachronism". *Business Lawyer* Vol. 16, No. 3, 4.1961, pp. 550–576, 550; See also Axley, Ralph E.: "The Case Against Cumulative Voting". *Wisconsin Law Review*, Vol. 1950, No. 2, 1950, pp. 278–287, 283.

Thus, cumulative voting was perceived as increasing the risk of a hostile takeover bid. The danger created by cumulative voting was described whereby "even if raiders are not able to gain immediate control of the targets, board representation gives them access to confidential internal corporate information and creates the possibility of disruption at the board level...."[195] Consequently, management's willingness to change the corporate domicile to avoid cumulative voting had a significant impact on the decision of several states to shift to permissive regimes.[196] In this respect, business elites needed a credible board-centered governance mechanism to address performance issues in substitution for the market-centered approach[197] associated with the hostile tender offer. Managers turned to the monitoring board and independent directors as a critical element in the intellectual and legal architecture necessary to preserve managerial autonomy against the pressure of the market in corporate control and a substitute for greater government intervention in the wake of scandals,[198] despite the encroachment on managerial autonomy.[199] The court also regarded an independent director – who was most likely to resist management's self-interested strategies that undermined the shareholders' welfare[200] – as

---

195 Fleischer A. / Sussman A.R. / Lesser H.: *Takeover Defense.* Prentice Hall Law & Business: 4th Edition, 1990, p. 457; Mitchell M.L. / Mulherin J.H. / Netter J.M., Poulsen A.B.: "Shark Repellents and Managerial Myopia: An Empirical Test". *The Journal of Political Economy,* Vol. 98, No. 5, 10.1990, pp. 1108–1117.

196 A survey of the Fortune 500 in 1992 found eleven firms that had shifted corporate domicile to Delaware in the mid-1980s to avoid cumulative voting. The timing correlates rather well with the shifts by nine states from mandatory to permissive regimes in the late 1980s. See Gordon, Jeffrey N.: *What is Relational Investing and How Cumulative Voting Can Play a Role.* (Columbia University Center for Law & Economic Studies Working Paper No. 97). New York: Center for Law and Economic Studies, Columbia University School of Law, 1993.

197 See Gordon, Jeffrey N.: "The Rise of Independent Directors in the United States, 1950–2005: Of Shareholder Value and Stock Market Prices". *Stanford Law Review,* Vol. 59, No. 6, 2007, pp. 1465–1568, 1522.

198 See Gordon, Jeffrey N.: "The Rise of Independent Directors in the United States, 1950–2005: Of Shareholder Value and Stock Market Prices". *Stanford Law Review,* Vol. 59, No. 6, 2007, pp. 1465–1568, 1472.

199 "The courts have historically been reluctant to expose corporate fiduciaries to potentially astronomical liabilities unless the underlying conduct strikes them as morally egregious. As a result, the traditional duty of due care is likely to be enforced by courts only if liabilities are reduced to a reasonable level by imposing a ceiling on maximum liability." See Coffee, John C. / Schwartz, Donald E.: "The Survival of the Derivative Suit: An Evaluation and a Proposal for Legislative Reform". *Columbia Law Review,* Vol. 81, No. 2, 3.1981, pp. 261–336, 316–318.

200 See Gordon, Jeffrey N.: "Corporations, Markets, and Courts". *Columbia Law Review,* Vol. 91, No. 8, 12.1991, pp. 1931–1988, 1961; Palmiter, Alan R.: "Reshaping the Corporate Fiduciary Model: A Director's Duty of Independence". *Texas Law Review,* Vol. 67, No. 7, 1989, pp. 1351–1464, 1368; Easterbrook, Frank H. / Fischel, Daniel R.: "The Proper Role of a Target's Management in Responding to a Tender Offer".

a relatively low-cost mechanism for corporate governance than a hostile takeover. According to Unocal Corp. v. Mesa Petroleum Co., the Delaware courts stressed the role of independent directors in approving the takeover defense by holding that the presence of an independent board majority shifted the burden of proof from the directors to the tender offeror, because without any conflict directors could exercise independent business judgment.[201] Moran also found that the proof that directors' action was reasonable was "materially enhanced ... where ... a majority of the board favoring the proposal consisted of independent directors".[202] Thus, it

---

Harvard Law Review, Vol. 94, No. 6, 1981, pp. 1161–1204, 1169; Johnson, Jennifer J. / Siegel, Mary: "Corporate Mergers: Redefining the Role of Target Directors". *University of Pennsylvania Law Review*, Vol. 136, No. 2, 12.1987, pp. 315–416, 379; Polk v. Good, 507 A.2d 531, 537 (Del. 1986) ("The presence of the 10 outside directors on the Texaco board, coupled with the advice rendered by the investment banker and legal counsel, constitute a prima facie showing of good faith and reasonable investigation."); Panter v. Marshall Field & Co., 646 F.2d 271, 294 (7th Cir.) (noting that presumption of good faith afforded by business judgment rule heightens when independent outside directors compose the majority of the board), cert. denied, 454 US 1092 (1981); Enterra Corp. v. SGS Associates, 600 F. Supp. 678, 685 (E.D. Pa. 1985); Ivanhoe Partners v. Newmont Mining Corp., Nos. 9281, 9221 (Del. Ch. Oct. 15, 1987) (noting favorably that a majority of the board members who enacted defensive tactics were outside independent directors); Puma v. Marriott, 283 A.2d 693, 696 (Del. Ch. 1971) (noting that the sole interest of outside independent directors is "the furtherance of the corporate enterprise").

201 Unocal Corp. v. Mesa Petroleum Co, 493 A.2d 946 (Del. 1985).

202 Moran v. Household Int'l, Inc., 500 A.2d 1346, 1356 (Del. 1985) (noting the proof that directors satisfied Unocal standards was "materially enhanced" when "a majority of the board favoring the proposal consisted of outside independent directors" who otherwise acted in accordance with those standards); See also Panter v. Marshall Field & Co., 646 F.2d 27I, 294 (7th Cir.), cert. denied, 454 US 1092 (1981); Martin Marietta Corp. v. Bendix Corp, 549 F. Supp. 623, 634 (D. Md. 1982); Paramount Communications, Inc. v. Time Inc., 571 A.2d 1140, 1154 (Del. 1989); Mills Acquisition Co. v. MacMillan, Inc., 559 A.2d 1261, 1287 (Del. 1988) ("In the absence of self-interest, and upon meeting the enhanced duty mandated by Unocal, the actions of an independent board of directors in designing and conducting a corporate auction are protected by the business judgment rule."), appeal dismissed, 548 A.2d 498 (1988); Revlon, Inc. v. MacAndrews & Forbes Holdings, Inc., 506 A.2d 173, 176 n.3 (Del. 1985) (rejecting to apply "certain presumptions that generally attach to the decisions of a board whose majority consists of truly outside independent directors" when evidence was at best unclear as to directors' independence); Gelfond, Sebastian: "Reevaluating the Duties of Target Management in a Hostile Tender Offer". *Boston University Law Review*, Vol. 60, No. 3, 1980, pp. 403–473, 470–472 (adoption of defensive tactics by independent directors with professional financial assistance allows application of the business judgment rule). If a majority of the current board was not independent, the board would appoint a special committee composed primarily of outside directors in order to respond to

appears that there was a substantial decline in the number of unsolicited tender offers beginning in the 1990s. At the same time, there was a shift toward corporate boards with a majority of outside directors. The increase in independent directors could be attributed to the failure of the market for corporate control as a corrective measure against managerial inefficiency. Rather than market of corporate control and cumulative voting, the independent board helped to lock in shareholder value as the guide for management behavior. The fact is that the most important development of independent directors occurred in the 1990s as part of the post-hostile bid settlement among institutional investors, managers and boards.[203]

II. Re-concentrated Corporate Ownership

In the US, there has been a recent re-concentration of ownership in the hands of institutional investment intermediaries, which gives rise to "the agency costs of agency capitalism." Even if the prevailing ownership structures in the US are less concentrated than in continental Europe, this feature of the American system is sometimes overestimated. Recent literature has questioned how diffused share ownership in the US really is, observing that this idea might largely be "a myth".[204] In 1950, the Berle-Means description advanced some twenty years earlier remained accurate. Equities were still predominantly held by households, whereas institutional investors – including pension funds – held only approximately 6.1% of US equities.[205] However, by 1980, the distribution of shareholdings began to shift away from households toward institutions. At that time, institutional investors held 28.4%

the tender offer; Simpson, Scott V.: "The Emerging Role of the Special Committee – Ensuring Business Judgment Rule Protection". *Business Lawyer*, Vol. 43, No. 2, 1988, pp. 665–690, 674; Veasey, E. Norman: "The New Incarnation of the Business Judgment Rule in Takeover Defenses". *Delaware Journal of Corporate Law*, Vol. 11, No. 2, 1986, pp. 503–512, 510–511 (Outside directors do not hold lucrative management positions, so a majority of the special committee would have much less of a conflict of interest than the full board would); Matheson, John H. / Norberg, Jon: "Hostile Share Acquisitions and Corporate Governance: A Framework for Evaluating Anti-takeover Activities". *University of Pittsburgh Law Review*, Vol. 47, 1986, pp. 407–491, 409 ("It may be part of management's duty to actively resist proposals that management does not consider to be in the best interests of the shareholders.").

203 Gordon, Jeffrey N.: "The Rise of Independent Directors in the United States, 1950–2005: Of Shareholder Value and Stock Market Prices". *Stanford Law Review*, Vol. 59, No. 6, 2007, pp. 1465–1568, 1477.

204 See Holderness, Clifford G.: "The Myth of Diffuse Ownership in the United States". *The Review of Financial Studies*, Vol. 22, No. 4, 2009, pp. 1377–1408, 1406.

205 See Tonello, Matteo / Rabimov, Stephan: "The 2010 Institutional Investment Report: Trends in Asset Allocation and Portfolio Composition". The Conference Bd., Inc., 2010, p. 22 table 10, retrieved 22.2.2013, from http://ssrn.com/abstract=1707512 (on file with the Columbia Law Review).

of US equities.[206] By 2009, institutional investors held 50.6% of all US public equities and 73% of the equity of the thousand largest US corporations.[207] By this, we mean that the beneficial owners of US equity confront two agency relationships: between the portfolio company management and the institutional record holder and between the record holder and the beneficial owner.[208] In 2011, institutional investors owned over 70% of the outstanding stock of the thousand largest US public corporations.[209] This ownership change occurred due to: (i) political decisions to privatize the provision of retirement savings and the funding requirement of such a provision; and (ii) capital market developments that favor investment intermediaries offering low-cost diversified investment vehicles. To cite the data from a research conducted by Clifford Holderness, 53% of US public corporations have a single family as a blockholder, versus 59% of the non-US firms examined. The average ownership percentage of these blockholders is 32% in the United States, versus 36% in other countries. The difference – at least according to this empirical evidence – is not as profound as it is commonly believed. In addition, owing to antitakeover devices and other legal mechanisms that can be adopted to protect the current management and the shareholders' coalition that support them in the US, it can be very difficult for minority shareholders to challenge a blockholder holding even a 30% stake in a listed corporation.[210]

The re-concentration of ownership of US equities in intermediary institutions has resulted in conflicting views of the corresponding governance structure. On the one hand, the concentration of ownership holds out the possibility that the institutions will – like Pinocchio – come to act like real boys, like "real" owners and actively

206 See Tonello, Matteo / Rabimov, Stephan: "The 2010 Institutional Investment Report: Trends in Asset Allocation and Portfolio Composition". The Conference Bd., Inc., 2010, p. 22 table 10, retrieved 22.2.2013, from http://ssrn.com/abstract=1707512 (on file with the Columbia Law Review).

207 See Tonello, Matteo / Rabimov, Stephan: "The 2010 Institutional Investment Report: Trends in Asset Allocation and Portfolio Composition". The Conference Bd., Inc., 2010, p. 22 table 10, retrieved 22.2.2013, from http://ssrn.com/abstract=1707512 (on file with the Columbia Law Review). For a time series of institutional ownership between 1950 and 2004, see Gordon, Jeffrey N.: "The Rise of Independent Directors in the United States, 1950–2005: Of Shareholder Value and Stock Market Prices". *Stanford Law Review*, Vol. 59, No. 6, 2007, pp. 1465–1568, 1568; Gillian, Stuart L. / Starks, Laura T.: "The Evolution of Shareholder Activism in the United States". *Journal of Applied Corporate Finance*, Vol. 19, No. 1, 2007, pp. 55–73, 57.

208 See Gilson, Ronald J. / Gordon, Jeffrey N.: "The Agency Costs of Agency Capitalism: Activist Investors and the Revaluation of Governance Rights". *Columbia Law Review*, Vol. 113, No. 4, 5.2013, pp. 863–927, 867.

209 See IRRC: *Controlled Companies in the Standard & Poor's 1500: A Ten Year Performance and Risk Review*, 10.2012, pp. 9–10.

210 See Holderness, Clifford G.: "The Myth of Diffuse Ownership in the United States". *The Review of Financial Studies*, Vol. 22, No. 4, 2009, pp. 1377–1409, 1396.

supervise the performance of professional management.[211] On the other hand, institutions have continually failed to play this role: despite the urging of academics and regulators, they remain stubbornly responsive yet not proactive.[212] A comprehensive 1998 survey conducted by Bernard S. Black found that institutions devoted little effort to monitoring management and rarely conducted proxy solicitations or put forward shareholder proposals, nor did they seek to elect representatives onto boards of directors; by contrast, they typically disclaimed the ability or desire to decide company-specific policy questions.[213] Roberta Romano has shown that public pension funds face political constraints that are likely to prevent them from serving very effectively as corporate managers.[214] Parrino, Sias and Starks find that many institutional investors still vote with their feet by selling their shares when they are dissatisfied with corporate decisions.[215] Jack Coffee has pointed out that the long-term, relational investment requiring institutional investors to have a voice in corporate governance may be too costly for such investors because it will entail a sacrifice of liquidity.[216] Even ardent proponents of institutional investor activism thus concede that institutions are unlikely to be involved in day-to-day corporate matters.[217] Jill Fisch has argued that institutional investors may not find it rational to engage in so-called "relational investing" unless they are given special benefits,

---

211 See Gilson, Ronald J. / Gordon, Jeffrey N.: "The Agency Costs of Agency Capitalism: Activist Investors and the Revaluation of Governance Rights". *Columbia Law Review*, Vol. 113, No. 4, 5.2013, pp. 863–927, 888.

212 See Gilson, Ronald J. / Kraakman, Reinier: "Reinventing the Outside Director: An Agenda for Institutional Investors". *Stanford Law Review*, Vol. 43, No. 4, 4.1991, pp. 863–906, 881–885.

213 Most importantly, the review found "no strong evidence of a correlation between firm performance and percentage of shares owned by institutions." See Black, Bernard S.: "Shareholder Activism and Corporate Governance in the United States". *New Palgrave Dictionary of Economics and the Law*, Vol. 3, 1998, pp. 459–465, 462.

214 See Romano, Roberta: "Public Pension Fund Activism in Corporate Governance Reconsidered". *Columbia Law Review*, Vol. 93, No. 4, 1993, pp. 795–853, 796.

215 See Parrino, Robert / Richard W. Sias / Laura T. Starks: "Voting with Their Feet: Institutional Ownership Changes around Forced CEO Turnover". *Journal of Financial Economics*, Vol. 68, No. 1, 2003, pp. 3–46, 43; "Because institutional investors are generally profit maximizers, they will not engage in an activity the costs of which exceed the benefits. On the benefit side of the equation, corporate governance activism is unattractive because in many cases, activism is unlikely to avail." See Bainbridge, Stephen M.: *The New Corporate Governance in Theory and Practice.* Oxford University Press: 7.2008, p. 208.

216 See Coffee, John C.: "Beyond the Shut-Eyed Sentry: Toward a Theoretical View of Corporate Misconduct and an Effective Legal Response". *Virginia Law Review*, Vol. 63, No. 7, November, 1977, pp. 1099–1278, 1271.

217 See Bainbridge, Stephen M.: *The New Corporate Governance in Theory and Practice.* Oxford University Press: 7.2008, p. 208.

which they are unlikely to receive.[218] Greenwood argues that hedge fund managers are generally ill-suited to make operational business decisions and – due to their short-term focus – are unlikely "to devote time and energy to a task delivering long-term value, because there are no guarantees that the effort will pay off, or that other shareholders would recognize the increase in value by paying a higher price per share". Instead, they mainly profit from transactions in corporate control rather than corporate governance activism because "hedge funds are better at identifying undervalued companies, locating potential acquirers for them, and removing opposition to a takeover"[219].

Capital market evolution has concentrated governance rights in fewer hands, despite continually urging conversely appears to have little interest in playing or in the capacity to play an active stewardship role in portfolio company governance. A new set of agency costs arises because in addition to the divergence between the interests of record owners and the firm's managers, divergence exists between the interests of record owners – the institutional investors – and the beneficial owners of those institutional stakes. Gompers, Ishii and Metrick contribute to the accumulating empirical evidence that controlling minority shareholder structures are associated with increased agency costs and reduced firm value.[220] The business model of key investment intermediaries like mutual funds[221] – which focuses on increasing assets under management through superior relative performance – undermines their incentive and competence to engage in the active monitoring of portfolio company performance. Such investors will be "rationally reticent", namely willing to respond to governance proposals but not to propose them.[222] First, mutual funds are potentially powerful: given the concentration in the mutual

218 See Fisch, Jill E.: "Taking Boards Seriously". *Cardozo Law Review*, Vol. 19, No. 1–2, 1997–1998, pp. 265–290, 265.

219 See Greenwood, Robin: *The Hedge Fund as Activist.* HBR Working Knowledge: 22.8.2007; His hypothesis was confirmed by his study incorporating over 1,000 cases of hedge fund activism, which found that "targets of investor activism earn high returns only for the subset of events in which the activist successfully persuades the target to merge or get acquired." See Bainbridge, Stephen M.: *The New Corporate Governance in Theory and Practice.* Oxford University Press: 7.2008, p. 207.

220 See Bebchuk, Lucian A. / Weisbach, Michael S.: "The State of Corporate Governance Research". *The Review of Financial Studies*, Vol. 23, No. 3, Corporate Governance, 3.2010, pp. 939–961, 949.

221 The peculiar position of institutional investors in the re-concentration of ownership of US public corporations can most easily be seen from the governance role played by mutual funds, both owing to their size and homogeneity and due to the extensive information available concerning their governance activities.

222 Gilson, Ronald J. / Gordon, Jeffrey N.: "The Agency Costs of Agency Capitalism: Activist Investors and the Revaluation of Governance Rights". *Columbia Law Review*, Vol. 113, No. 4, 5.2013, pp. 863–927, 863.

fund industry,[223] 25 mutual fund families hold the voting rights for some 18.75% of outstanding US equities.[224] By any measure, mutual funds have the power to be a significant force in the governance of large US corporations. Second, mutual funds are at least on the surface anything but proactive. For example, during the 2009 proxy season, the proxy statements of Russell 3000 corporations contained 20,434 proposals to be voted upon by shareholders. Of these, shareholders proposed 646 (3.2% of all proposals), whereas the remainder were proposed by management. In turn, during the 2007 to 2009 proxy seasons, mutual funds proposed only 84 (4.5% of all shareholder proposals).[225]

Third, while mutual funds are not proactive, they are not passive in the Berle-Means sense: they very frequently oppose management on core corporate governance issues. The most extreme example concerns voting on antitakeover matters – poison pills and staggered boards – and illustrates the extent to which mutual funds vote against management recommendations when the issue is presented to them. Over the 2004 and 2005 proxy seasons, mutual funds voted in favor of shareholder proposals to require shareholder approval before adopting a poison pill almost 80% of the time and in favor of proposals to declassify the board of directors 90% of the time.[226] The same results appear for the 2003–2008 period: mutual fund voting in favor of shareholder proposals to declassify the board reached 87.4%[227] and 68.4% with respect to shareholder proposals to require shareholder approval for a poison pill.[228]

Professor Gordon proposed that the institutional investors could revive cumulative voting by electing independent directors. Gordon's argument is based upon the fact that the market for corporate control through the tender offer was eliminated, while institutional investors emerged as a force in the world of corporate

---

223 See Gilson, Ronald J. / Gordon, Jeffrey N.: "The Agency Costs of Agency Capitalism: Activist Investors and the Revaluation of Governance Rights". *Columbia Law Review*, Vol. 113, No. 4, 5.2013, pp. 863–927, 886.

224 The calculation is based on the following two facts: in 2011, the largest twenty-five mutual fund families represented 73% of mutual fund assets under management. Investment Company Institute: *Investment Company Fact Book – A Review of Trends and Activity in the U.S. Investment Company Industry*. 52nd Edition, 2012, p. 12 fig.1.5.

225 See Investment Company Institute: *Investment Company Fact Book – A Review of Trends and Activity in the U.S. Investment Company Industry*. 52nd Edition, 2012, p. 8, fig.6.

226 See Morgan, Angela / Poulsen, Annette B. / Wolf, Jack G. / Yang, Tina: "Mutual Funds as Monitors: Evidence from Mutual Fund Voting". *Journal of Corporate Finance*, Vol. 17, No. 4, 9.2011, pp. 914–928, 920, table 2.

227 See Cotter, James / Palmiter, Alan / Thomas, Randall: "ISS Recommendations and Mutual Fund Voting on Proxy Proposals". *Villanova Law Review*, Vol. 55, No. 1, 55, 2010, pp. 1–56, 38.

228 See James Cotter, Alan Palmiter, Randall Thomas, ISS Recommendations and Mutual Fund Voting on Proxy Proposals, Villanova Law Review, Vol. 55, No. 1, 55, 2010, pp. 1–56, 44 table 5A.

governance. He holds that although cumulative voting could be used for self-serving purposes by a minority interest, the institutions – which on aggregate own more than 50% of the stock in many large corporations and serve as long-term investors in the firm-owners rather than as short-term traders or arbitrageurs – would be "well motivated" and could take a "board composition" approach to monitor the corporate governance and may attempt to take advantage of cumulative voting.[229] They are likely to use powers added by cumulative voting to pursue strategies that will increase share values, produce gains that are common to all shareholders and exert influence to enhance the quality, independence and accountability of the board, rather than intervening in business decision-making.[230] Furthermore, minority representation on the board could increase the likelihood of shareholders who launch a proxy fight to obtain at least a partial victory. This might strengthen the voice and monitoring function of institutional investors, leading to increased participation and improved directors' accountability.[231]

In recent years, due to the increasing role of institutional investors, the concern for self-referential and unaccountable boards has gained momentum and prompted several important reforms concerning minority shareholders' representatives, although these new rules at the state and federal levels mainly focus on shareholders' access to corporate proxy statements rather than on adopting cumulative voting. First, the state passed the North Dakota Publicly Traded Corporation Act (NDPTCA) of 2007, a decidedly "shareholders friendly" statute designed to facilitate a more active role for stockholders in the process of selecting the directors. Five key provisions characterize the new North Dakota statute: shareholders' access to corporate proxy statements, majority voting in directors' elections, shareholders' advisory vote on executive compensation, limitations of supermajority rules and anti-takeover provisions. Furthermore, in 2009, Delaware responded by amending Sections 112 and 113 of the state's General Corporation Law (hereinafter "DGCL") to explicitly allow a corporation to adopt shareholder-empowering rules analogous to those available under the NDPTCA. However, none of those amendments introduced a significant change to Delaware law because even before their enactment, the bylaws or charter could equally provide for proxy access and proxy expense reimbursement.[232] Finally, on May 20, 2009, the Securities and Exchange Commission (SEC) approved a proposed amendment to the existing proxy rules, with the intention of facilitating shareholders' nominations of directors. Pursuant to the amendment of Exchange Act Rule 14a-8(i) (8), shareholders meeting the minimum

---

229 See Gordon, Jeffrey N.: "Institutions as Relational Investors: A New Look at Cumulative Voting". *Columbia Law Review*, Vol. 94, No. 1, 1.1994, pp. 124–192, 127.

230 See Gordon, Jeffrey N.: "Institutions as Relational Investors: A New Look at Cumulative Voting". *Columbia Law Review*, Vol. 94, No. 1, 1.1994, pp. 124–192, 127.

231 Ventoruzzo, Marco: "Empowering Shareholders in Directors' Elections: A Revolution in the Making". *European Company and Financial Law Review*, Vol. 8, No. 2, 6.2011, pp. 105–144, 142.

232 CA, Inc. v. Afscme Employees Pension Plan, 953 A.2d 227(Del. 2008).

holding and tenure requirements are allowed to access the company's proxy material to propose bylaws amendments concerning the procedures of nominating directors.[233] This procedure merely made it possible for shareholders to support the adoption of cumulative voting or other similar arrangements that might facilitate the appointment of a more diverse board of directors.[234] During the 2009 proxy season, 28 proposals for adopting cumulative voting for directors' elections were presented.[235] While almost one-quarter of all the outstanding shareholders voted in favor of cumulative voting on average, as a matter of fact, none of the proposals to adopt cumulative voting were approved.[236]

C. Non-Adoption of Cumulative Voting in the EU

The adoption of independent directors according to the Commission Recommendation has triggered the issue that the EU Green Paper of 2011 proposed in question (21) by stating that "Do you think that minority shareholders need additional rights to represent their interests effectively in companies with controlling or dominating shareholders?"[237] A positive answer would justify the recourse to multiple-winner voting systems[238] such as cumulative voting. However, as reported in the Feedback Statement on the consultation, the vast majority of respondents – who share the view that minority shareholders are already sufficiently protected[239] – are opposed to board representation of minority shareholders, arguing that additional rights

---

233 "Under the new rule, proxy proposals that would disqualify a director standing for election, remove her before end of her term or affect in other ways the outcome of an election could still be excluded by the corporation." See Ventoruzzo, Marco: "Empowering Shareholders in Directors' Elections: A Revolution in the Making". *European Company and Financial Law Review*, Vol. 8, No. 2, 6.2011, pp. 105–144, 122.

234 Ventoruzzo, Marco: "Empowering Shareholders in Directors' Elections: A Revolution in the Making". *European Company and Financial Law Review*, Vol. 8, No. 2, 6.2011, pp. 105–144, 121.

235 Ventoruzzo, Marco: "Empowering Shareholders in Directors' Elections: A Revolution in the Making". *European Company and Financial Law Review*, Vol. 8, No. 2, 6.2011, pp. 105–144, 129.

236 Ventoruzzo, Marco: "Empowering Shareholders in Directors' Elections: A Revolution in the Making". *European Company and Financial Law Review*, Vol. 8, No. 2, 6.2011, pp. 105–144, 130.

237 *EU Green Paper of 2011*, p. 17.

238 Davies, Paul L. / Hopt, Klaus J.: "Corporate Boards in Europe – Accountability and Convergence". *American Journal Comparative Law*, Vol. 61, No. 2, 2013, pp. 301–375, 338.

239 "Many respondents advanced two arguments in particular: one being that additional rights are only increase the potential for abuse by minority shareholders and are contrary to shareholders equality; the other that minority shareholders do not form a homogenous group." Feedback Statement, p. 22.

are merely likely to increase the potential for abuse and that granting them would be contrary to shareholder equality.[240] Thus, the EU Action Plan does not mention this system.

I. Non-executive or Supervisory Directors of Listed Companies

The purpose of independent representatives is to monitor the management by playing an effective role in key areas where the potential for conflict of interest is particularly high, as well as to balance the power of controlling shareholders and minority shareholders – rather than merely protecting the latter – to ensure that no individual or small group of individuals can dominate decision-making on the part of these bodies.[241] Article 4 stipulates the number of independent directors: a sufficient number of independent non-executive or supervisory directors should be elected to the (supervisory) board of companies to ensure that any material conflict of interest involving directors will be properly dealt with. In fact, according to an European survey by Heidrick and Struggles, fewer independent directors are found in Europe.[242] Despite the existence of considerable variation across European countries, there seems to have been no structural change in board independence levels in recent years, with the average board independence in European Firms remaining stable at 34% from 2004 to 2010.[243] In the Netherlands, 75% of all supervisory board members were independent, as well as 72% in Finland, 62% in Switzerland, 61% in the United Kingdom, 51% in Norway and 48% in Italy.[244] Countries below the European

---

240 See Feedback Statement, p. 16. Cumulative voting has been criticized for in fact allowing greater power to directors who are either shareholders themselves or hold the proxies of smaller shareholders. Gordon, Jeffrey N.: "Institutions as Relational Investors: A New Look at Cumulative Voting". *Columbia Law Review*, Vol. 94, No. 1, 1.1994, pp.124–192, 142–160; More obviously, cumulative voting cannot help the typical public shareholder in a listed company, who holds far less than the minimum proportion – one divided by the total number of directors – required to elect a single director. Clarke, Donald C.: "Nothing but Wind? The Past and Future of Comparative Corporate Governance". *American Journal of Comparative Law*, Vol. 59, No. 1, 2011, pp. 75–110, 89.

241 See Davies, Paul L. / Hopt, Klaus J.: "Corporate Boards in Europe – Accountability and Convergence". *American Journal Comparative Law*, Vol. 61, No. 2, 2013, pp. 301–375, 323.

242 See Heidrick, Struggles: *European Corporate Governance Report 2011: Challenging Board Performance*. p. 42, figure 35.

243 See Ferreira, Daniel / Kirchmaier, Tom: "Corporate Boards in Europe: size, independence and gender diversity". In: Belcredi, Massimo / Ferrarini, Guido (eds.): *Boards and shareholders in European listed companies: facts, context and post-crisis reforms*. International Corporate Law and Financial Market Regulation. Cambridge University Press: 2.2014, pp. 191–223, 198.

244 See Heidrick, Struggles: *European Corporate Governance Report 2011: Challenging Board Performance*. p. 42, figure 35.

average of 43% independent directors included France and Sweden (40%), Austria (36%), Spain (33%), Belgium (32%), Denmark (30%) and finally Germany (21%), which had the lowest ratio of independent directors in the survey.[245] Nonetheless, when the concept of independent director was incorporated into the corporate governance codes, there was a considerable convergence in the EU,[246] despite the fact that this caused considerable difficulties for countries with a concentrated shareholder structure such as Germany regarding independence from a controlling shareholder; indeed, this issue caused some resistance. In Germany, according to the GCGC, the recommendation is simply that "the supervisory board shall include what it considers an adequate number of independent members", without specifying a specific number of independent directors.[247]

1. *Independence and Controlling Shareholders*

According to Commission Recommendation (18), "corporate governance codes adopted in the Member States recognize the need for a significant proportion of non-executive or supervisory directors to be independent, that is to say, free of any material conflict of interest. Independence is most often understood as the absence of close ties with management, controlling shareholders or the company itself." Article 13.1 provides that "a director should be considered to be independent only if he is free of any business, family or other relationship, with the company, its controlling shareholder or the management of either, that creates a conflict of interest such as to impair his judgment."[248]

In the absence of any common understanding of what independence precisely entails, Commission Recommendation (18) proposes that "it is appropriate to provide a general statement describing what the general objective is. Provision should also be made to cover a (non-exhaustive) number of situations, involving the relationships or circumstances usually recognized as likely to generate a material conflict of interest, which Member States must duly consider when introducing at national level the criteria to be used by the (supervisory) board. The determination of what constitutes independence should principally be an issue for the (supervisory) board itself to determine. When the (supervisory) board applies the independence criteria, it should focus on substance rather than form." Article 13.2 provides that a number of criteria for assessing the independence of directors should be adopted at the national level,

245 See Heidrick, Struggles: *European Corporate Governance Report 2011: Challenging Board Performance.* p. 42, figure 35.

246 See more generally, Martynova M. / Renneboog L.: "Evidence on the international evolution and convergence of corporate governance regulations". *Journal of Corporate Finance,* Vol. 17, No. 5, 2011, pp. 1531–1557, 1531.

247 *GCGC,* Article 5.4.2.

248 *Commission Recommendation,* Article 13.1.

taking into account the guidance set out in Annex II,[249] which identifies a number of situations reflecting the relationships or circumstances usually recognized as

249 Commission Recommendation, Annex II Profile of independent non-executive or supervisory directors: It is not possible to list comprehensively all threats to directors' independence; the relationships or circumstances which may appear relevant to its determination may vary to a certain extent across Member States and companies, and best practices in this respect may evolve over time. However, a number of situations are frequently recognized as relevant in helping the (supervisory) board to determine whether a non-executive or supervisory director may be regarded as independent, even though it is widely understood that assessment of the independence of any particular director should be based on substance rather than form. In this context, a number of criteria, to be used by the (supervisory) board, should be adopted at national level. Such criteria, which should be tailored to the national context, should be based on due consideration of at least the following situations:
(a) not to be an executive or managing director of the company or an associated company, and not having been in such a position for the previous five years;
(b) not to be an employee of the company or an associated company, and not having been in such a position for the previous three years, except when the non-executive or supervisory director does not belong to senior management and has been elected to the (supervisory) board in the context of a system of workers' representation recognized by law and providing for adequate protection against abusive dismissal and other forms of unfair treatment;
(c) not to receive, or have received, significant additional remuneration from the company or an associated company apart from a fee received as non-executive or supervisory director. Such additional remuneration covers in particular any participation in a share option or any other performance-related pay scheme; it does not cover the receipt of fixed amounts of compensation under a retirement plan (including deferred compensation) for prior service with the company (provided that such compensation is not contingent in any way on continued service);
(d) not to be or to represent in any way the controlling shareholder(s) (control being determined by reference to the cases mentioned in Article 1(1) of Council Directive 83/349/EEC (1));
(e) not to have, or have had within the last year, a significant business relationship with the company or an associated company, either directly or as a partner, shareholder, director or senior employee of a body having such a relationship. Business relationships include the situation of a significant supplier of goods or services (including financial, legal, advisory or consulting services), of a significant customer, and of organizations that receive significant contributions from the company or its group;
(f) not to be, or have been within the last three years, partner or employee of the present or former external auditor of the company or an associated company;
(g) not to be executive or managing director in another company in which an executive or managing director of the company is non-executive or supervisory director, and not to have other significant links with executive directors of the company through involvement in other companies or bodies;

being likely to generate material conflict of interest. The EU Green Paper 2011 does not touch upon independence as a discussion theme and mentions it just once as one of the "broad set of criteria" for the selection of non-executive board members. According to the Report on the application by the Member States of the EU of the Commission Recommendation on the role of non-executive or supervisory directors of listed companies and on the committees of the (supervisory) board (hereinafter "the Report"),[250] all Member States now require or recommend the presence of independent directors in (supervisory) boards, although differences in the definition of independence make standards uneven.[251] Several Member States apply the entire set of independence criteria contained in the Commission Recommendation[252] and a considerable number of Member States recommend almost all the independence criteria.[253] However, in some Member States, there is only a general definition in place, whereas no independence criteria have been specified or there are only very general criteria in place (e.g. Slovakia, Malta and Germany).[254]

In particular, it is worth examining their role in the German corporate governance system to show that independence from management does not necessarily lead to the protection of shareholder interests. Germany adopts the independence requirements for supervisory board by GCGC, in which Article 5.4.2 provides that the supervisory board shall include what it considers an adequate number of independent members. Within the meaning of this recommendation, a supervisory board member is not to be considered independent in particular if he/she has personal or business relations with the company, its executive bodies, a controlling shareholder or an enterprise associated with the latter that may cause a substantial and not merely temporary conflict of interests. Not more than two former members of the management board shall be members of the supervisory board and supervisory board members shall not exercise directorships or similar positions or advisory tasks

---

(h) not to have served on the (supervisory) board as a non-executive or supervisory director for more than three terms (or, alternatively, more than 12 years where national law provides for normal terms of a very small length);
(i) not to be a close family member of an executive or managing director, or of persons in the situations referred to in points (a) to (h);

250 The Report, p. 10. The report is based on the replies of Member States to a Commission questionnaire as well as on the examination of national corporate governance codes of 21 Member States, aiming at evaluating whether Member States have put in place the necessary framework in order to give effect to the main principles of the Recommendation.

251 A comprehensive survey among European Members States in 2009 concluded that "there are considerable discrepancies in the stringency of independence definitions from one Member State to the other". European Commission, Study on Monitoring and Enforcement Practices in Corporate Governance in the Member States, September 23th, 2009, p. 75.

252 E.g. Poland, Belgium, Estonia, Latvia, Lithuania and Luxemburg.

253 The Report, p. 7.

254 The Report, p. 7.

for important competitors of the enterprise. Furthermore, Article 5.4.4 of GCGC and Article 100 (2) of AktG provides a cooling-off period for management board members who may not become members of the supervisory board of the company within two years after the end of their appointment unless they are appointed upon a motion presented by shareholders holding more than 25% of the voting rights in the company. In the latter case, the appointment to the chairmanship of the supervisory board shall be an exception to be justified to the General Meeting. However, it is by no means intended that supervisors should be independent of all outside influence and exercise their judgment in pristine isolation from the world around them. Nonetheless, these requirements mainly focus on the supervisors' independence from management rather than the independence from controlling shareholders. In this sense, German corporate law seems to be clearer about the functions of independent directors (or their equivalent) than US federal law, which mainly seeks to ensure that a certain number of directors are not beholden to management.[255]

On the one hand, the Commission Recommendation confines itself to treating a representative of a controlling shareholder as not independent.[256] It aims to ensure that independent directors do not solely represent the interests of the controlling shareholder as these may – under certain circumstances – not be in line with those of minorities. Such a requirement has not been fully endorsed in all Member States, especially in countries where controlling shareholder and family enterprises are typical.[257] In some jurisdictions, the absence of business and personal relationships with significant shareholders is required for some – but not all – independent directors.[258] For example, the Swedish corporate governance code recommends that at least two of the directors who are independent of the company and its management (this should be the majority) have to be independent of the major shareholders. Other jurisdictions, such as the French corporate governance code[259], either offer a narrow

---

255 Hopt, Klaus J.: „Unternehmensführung, Unternehmenskontrolle, Modernisierung des Aktienrechts – Zum Bericht der Regierungskommission Corporate Governance". In: Hommelhoff, Peter / Lutter, Marcus / Schmidt, Karsten / Schön, Wolfgang / Ulmer, Peter (eds.): Corporate Governance – Gemeinschaftssymposium der Zeitschriften ZHR/ZGR. Heidelberg: Verlag Recht und Wirtschaft, 2002, supplement to ZHR no. 71, p.61.

256 Commission Recommendation, Annex II, no. 1 (d).

257 The Report, p. 7.

258 Mähönen, Jukka T.: "Finland – Corporate Governance: Nordic Tradition with American Spices". In: Fleckner, Andreas M. / Hopt, Klaus J. (eds.): *Comparative Corporate Governance: A Functional and International Analysis*. Cambridge University Press: 2013, pp. 393–443; Rolf, Skog / Sjöman, Erik: "Corporate boards in Sweden". In: Davies, Paul / Hopt, Klaus / Nowak, Richard / van Solinge, Gerard (eds.): *Corporate Boards in Law and Practice*. Oxford University Press: 2013, pp. 617–652.

259 For instance, directors in France representing major shareholders of the corporation may be considered as independent, if those shareholders do not take part in the control of the corporation. See *French Corporate Governance Code* Article 9.5.

definition of independence from "main shareholders"[260] or require an analysis of independence-in-fact.[261] Moreover, some codes refer to "controlling shareholders"[262] while others to "majority shareholders"[263] or "significant shareholders" holding more than 5% of the voting shares[264] or 10% of the same[265]. As is expressly noted in some of the national analyses, the recommendations on board composition do not, in fact, prevent a controlling shareholder from appointing a majority of the board who are linked to that controlling shareholder.[266] In continental Europe, the creation of independent boards is problematic. In most member states, controlling shareholders retain the power to appoint and dismiss both the board and the management of the company. Thus, the effectiveness of adopting US style board independence

---

260 For example, the Corporate Governance Code in the Netherlands excludes independence for directors holding at least 10% of the shares in the concerned company, although it does not consider the case of directors' business and personal relationship with significant shareholders. Van Bekkum, Jaron / Hijink, Steven / Micheal C. / Schouten, Jaap W.: "Netherlands-Corporate governance in the Netherlands". In: Fleckner, Andreas M. / Hopt, Klaus J. (eds.): *Comparative Corporate Governance: A Functional and International Analysis.* Cambridge University Press: Winter, 2013, pp. 648–701.

261 In Germany, business and personal ties with the corporation, its managers and controlling shareholders exclude independence only when they may result in "substantial and not temporary conflict of interests". GCGC Article 5.4.2 provides that the supervisory board shall include what it considers an adequate number of independent members. Within the meaning of this recommendation, a supervisory board member is not to be considered independent in particular if he/she has personal or business relations with the company, its executive bodies, a controlling shareholder or an enterprise associated with the latter that may cause a substantial and not merely temporary conflict of interests. Not more than two former members of the Management Board shall be members of the supervisory board and supervisory board members shall not exercise directorships or similar positions or advisory tasks for important competitors of the enterprise.

262 See GCGC, Article 5.4.2.

263 See *French Corporate Governance code,* Amended in June 2013, Article 8.5.

264 See *Spanish Corporate Governance Code,* Article 5.5.1.

265 See *Dutch Corporate Governance Code,* Article III.2.2; *Belgium Corporate Governance Code,* Article 2.4; Davies, Paul L. / Hopt, Klaus J.: "Corporate Boards in Europe – Accountability and Convergence". *American Journal Comparative Law,* Vol. 61, No. 2, 2013, pp. 301–375, 324.

266 In Sweden, the nomination committee and plurality voting requirements tend in the same direction. In Belgium, if there is a controlling shareholder, non-independent non-executives are always in the majority. See Davies, Paul L. / Hopt, Klaus J.: "Corporate Boards in Europe – Accountability and Convergence". *American Journal Comparative Law,* Vol. 61, No. 2, 2013, pp. 301–375, 324.

rules to ensure independent audit committees – where the board remains exposed to controlling shareholder influence – is likely to yield few benefits.[267]

On the other hand, the purpose of adopting independent directors is to mitigate the agency problem between controlling and minority shareholders, although controlling shareholders often run the hiring process either directly or through their representatives in the board and in controlled corporations, nomination committees submit to the board the names of candidates suggested to them by controlling shareholders, who will ultimately approve the board proposals in the general meeting.[268] The role of independent directors is substantially that of expressing opinions on issues, albeit upon which the entire board will decide, often under the influence of controlling shareholders. In a similar scenario, the protection afforded by independent directors to minority shareholders vis-à-vis controlling shareholders is negligible.[269] In principle, the role of independent directors in controlled corporations is different from that in widely held corporations, because controlling shareholders substantially perform some of the functions that independent directors exercise when shareholders are diffuse, such as making the core decisions concerning executive remuneration and the selection of board candidates.[270] In practice, the board's role is often reduced to ratifying the pay terms and conditions negotiated in advance by the controlling shareholders with the executives.[271] As María Gutiérrez Urtiaga and Maribel Saez argue, independent directors have played a limited role in companies with concentrated ownership structures because in most jurisdictions they are appointed by the controlling shareholder. It is doubtful that a careful and selective approach towards independence and conflicts of interests will suffice to adequately strengthen market confidence.[272] Independent directors may be affiliated with the controlling shareholders even if they hold no

267 See Coffee, John C.: "A Theory of Corporate Scandals: Why the US and Europe Differ". *Oxford Rev of Economic Policy*, Vol. 21, No.2, 2005, pp. 198–211.

268 See Ferrarini, Guido / Filippelli, Marilena: "Independent directors and controlling shareholders around the world". *ECGI Working Paper* N. 258/2014, 5.2014, p. 26.

269 See Ferrarini, Guido / Filippelli, Marilena: "Independent directors and controlling shareholders around the world". *ECGI Working Paper* N. 258/2014, 5.2014, p. 33.

270 In most countries and especially in Europe, the audit committee comprises independent directors. See Ferrarini, Guido / Filippelli, Marilena: "Independent directors and controlling shareholders around the world". *ECGI Working Paper* N. 258/2014, 5.2014, p. 33.

271 See Ferrarini, Guido / Filippelli, Marilena: "Independent directors and controlling shareholders around the world". *ECGI Working Paper* N. 258/2014, 5.2014, p. 26, 32; Guido A. Ferrarini, Niamh Moloney, Executive Remuneration in the EU: The Context for Reform, Oxford Review Economic Policy, Vol. 21, No. 2, 2005, pp. 304–323.

272 See Hopt, Klaus J.: „Unternehmensführung, Unternehmenskontrolle, Modernisierung des Aktienrechts – Zum Bericht der Regierungskommission Corporate Governance". In: Hommelhoff, Peter / Lutter, Marcus / Schmidt, Karsten / Schön, Wolfgang / Ulmer, Peter (eds.): Corporate Governance – Gemeinschaftssymposium der Zeitschriften ZHR/ZGR. Heidelberg: Verlag Recht und Wirtschaft, 2002, supplement to ZHR no. 71, p. 61.

other positions in the firm, rather than being truly independent of the controlling shareholders.[273] There is no evidence that independent directors are less likely to collude with controlling shareholders or that they are more able to thwart expropriation activities by controlling shareholders. Owing to their affiliation with the controlling shareholders, such directors cannot serve as an effective force to mitigate expropriation of the controlling shareholders and the controlling shareholders may even make important corporate decisions without consulting the board.[274]

In the "Deconstructing Independent Directors", María Gutiérrez and Maribel Sáez have shown the inefficiencies of the institution of independent directors – especially in jurisdictions with ownership concentration – despite its success among legislators. In their view, if the EU continues to take the desirability of independent directors for granted as the best mechanism to solve agency problems in corporations, it may bring more costs than benefits. While the existence of independent directors may not solve the problems, it may appear to do so. Therefore, insiders can pack the boards with independents to protect themselves from critics and stronger legal action. The intense focus on independent directors deflects attention from other solutions that could be more effective.[275]

There are more profound issues behind the conflicts between independent directors and controlling shareholders. The Anglo-American drive towards shareholder value in the European corporate governance debate and in the context of legislative reform seems to rest upon an underlying assumption that dispersed shareholding in a company (typically in the US) is good,[276] while concentrated ownership – which is often a poor substitute for markets – can have a negative effect on the economy and does not provide the best financing for companies.[277] However, there does not seem to be any empirical basis for stating that blockholder control per se is bad

273 See Peng M.W.: "Outside directors and firm performance during institutional transitions". *Strategic Management Journal*, Vol. 25, No. 5, 2004, pp. 453–471.

274 See Chen, Victor Zitian / Li, Jing / Shapiro, Daniel M.: "Are OECD-prescribed "good corporate governance practices" really good in an emerging economy?". *Asia Pacific Journal of Management*, Vol. 28, No. 1, 2011, pp. 115–138, 122; Fich, E.M.: "Are some outside directors better than others? Evidence from director appointments by Fortune 1000 firms". *Journal of Business*, Vol. 78, No. 5, 2005, pp. 1943–1971, 1969.

275 Gutiérrez, María / Sáez, Maribel: "Deconstructing Independent Directors". *Journal of Corporate Law Studies*, Vol. 13, No. 1, 4.2013, pp. 63–94, 94.

276 Shleifer, Andrei / Vishny, Robert W.: "A Survey of Corporate Governance". *Journal of Finance*, Vol. 52, No. 2, 1997, pp. 737–783, 739.

277 See generally Cheffins, Brian R.: "Corporate Law and Ownership: A Darwinian Link?". *University of New South Wales Law Journal*, Vol. 25, No. 2, 6.2002, pp. 346–388; Ma Gengxin: "Wanshan Woguo Shangshi Gongsi Duli Dongshi Zhidu Jianshe de Sikao" [Some Thoughts on Perfecting the Construction of the Independent Director System in China's Listed Companies]. *Zheng-Fa Luntan* [Political-Legal Forum], Vol. 20, No. 6, 2002, p. 62.

and regulatory measures should be adopted against it.[278] On the one hand, when countries had different ownership structures at earlier points in time – owing to their different circumstances at the time, or even due to historical accidents – these differences might persist at later points in time even if their economies have otherwise become quite similar. Given this path dependence, a country's pattern of ownership structures at any point in time partly depends on the patterns that it had earlier.[279] As Enriques and Volpin put it:

> *Indeed, a cynical observer might argue that when European policymakers adopt US-style solutions designed to tackle managerial agency problems, they can appear to be doing something to reform European corporate governance while actually leaving the rents of Europe's dominant shareholders perfectly intact.*[280]

The efficient ownership structure for a company is often path dependent, first because the relative efficiency of alternative ownership structures partly depends on the structures with which the company and/or other companies in its environment started, due to sunk adaptive costs, network externalities, complementarities and multiple optima. Second, existing corporate structures might well have persistence power due to internal rent-seeking, even if they cease to be efficient. Those parties who participate in corporate control under an existing structure might have the incentive and power to impede changes that would reduce their private benefits of control even if the change would be efficient.[281] As long as those who can block structural transformation do not bear the full costs of persistence or do not capture the full benefits of an efficient move, inefficient structures that are already in place might persist.[282] Even if certain goals have converged, it does not mean that the law or functional equivalents will converge. The recent wholesale adoption of rules may be a reaction to the crisis created by different scandals. In fact, they may not

278 Bolton, Patrick / Becht, Marco / Röell, Alisa: "Corporate governance and control". In: Constantinides G.M. / Harris M. / Stulz R. M. (eds.): *Handbook of the Economics of Finance*. Elsevier: 1st Edition, Vol. 1, chapter 1, 2003, pp. 1–109, 7.

279 Bebchuk, Lucian A. / Roe, Mark J.: "A Theory of Path Dependence in Corporate Ownership and Governance". *Stanford Law Review*, Vol. 52, No. 1, 11.1999, pp. 127–170, 129.

280 Enriques, Luca / Volpin, Paolo: "Corporate Governance Reforms in Continental Europe". *Journal of Economic Perspectives*, Vol. 21, No. 1, 2007, pp. 117–140, 138.

281 See Bebchuk, Lucian A. / Roe, Mark J.: "A Theory of Path Dependence in Corporate Ownership and Governance". *Stanford Law Review*, Vol. 52, No. 1, 11.1999, pp. 127–170, 130.

282 See Bebchuk, Lucian A. / Roe, Mark J.: "A Theory of Path Dependence in Corporate Ownership and Governance". *Stanford Law Review*, Vol. 52, No. 1, 11.1999, pp. 127–170, 130.

be productive, especially when adopted without regard to the local conditions such as the ownership structure.[283]

On the other hand, Gilson has shown that we should distinguish between efficient and inefficient controlling shareholders.[284] Despite research indicating that family-controlled firms underperform compared to non-family-controlled firms – at least when control is passed on to the founder's child – several recent contributors have found surprisingly positive results for family-controlled firms, particularly when the family actually manages the firm as opposed to having formal control and not exercising it, and especially in the case of companies in Continental Europe.[285] Family control helps to protect shareholders' interests against managerial abuses, since the controlling owner and the manager are often the same person. Moreover, the controlling family is likely to commit more human capital to the firm and care more about its long-run value.[286]

From the relationship between controlling shareholders and independent directors in the EU, we can see that both the legal protection of investors and some form of concentrated ownership are essential elements of a good corporate governance system. Concentrated ownership – through large share holdings, takeovers and bank finance – is also an almost universal method of control that helps investors to get their money back. Large investors appear to be necessary to force managers to distribute profits. These investors require at least some basic legal rights – such as the voting rights or the power to pull collateral – to exercise their power over the management. If small investors are to be attracted to the business of financing companies, they also require some legal protection against expropriation by both the managers and large investors. Legal protection and large investors are complementary in an effective corporate governance system.[287]

---

283 See Enriques, Luca: "Bad Apples, Bad Oranges: A Comment from Old Europe on Post-Enron Corporate Governance Reforms". *Wake Forest Law Review*, Vol. 38, No. 3, 2003, pp. 911–935, 934–945; Bratton, William / McCahery, Joseph A.: "Comparative Corporate Governance and the Theory of the Firm: The Case Against Global Cross Reference". *Columbia Journal of Transnational Law*, Vol. 38, No. 2, 1999, pp. 213–298, 258–265.

284 See Gilson R.J.: "Controlling Shareholders and Corporate Governance: Complicating the Comparative Taxonomy". *Harvard Law Review*, Vol. 119, No. 6, 4.2006, pp. 1641–1679, 1645.

285 See Enriques, Luca / Volpin, Paolo: "Corporate Governance Reforms in Continental Europe". *Journal of Economic Perspectives*, Vol. 21, No. 1, 2007, pp. 117–140, 122; Barontini R. / Caprio L.: "The Effect of Family Control on Firm Value and Performance: Evidence from Continental Europe". *European Financial Management*, Vol. 12, No. 5, 2006, pp. 689–723, 690.

286 See Bertrand, Marianne / Schoar, Antoinette: "The Role of Family in Family Firms". *Journal of Economic Perspectives*, Vol. 20, No. 2, 2006, pp. 73–96.

287 See Shleifer, Andrei / Vishny, Robert W.: "A Survey of Corporate Governance". *Journal of Finance*, Vol. 52, No. 2, 1997, pp. 737–783, 769.

2. *Independence and Employee Codetermination*

There is a special system in the German stakeholder-centered model of corporate governance, namely the codetermination system. The strong labor codetermination is reinforced by the duty of management to take into account the coalition of interests between shareholders and stakeholders, including those of employees and even the public interest.[288] There is a view that employee codetermination constitutes the reason against mandatory representation of minority shareholders on the board, since it would even further split up the shareholder side of the board and minority representation may lead to high levels of intra-board conflict.[289] In Germany, first, through the Mining, Iron and Steel Industry Codetermination Act of 1951 (generally known as the Montan-Mitbestimmungsgesetz), the system of parity employee representation or parity codetermination at the supervisory board level was made compulsory for all industries involved in the mining, iron, coal and steel industry. Second, according to the Codetermination Act of 1976 (Mitbestimmungsgesetz, 1976 (MitbestG (1976)), another kind of codetermination was introduced outside the mining, coal, iron and steel industries. All public limited companies (Aktiengesellschaften: AGs), private companies (Gesellschaften mit beschränkter Haftung (GmbHs)), companies with one or more general partners but limited by shares (Kommanditgesellschaften auf Aktien: KGaAs) and cooperatives (Genossenschaften)[290] are subject to the MitbestG (1976), provided that they have more than 2,000 employees[291]. Therefore, the MitbestG (1976) has the widest general application across German industry and commerce. Half of the seats on the supervisory board are reserved for the representatives of the shareholders, while the representatives of the employees take up the other half of the seats.[292] Third, AGs and GmbHs with more than 500 employees were then made subject to the Betriebsverfassungsgesetz (1952) (hereinafter "BetrVG"), which provides that only one-third of the seats of those companies are reserved for the employee representatives, while the other two-thirds are filled by representatives of the shareholders to be elected in the shareholders' meeting.[293] In 2009, about 1,500 companies (695 stock corporations) were subject to third-parity

288 See Mülbert, Peter O.: „Shareholder Value aus rechtlicher Sicht". *Zeitschrift für Unternehmens- und Gesellschaftsrecht*, 1997, Vol. 26, No. 2, pp. 129 –172, 130.

289 See Hopt, Klaus J.: "Comparative Corporate Governance: The State of the Art and International Regulation". *American Journal of Comparative Law*, Vol. 59, No. 1, 2011, pp. 1–83, 27.

290 See MitbestG, Article 1 (1) 1 (1976).

291 See MitbestG, Article 1 (4) 1 (1976).

292 See MitbestG, Article 7 (1) (1976).

293 See BetrVG, Article 76 (1) (1952).

codetermination[294] and about 700 companies (280 stock corporations) were subject to quasi-parity codetermination[295].

The situation in countries with labor codetermination at the board level is more problematic and sometimes strongly politicized. Certain investors keep away from Germany because they are afraid of the German codetermination, which is largely unknown to them. First, codetermination may have a distorting impact on the general corporate governance function of the board. Codetermination – at least codetermination at parity – leads to a division between the two camps ("benches"). The employee members regularly meet previously in a caucus and tend to discuss and vote as a single body, unless there is a special representative for leading employees. This is different from the shareholder side, although the GCGC recommends that they also have separate pre-meetings. The distorting effect may be even stronger if the unions have their own representatives on the board. While the unions tend to have a broader view, which may be useful for the board in some cases, they may bring in labor interests from outside the company that are not in the interest of the company and the shareholders. Overall, this polarization by cementing "benches" is rather negative. Whether this distorting effect can be avoided by having independent directors is doubtful, even if the employee side were also to have independent directors.[296]

Second, codetermination may also have an effect on external corporate governance, i.e. on the takeover market. Indeed, codetermination is sometimes considered one of the many structural obstacles to the development of a lively takeover market. Among German companies, hostile takeovers were essentially non-existent: the first case came in 1997 when the steel giant Krupp launched a hostile takeover bid against its rival Thyssen. After worker protests and a public outcry over conflict of interest at Deutsche Bank – which advised Krupp on the takeover despite also sitting on Thyseen's supervisory board – Chancellor Schroeder intervened. He reminded the parties that a hostile transaction was contrary to Germany's implicit norms of behavior and successfully encouraged the firms to form a joint venture.[297] The

---

294 See Bayer, Walter / Hoffmann, Thomas: „AG-Report: Aktienrecht in Zahlen, Drittelbeteiligung der Arbeitnehmer im Aufsichtsrat". *Sonderteil Der Zeitschrift Die Aktiengesellschaft*, 2010, pp. 151, 153.

295 See Hans-Böckler-Stiftung: *Statistiken zur Mitbestimmungslandschaft*, retrieved 10.4.2014, from http://www.boeckler.de/38347.htm.

296 "The German Code Commission has been criticized for this and in its May 2012 changes has abolished this recommendation and merely states that this can be done." See Davies, Paul L. / Hopt, Klaus J.: "Corporate Boards in Europe – Accountability and Convergence". *American Journal Comparative Law*, Vol. 61, No. 2, 2013, pp. 301–375, 344.

297 See Milhaupt, Curtis J. / Pistor, Katharina: *The Mannesmann Executive Compensation Trial in Germany, Law and Capitalism: What Corporate Crises Reveal about Legal Systems and Economic Development around the World.* University of Chicago Press: 2008, pp. 70–86, 78.

Vodafone bid against Mannesmann marked the first time that a foreign company launched a hostile takeover bid against a flagship German firm.[298] The takeover battle between Porsche and VW proves that German codetermination is embedded in a carefully spun social web of different interests: a web in which the power of trade unions and employee representatives appears as an unshakeable bedrock.[299]

This is because both management and labor have an incentive to fight off hostile takeovers that may result in installing new management and cutting down labor costs and jobs at home.[300] In many instances when a foreign company refrains from a hostile takeover, the opportunity is missed to replace an inefficient management with a competent one because the appointment of management board members is undertaken by the supervisory board, which – also comprising employees – may be reluctant to agree on replacing the excising management board members.[301] As a result, amicable mergers between German and non-German companies very rarely take place. Foreign investors will be reluctant to choose a German co-determined company if global markets offer alternative investments not subject to codetermination. If the workforce takes its tasks seriously, it will seldom be prepared to support cross-border restructuring, which, in most cases, ushers in the danger that jobs will be lost to entities outside the country. It is striking – and hardly understood by an international observer – that the German reform agenda excludes codetermination almost as a matter of political principle. The British journal, The Economist, was no less blunt. Under the headline "Germany's codetermination rules should go", it argued that codetermination blocked firms from making the decisions that they needed to make to survive in tougher market conditions. When German companies tried to remain competitive on world markets by cutting costs and shifting production to cheaper countries, they often met fierce resistance from their own supervisory boards.

---

298 See Milhaupt, Curtis J. / Pistor, Katharina: *The Mannesmann Executive Compensation Trial in Germany, Law and Capitalism: What Corporate Crises Reveal about Legal Systems and Economic Development around the World.* University of Chicago Press: 2008, pp. 70–86, 78.

299 See Plessis J.J. Du / Großfeld B. / Luttermann C. / Saenger I. / Sandrock O.: *German Corporate Governance in International and European Context.* Springer: 2nd Edition, 2012, p. 185.

300 See Davies, Paul L. / Hopt, Klaus J.: "Corporate Boards in Europe – Accountability and Convergence". *American Journal Comparative Law,* Vol. 61, No. 2, 2013, pp. 301–375, 344.

301 A particularly "bitter" poison pill is now contained in S 33 (1) sentence 2 third alternative of the Wertpapier-Übernahme-Gesetz (Act on Takeovers) of 20 December 2001, which entered into effect on 1 Jan 2002 but was repealed in July 2006. It allowed the board of directors of a company that was the target of a hostile takeover to take measures with the approval of the supervisory board to frustrate the takeover. This could provoke the formation of a calamitous alliance between the board of directors and a co-determined supervisory board, which acted to the detriment of the rights catalogue of the German Federal Constitution (guarantee of the protection of property).

The Economist commented, "so, codetermination looks like the latest convenient example of what is wrong with business in Germany" and proceeded to ask: "Should the legal requirement for worker participation now be abandoned?"[302]

Despite becoming evident during recent years that the shortcomings of German codetermination have increasingly become a subject of public discussions and that a struggle has started concerning how to reshape German codetermination, this far-reaching codetermination regime and its accompanying vested interests are so deeply rooted in the country that Germany has held up EU efforts to harmonize national company laws on board composition or provide EU forms of incorporation.[303] The outstanding fact about employee representation systems in recent years is the absence of formal changes,[304] despite the measures being adopted: "promoting corporate disclosure, market-oriented accounting, performance-oriented executive remuneration and more flexible use of corporate equity"[305]. Path dependence has set up structures that are not easily changed and there may be forces within a country with powerful interests in preserving the system in place. As a result of a particular path, complementary institutions make it more difficult to foster change. Thus, keeping existing systems may in fact be an efficient result.[306] The employee codetermination has become the most significant obstacle against the spread of the shareholder-centered model in the EU. For example, the European Commission was unable to introduce a "board neutrality rule" prohibiting the management of a target company from taking any action that might result in the frustration of a takeover bid for this company without obtaining post-bid shareholder approval for the specific defensive measure in the Takeover Directive on a mandatory basis, although it

302 "Together they stand". *The Economist*, 16.7.2005, p. 14, p. 14.

303 "This far-reaching codetermination system is path-dependent and has its origins in the post-World War I (1922) and post-World War II (1950/1952/1976) eras when the forces of capital and labor had to jointly rebuild Germany's industry after the two wars." Milhaupt, Curtis J. / Pistor, Katharina: *Law and Capitalism: What Corporate Crises Reveal about Legal Systems and Economic Development around the World.* University of Chicago Press: 2008, p. 84.

304 "Contrary to what the convergence thesis might predict, there has been no significant downgrading of the representation requirements in the European jurisdictions." Davies, Paul L. / Hopt, Klaus J.: "Corporate Boards in Europe – Accountability and Convergence". *American Journal Comparative Law*, Vol. 61, No. 2, 2013, pp. 301–375, 345; Hopt, Klaus J.: „Gemeinsame Grundsätze der Corporate Governance in Europa?". *Zeitschrift für Unternehmens- und Gesellschaftsrecht*, Vol. 29, No. 6, 2000, pp. 798–809.

305 "To date, we have to admit, all the many efforts of reform within Germany have failed." See Davies, Paul L. / Hopt, Klaus J.: "Corporate Boards in Europe – Accountability and Convergence". *American Journal Comparative Law*, Vol. 61, No. 2, 2013, pp. 301–375, 342.

306 See Bebchuk, Lucian A. / Roe, Mark J.: "A Theory of Path Dependence in Corporate Ownership and Governance". *Stanford Law Review*, Vol. 52, No. 1, 11.1999, pp. 127–170, pp. 127.

had to allow the member states to opt out of this rule as well as the encompassing breakthrough rule and introduce a reciprocity exception, owing to a lack of political consensus in the highly sensitive topic of hostile takeovers.[307] Consequently, the

307 The resulting "Takeover Directive" was a compromise with many options, choices and discretions for the Member States by providing a "menu" of federal rules for takeovers. For the history of the Takeover Directive, see Gilson, Ronald J.: "The Political Ecology of Takeovers: Thoughts on Harmonizing the European Corporate Governance Environment". *Fordham Law Review*, Vol. 61, No. 1, 1992, pp. 161–192; Kirchner C. / Painter R.W.: "Takeover Defenses under Delaware Law, the Proposed Thirteenth EU Directive and the New German Takeover Law: Comparison and Recommendations for Reform". *The American Journal of Comparative Law*, Vol. 50, No. 3, Summer 2002, pp. 451–476; Clarke B.: "Takeover Regulation: Through the Regulatory Looking Glass". *German Law Journal*, Vol. 8, No. 4, 2007, pp. 381–426. In the Takeover Directive, Article 9(2) provides that during the period referred to in the second sub-paragraph, the board of the offeree company shall obtain the prior authorization of the general meeting of shareholders given for this purpose before taking any action, other than seeking alternative bids, which may result in the frustration of the bid and in particular before issuing any shares which may result in a lasting impediment to the offeror's acquiring control of the offeree company. Such authorization shall be mandatory at least from the time the board of the offeree company receives the information referred to in the first sentence of Article 6(1) concerning the bid and until the result of the bid is made public or the bid lapses. Member States may require that such authorization be obtained at an earlier stage, for example as soon as the board of the offeree company becomes aware that the bid is imminent. Article 12(1) provides that Member States may reserve the right not to require companies as referred to in Article 1(1) which have their registered offices within their territories to apply Article 9(2) and (3) and/or Article 11. Article 12 further provides that (2) where Member States make use of the option provided for in paragraph 1, they shall nevertheless grant companies which have their registered offices within their territories the option, which shall be reversible, of applying Article 9(2) and (3) and/or Article 11, without prejudice to Article 11(7). The decision of the company shall be taken by the general meeting of shareholders, in accordance with the law of the Member State in which the company has its registered office in accordance with the rules applicable to the amendment of the articles of association. The decision shall be communicated to the supervisory authority of the Member State in which the company has its registered office and to all the supervisory authorities of Member States in which its securities are admitted to trading on regulated markets or where such admission has been requested; (3) Member States may, under the conditions determined by national law, exempt companies which apply Article 9(2) and (3) and/or Article 11 from applying Article 9(2) and (3) and/or Article 11 if they become the subject of an offer launched by a company which does not apply the same Articles as they do, or by a company controlled, directly or indirectly, by the latter, pursuant to Article 1 of Directive 83/349/EEC; (4) Member States shall ensure that the provisions applicable to the respective companies are disclosed without delay; (5) Any measure applied in accordance with paragraph 3 shall be subject to the

boards in Germany, the Netherlands, Belgium, Poland and other countries have wide possibilities for shielding themselves from being held accountable by means of unfriendly takeovers.[308]

Thus, the approach of the Commission Recommendation in terms of treating employee representatives as putatively independent has little to commend, especially given that a director appointed by a controlling shareholder is not treated as independent.[309] The Commission Recommendation provides in its Annex that *employees* and persons who were employees for the previous three years cannot be considered independent unless they have been elected to the board in the context of a workers' representation system recognized by law and provided that they do not belong to senior management.[310] Regarding national rules for companies without labor codetermination, the Commission Recommendation is generally followed. The UK, French and Dutch corporate governance codes are more severe by

---

authorisation of the general meeting of shareholders of the offeree company, which must be granted no earlier than 18 months before the bid was made public in accordance with Article 6(1).

308 See Davies P. / Schuster, Edmund – Philipp / Van de Walle de Ghelcke, Emilie : "The Takeover Directive as a Protectionist Tool?". In: Bernitz, Ulf / Ringe, Wolf-Georg (eds.): *Company Law and Economic Protectionism: New Challenges to European Integration.* Oxford University Press: 2010, p. 105–157, 115. Gesetz zur Regelung von öffentlichen Angeboten zum Erwerb von Wertpapieren und von Unternehmensübernahmen (hereafter "WpÜG"), December 2001. Article 33(1) provides that after publication of the decision to make an offer and until the publication of the result pursuant to section 23 (1) sentence 1 no. 2, the board of management of the target company may not take any actions which could prevent the success of the offer. This does not apply to actions which a prudent and conscientious manager of a company not affected by a takeover bid would have taken, to endeavors to find a competing offer, or to actions consented to by the supervisory board of the target company. Article 33(2) provides that if the general meeting authorizes the board of management prior to the period referred to in subsection 1 sentence 1 to take actions falling within the competence of the general meeting in order to prevent the success of takeover bids, such actions shall be specified in detail in the authorization. The resolution by the general meeting requires a majority of at least three quarters of the share capital represented at the vote; the articles of association may provide for a larger majority and further requirements. Any actions by the board of management on the basis of an authorization pursuant to sentence 1 shall require the consent of the supervisory board. Article 33, WpÜG. Davies P. / Schuster, Edmund – Philipp / Van de Walle de Ghelcke, Emilie : "The Takeover Directive as a Protectionist Tool?". In: Bernitz, Ulf / Ringe, Wolf-Georg (eds.): *Company Law and Economic Protectionism: New Challenges to European Integration.* Oxford University Press: 2010, p. 105–157, 116.

309 See Davies, Paul L. / Hopt, Klaus J.: "Corporate Boards in Europe – Accountability and Convergence". *American Journal Comparative Law*, Vol. 61, No. 2, 2013, pp. 301–375, 341.

310 Commission Recommendation, Annex II no. 1 (b).

taking into account five previous years.[311] In Germany, decisions by the courts do not make this issue clear and most academics argue that employee representatives are not independent.[312] In a recent survey, advisor Heidrick and Struggles classifies employee representatives as a distinct category, leading to much less than half of all supervisory directors being considered independent in Germany.[313]

II. Proportional Voting and Slate Voting

There are some arguments against adopting cumulative voting at the level of EU corporate law. First, board election rules in Europe are largely in the shareholders' domain: assuming that minority representation grants superior investor protection, it is unclear why this has not yet emerged as a widespread market solution. Consequently, a call for regulation is not clearly justified. Moreover, even if a case for regulation can be established, it remains to be seen whether election rules should be mandated or take an enabling form, aimed at removing possible regulatory obstacles to minority representation.[314] Second, a rule granting board representation to minority shareholders may influence benefits and costs of activism.[315] The true extent to which board election rules may affect such courts remains unclear. Direct costs include expenses (the time of senior executives involved in activities such as the selection of candidates, coordination with other shareholders, plus out-of-pocket expenses for proxy solicitation and other campaign costs) that are necessary to successfully present a list of candidates. Indirect costs are less visible – yet not less real – and may include limitations to trading implied by market abuse regulation, sub-optimal diversification and legal liability for acting in concert and potential litigation costs.[316]

Furthermore, in terms of the representation of minority shareholders, there are two European original systems that are regarded as better than cumulative voting, namely the proportional voting in Spain and the slate voting system in

311 See Davies, Paul L. / Hopt, Klaus J.: "Corporate Boards in Europe – Accountability and Convergence". *American Journal Comparative Law*, Vol. 61, No. 2, 2013, pp. 301–375, 340.

312 See Hopt Klaus J. / Markus Roth: *Aktiengesetz: Grosskommentar*. de Gruyter Recht: 4th Edition, 2011, Article 100, no. 90.

313 See Heidrick, Struggles: *European Corporate Governance Report 2011: Challenging Board Performance*. p. 42, figure 35.

314 See Belcredi, Massimo / Bozzi, Stefano / Di Noia, Carmine: "Board elections and shareholder activism: the Italian experiment, Boards and Shareholders in European Listed Companies: Facts, Context and Post-crisis Reforms". In: Belcredi, Massimo / Ferrarini, Guido (eds.): *International Corporate Law and Financial Market Regulation*. Cambridge University Press: 2013, p. 377.

315 See Enriques, Luca / Volpin, Paolo: "Corporate Governance Reforms in Continental Europe". *Journal of Economic Perspectives*, Vol. 21, No. 1, 2007, pp. 117–140.

316 See Pozen, Robert C.: *Insitutional Perspective on Shareholder Nomination of Corporate Directors*. Harvard Law School – John M. Olin Center for Law, Economics and Business: Discussion Paper Series No. 429, 8.2003.

Italy.[317] Article 137 of the Spanish Ley des Sociedades Anonimas argues the right of a minority of shareholders to appoint directors in proportion to their stake in the capital of the corporation. For example, if a corporation has a board of directors of nine members, shareholders owning 10% of the shares can require the appointment of one representative to the board. In Italian corporate law, Article 147 of the Consolidated Law on Financial Markets provides that shareholders holding a minimum threshold of shares – which is inversely proportional to the market capitalization of the corporation and varies from 0.5% to 4.5% – can present lists of candidates for the election onto the board. According to the Italian scholars, the list voting is preferable to cumulative voting[318] because in comparison with cumulative voting it offers a more stable, clear and assured mechanism for a limited representation of minority shareholders on the board and represents a sensible compromise between the total absence of minority representation that characterizes today's boards and the potentially more extreme and less predictable effects of cumulative voting.[319] "The increased yet limited diversity on the board could improve directors' accountability to shareholders and enhance the monitoring and controlling role of the board in the interest of a broader number of shareholders. The concern for the development of disruptive conflicts on the board seems quite limited, especially in the light of the non-managerial role played by the modern board of directors."[320]

In fact, Italy has made considerable progress to promote and defend shareholder rights and improve transparency in recent years. In particular, minority shareholders now have a direct role in selecting at least one member of the board and the board of auditors.[321] Since 2007, a slate vote mechanism is mandated for the appointment of directors for all listed companies. Directors are appointed based upon slates (*i.e.* lists of candidates) presented by shareholders owning a minimum threshold of the share capital. The threshold is determined annually by Consob, taking into account the company's capitalization, free float and ownership structure. Each list of candidates must indicate which director meets independence standards set by the law and/or the Code of Corporate Governance. At least one board member must

317 See Murphy, Michael E.: "The Nominating Process for Corporate Boards of Directors – A Decision-Making Analysis". *Berkeley Business Law Journal*, Vol. 5, No. 2, 2008, pp. 131–193, 183.

318 See Ventoruzzo, Marco: "Empowering Shareholders in Directors' Elections: A Revolution in the Making". *European Company and Financial Law Review*, Vol. 8, No. 2, 6.2011, pp. 105–144, 137.

319 See Ventoruzzo, Marco: "Empowering Shareholders in Directors' Elections: A Revolution in the Making". *European Company and Financial Law Review*, Vol. 8, No. 2, 6.2011, pp. 105–144, 140.

320 See Ventoruzzo, Marco: "Empowering Shareholders in Directors' Elections: A Revolution in the Making". *European Company and Financial Law Review*, Vol. 8, No. 2, 6.2011, pp. 105–144, 140.

321 OECD: *Assessment and Recommendations, in Related Party Transactions and Minority Shareholder Rights* (hereinafter "RPTs and MSR"), 2012, p. 117.

be elected from the minority slate that received the largest number of votes and who is not linked in any way, even indirectly, to the shareholders who presented or voted the list that came first by number of votes. Some companies such as privatized ones have reserved a higher number of board places for the minority slate (*i.e.* must be one-fifth of the board). Company bylaws establish the mechanisms according to which board seats are distributed among the slates presented. The questionnaire reports that more often than not, companies grant a majority premium to the slate receiving the highest number of votes, which takes all board seats aside from the quota reserved for minorities (one seat). However, a few companies adopt a proportional multi-winner system where any slate takes a number of board seats proportional to the votes that it receives. Box 6.2 outlines how votes are allocated within a slate.[322] An assessment of implementation carried out by Assonime in 2011 shows that companies where more than one slate of directors were presented in the 2007–2010 period account for almost 40% of the market. Moreover, minority slates are more frequently presented in blue chips and financial companies (generally characterized by higher ownership dispersion). Finally, minority slates are presented by shareholders classified as institutional investors – either Italian or foreign – in almost 20% of cases (*i.e.* in 8% of the market).[323]

322 OECD: RPTs and MSR, p. 113.
323 OECD: RPTs and MSR, p. 113.

Third Chapter: New Form of Cumulative Voting in China

The Company Law of 2005 has adopted cumulative voting from the US through Article 106 to protect minority shareholders and promote their motivation for corporate control as well as guarding against their opportunism and possible harassment of the majority. On December 28, 2013, the Company Law 2005 was amended further by the sixth Session of the Standing Committee of the Twelfth National People's Congress. Despite the provision of cumulative voting remaining, Article 106 has been changed into Article 105, adopting the permissive cumulative voting by stipulating: "When the shareholders' assembly elects directors or supervisors, it may, according to the articles of association or resolution of the shareholders' assembly, adopt a cumulative voting system. The term 'cumulative voting system' as mentioned in this Law refers to a system of voting by shareholders for the election of directors or supervisors at a session of the shareholders' assembly in which the shareholder can multiply his voting rights by the number of candidates and direct them all towards one candidate, director or supervisor."

Furthermore, in the Code – which is mandatory for all listed companies that have been melded into the listing rules of the two Stock Exchanges (Shanghai and Shenzhen Stock Exchange) and which serves as the major measuring standard for evaluating whether a listed company has a good corporate governance structure and whether major problems exist with the corporate governance structure of a listed company – the securities supervision and regulation authorities may instruct the company to make corrections in accordance with the Code. Article 31 provides: "The election of directors shall fully reflect the opinions of minority shareholders. A cumulative voting system shall be earnestly advanced in shareholders' meeting for the election of directors. Listed companies that are more than 30% owned by controlling shareholders shall adopt a cumulative voting system, and the companies that do adopt such a system shall stipulate the implementing rules for such cumulative voting system in their articles of association."[324]

A. Justification for the Adoption of Cumulative Voting

The purpose of China's import of cumulative voting is to shield minorities from the prejudice of both controlling shareholders and management and support the development of the capital market. Having originally been drafted as a way to protect minority shareholders from "overreaching" by a majority who could form rings to control absolutely and abuse and plunder the property of the minorities (by allowing a shareholder to multiply the number of votes he/she (hereinafter "he") has – as determined

324 The Code, Article 31.

by the number of shares he holds, the number of directors to be elected – and to cast all his votes for any one candidate or distribute his votes among the candidates in any way he chooses[325]), cumulative voting is absolutely regarded by Chinese legislation as a feasible institution to resolve the agency problem in PLCs with concentrated ownership. In essence, it enables minority stockholders to secure representation upon the corporation's board[326] and allows them to obtain direct contact with the business of the corporation and its management, observing the conduct of the corporate officers whom the directors may employ.[327] In the eyes of Chinese legislation, cumulative voting can strengthen the hand of minority shareholders, because if cumulative voting is used in the appointment of directors, minority shareholders can appoint directors of their choice to provide a fairer balance of interests within the board, which otherwise will almost exclusively be appointed by the majority shareholder.

The decline of cumulative voting in corporations of US does not mean that the system is absolutely redundant and outdated for other countries where the market, legal and cultural conditions are completely different from the US.[328] The corporate governance system in China is less developed and the Company Law of 2005 has just established the whole system by transplanting institutions from Germany and US, while the US has already long had sophisticated systems through the practice of legislation and court as well as corporations in corporate governance. In China, where ownership is highly concentrated, this market only disciplines the insiders of the relatively few companies that are widely held.[329] The active market for corporate control – which is the immediate cause for the decline of cumulative voting – does not exist in China, whereby since the first takeover event of Yanzhong Shiye by Baoan in 1993 and the promulgating of "Provisional Regulations on Stock Issuance Management", the market for corporate control has made considerable progress for more than 20 years, albeit remaining in its initial phase.[330] According to Article 3 of

325 Henn, Harry G. / Alexander, John R.: *Laws of Corporations and Other Business Enterprises.* West Publish Corporation: 3rd Edition, 1983, p. 495.

326 See Editors, Law Review: "Cumulative Voting: Removal, Reduction and Classification of Corporate Boards". The University of Chicago Law Review: Vol. 22, No. 3, Spring 1955, pp. 751–759,752.

327 Humphrys v. Winous Co., 133 N.E.2d 780, 782 (Ohio 1956).

328 Wenjia, Yan: "Cumulative Voting: In the US (Declining), in China (Rising) and the EU (Not-Adopted)". *ECFR*, Vol. 12, No. 1, 4.2015, pp. 79–109, 95.

329 See Rossi, Stefano / Volpin, Paolo: "Cross-Country Determinants of Mergers and Acquisitions". *Journal of Financial Economics*, Vol. 74, No. 2, 2004, pp. 277–304.

330 In 2008, takeover amounts reached a high point at 64.898 billion RMB and China became the country with most rapidly developing takeover market. In 2009, takeover events achieved new progress, reaching the fivefold of it in 2005 and ranked Top three in Global takeover market, according to the statistics provided by FactSet, and became one the most important takeover market. However, the market for corporate control in China is still less developed: in 2008, the global average transaction size was 93.1 million and 233 million Dollars in US, while it

"Administrative Rules on Acquisition of Listed Company", the purchaser may carry out the takeover of a listed company and gain the power to actually control the same by means of takeover by agreement, takeover by offer or centralized trading at competing prices on a stock exchange. Among the takeover cases from 2006 to 2010, the number of takeovers through agreements reached 3,657, of which only 22 related to takeover by offer.[331] The repealing of the split-share system[332] by Chinese security authorities in the summer of 2005 aimed to promote the stock dispersion and provide support for the growth of the market for corporate control, allowing takeover by offer to replace agreed acquisition – the negotiated takeover – which is triggered inside trading and may damage the interests of minority shareholders, remaining to be the primary measure for corporate control transactions. Thus, the role that hostile takeovers has played in improving corporate governance is quite limited in China. The possibility of cumulative voting's misuse in hostile takeover could not exist, while cumulative voting may enhance the market of corporate control's development based on the experience of the US. On the other side, China differs from many European countries in as much as the latter has powerful controlling shareholders who can effectively monitor the corporate governance and their own corporate governance measures for supporting minority shareholders, such as proportional voting and slate voting, which have worked for a long time.

B. Justifications for the Legislation Form

The Chinese corporate governance system generally adopts the institution through the opt-in form of permissive cumulative voting, although it requires the mandatory implement in PLCs with concentrated ownership, which is judged by whether there

---

was only 4,930,000 Dollars in China based on the statistics of Thompson Reuters. Retrieved 3.7.2013, from http://cn.wsj.com/gb/20100115/bch143704.asp.

331 CSMAR Solution: *Takeover and Restructure Database*, retrieved 25.6.2013, from http://www.gtarsc.com/.

332 The Chinese stock market can be classified into two broad categories according to their tradability on secondary markets before 2005. Non-tradable stocks include state shares, legal person shares and employee shares, while the tradable counterpart is held by diffuse shareholders. With respect to the official definition of the non-tradable part, state shares are held by government agencies or state-authorized organizations at either the central or local levels, whereas legal person shares are those owned by domestic institutions and enterprises with legal person status. This split-share system – which was a unique product from the very early stage of the Chinese stock market – was the result of a compromise between the need to privatize SOEs and the healthy, gradual development of the stock market by its nature. Wang, Wallace Wen-Yeu / Chen, Jian-Lin: "Bargaining for Compensation in the Shadow of Regulatory Giving: The Case of Stock Trading Rights Reform in China". *Columbia Journal of Asian Law*, Vol. 20, No. 298, 2006, pp. 298–356, 312–318; Kister, Sandra P.: "China's Share-Structure Reform: An Opportunity to Move Beyond Practical Solutions to Practical Problems". *Columbia Journal of Transnational Law*, Vol. 45, No. 1, 2006, pp. 312–363, 313.

are more than 30% of shares owned by controlling shareholders. For other PLCs with relatively dispersed ownership and unlisted joint stock companies, the Company Law does not mandate but allows cumulative voting as a choice. In such companies, the effect of cumulative voting is subject to the control of majority shareholders who can amend the charters to eliminate cumulative voting under the principal of "one share, one vote". According to Article 103 of the Company Law, the "opt in" and "opt out" clause of cumulative voting in articles is passed absolutely by two-thirds or more of the voting rights, which the shareholders who attend the meeting of the shareholders shall obtain from the shareholders' meeting. At the same time, if it is the resolution of the general meeting to adopt the system, the decision for the withdrawal of such a resolution requires more than half of the voting rights of the shareholders present.[333]

On the one hand, the permissive form of Company Law is consistent with the mainstream attitude in the US for cumulative voting. It is beneficial for the stability of the law and cumulative voting to accommodate the development of Chinese corporations because the law shall provide various systems of corporate governance as options for the corporations before an institution is proven to be absolutely effective for the improvement of corporate governance and the companies will select the optimal institutions through the competition between the corporations.[334]

On the other hand, the Code adopts cumulative voting by mandatory form for the companies with concentrated ownership. According to an investigation about the ownership of 1,135 PLCs in 2004, in 802 cases, the largest shareholder owns more than 30% and these companies account for 71% of the PLCs under investigation.[335] Based on this investigation, we can see that the intention of the Code permits only a small fraction of companies to obtain the chance to eliminate such a system and the majority of PLCs are strongly urged to adopt cumulative voting through their articles and resolutions of the general meeting. By the end of 2003, over half of the

333 Article 103 of Company Law rules that: "When a shareholder attends the shareholders' assembly, he shall have one voting right for each share he holds. However, the company has no voting right for its own shares it holds. When any resolution is to be made by the shareholders' assembly, it shall be adopted by shareholders representing more than half of the voting rights of the shareholders in presence. However, when the shareholders' assembly makes a decision to modify the articles of association or to increase or reduce the registered capital, or a resolution about the merger, division, dissolution or change of the company form, the resolution shall be adopted by shareholders representing 2/3 or more of the voting rights of the shareholders in presence."

334 Wenjia, Yan: "Cumulative Voting: In the US (Declining), in China (Rising) and the EU (Not-Adopted)". *ECFR*, Vol. 12, No. 1, 4.2015, pp. 79–109, 98.

335 See Rongqing, Ding / Hongzhen, Zhang: "Cong Guoji Bijiao Kan Woguo Guquan Jizhongdu" [Discussions on Corporate Concentrated Ownership of China from International View], *Shichang Zhoukan Caijing Luntan* [Market Weekly Economics], Vol. 11, 2004, pp. 23–24, 24.

listed companies with a majority shareholder owning more than 30% of the shares had incorporated cumulative voting provisions into their articles of association.[336]

The primary reason for this approach has largely been to ensure some degree of shareholder influence in corporate governance in PLCs with concentrated ownership as a result of that country's unique process of mass privatization. If the code allowed such corporations to opt out of cumulative voting, the system would have been avoided by controlling shareholders and the intention of cumulative voting would be frustrated. In detail, although an amendment requires approval through a shareholder vote, voting shareholders generally have little incentive to inform themselves. Indeed, the amendment must first be proposed by the board of directors, whose decision might have been made despite the operation of various market forces, not only through considerations of value maximization but also through the often different interests of managers and dominant shareholders.[337]

Furthermore, based on the view of the mandatory corporate governance provisions' adherents, allowing opt-outs with respect to an issue such as cumulative voting might lead to the adoption of value-decreasing opt-out amendments.[338] In 1984, Sanjai Bhagat and James Brickley addressed the question of how proposed charter amendments on cumulative voting affected wealth, finding that "cumulative voting can have a positive effect on firm value" and concluding that efforts to restrict cumulative voting rights were associated with negative stock price reactions by measuring each of 126 New York Stock Exchange (hereinafter "NYSE") companies' two-day stock returns during 1962–1982, when an amendment was proposed that either reduced or increased cumulative voting powers.[339] The study's findings were consistent with those of another study finding that "cumulative voting is an important element in proxy fights, which tend to benefit shareholders"[340]. Some other studies concerning the impact of the classified boards and restriction of

336 See Xu Qing: "Woguo Shangshi Gongsi Leiji Toupiao Zhidu Cunzai Quexian" [Loopholes Exist in the Cumulative Voting System of Chinese Listed Companies], *Shanghai Zhengquan Bao* [Shanghai Securities News], 16.9.2004.

337 See Bebchuk, Lucian A.: "Limiting Contractual Freedom in Corporate Law: The Desirable Constraints on Charter Amendments". *Harvard Law Review*, Vol. 102, No. 8, 6.1989, pp. 1820–1860, 1824.

338 See Bebchuk, Lucian A.: "Limiting Contractual Freedom in Corporate Law: The Desirable Constraints on Charter Amendments". *Harvard Law Review*, Vol. 102, No. 8, 6.1989, pp. 1820–1860, 1824.

339 The results indicated that amendments reducing the effect of cumulative voting were associated with negative stock price reactions (-.88 % average returns) around the announcement period. The strongest negative reaction was generated by proposals seeking the elimination of cumulative voting (-1.57 %) and classification of the board (-1.3 %). See Bhagat, Sanjai / Brickley, James A.: "Cumulative Voting: The Value of Minority Shareholder Voting Rights". *Journal of Law and Economics*, Vol. 27, No. 2, 1984, pp. 339–366, 353–355.

340 See Dodd, Graham / Warner, Jerold: "On Corporate Governance: A Study of Proxy Contests". *Journal of Financial Economics*, Vol. 11, No. 1, 1983, pp. 401–438, 436.

cumulative voting also indicate that the market reacts negatively to these provisions, particularly to those adopted during the takeover wave of the 1980s.[341]

However, the adoption of cumulative voting does not mean taking away any rights of the majority of the company.[342] Opportunistic behaviors by minority shareholders must also be checked and company law seeks to provide a sensible balance between the control rights of majority shareholders and minority shareholders' protection.[343] According to the classical separation of ownership and control perspective, a dominant or majority shareholder has both the incentive and ability to monitor management, whereby the firm is managed in a manner consistent with profit maximization.[344] On the one hand, fewer shareholders with larger stakes in a firm means that their own performance is intimately tied to the performance of the invested firm.[345] When shareholders are unable to dilute their holdings – as was the case for many years – there are also strong incentives to "supervise" in a manner consistent with shareholders' long-term commitments[346], monitoring a manager's performance, cooperating with other board members and appointing board representatives with the necessary skills and expertise.[347] One the other hand, with few large shareholders,

341 See Mahoney J.M. / Mahoney J.T.: "An empirical investigation of the effect of corporate charter anti-takeover amendments on stockholder wealth". *Strategic Management Journal*, Vol. 14, No. 1, 1993, pp. 17–31, 18; Mahoney J.M. / Murthy, C. Sundara / Mahoney J.T.: "The differential impact on stockholder wealth of various anti-takeover provisions". *Managerial and Decision Economics*, Vol. 17, No. 6, 1996, pp. 531–549, 545.

342 As Joseph Medill said: "The object of cumulative voting is not to cripple or injure the rights of the majority in any respect. Their power to control the offices of the company remains intact; but this is to protect the minority from being plundered and robbed out of house and home, their stock confiscated and lost for the want of some representative to look after their interest." See Medill, Joseph: "The floor speech". *Columbia Law Review*, Vol. 94, No.1, 1.1994, p. 143.

343 Black, Bernard S. / Kraakman, Reinier: "A Self-enforcing Model of Corporate Law". *Harvard Law Review*, Vol. 109, No. 8, 1996, pp. 1911–1982, 1952.

344 The term "blockholder" is used here to describe a shareholder of the company who – at least under normal circumstances – can exercise effective control over the company due to his shareholding. Davies P. / Schuster, Edmund – Philipp / Van de Walle de Ghelcke, Emilie : "The Takeover Directive as a Protectionist Tool?". In: Bernitz, Ulf / Ringe, Wolf-Georg (eds.): *Company Law and Economic Protectionism: New Challenges to European Integration.* Oxford University Press: 2010, p. 105–157, 119.

345 See Alchian A.A. / Demsetz H.: "Production, Information Costs and Economic Organization". *American Economic Review*, Vol. 62, No.5, 1972, pp. 777–795.

346 See Clark, Gordon L.: "Financial Valuation of the German Model: The Negative Relationship Between Ownership Concentration and Public Market Returns, 1997–2001". *Economic Geography*, Vol. 81, No. 1, 2005, pp. 11–29,16.

347 See Clark, Gordon L.: "Financial Valuation of the German Model: The Negative Relationship Between Ownership Concentration and Public Market Returns, 1997–2001". *Economic Geography*, Vol. 81, No. 1, 2005, pp. 11–29,16.

the costs of coordination are lower than when there are many shareholders[348] and large shareholders have the monetary means to exercise control by collecting information and monitoring management activities. The dominant shareholder can often control the board.[349] Therefore, the higher level of control – compared to diffuse ownership – leaves less room for managerial discretion and this may give a better firm performance. Thus, Listed Companies Department of Shanghai Stock Exchange published a document without legal enforcement on March 30, 2005, "Notice of Issuing Recommendations of Detailed Rules for the Implementation of Cumulative Voting in 'Articles of Companies'", in which Article X+2 provides that "before the determination of suitable candidates, board of directors and supervisors shall consult the top ten tradable shareholders of the company in writing."

C. Limitations of Cumulative Voting by the Company Law

More than ten years have passed since the adoption of cumulative voting by the Code. In 2012, the number of enterprises adopting cumulative voting had increased from 290 in 2011 to 438, accounting for only 18.8% of all PLCs.[350] This part will focus on the restrictions of cumulative voting by some provisions of the Company Law and seek strategies to resolve these problems.

I. Institutional Investors and Cumulative Voting

Despite the disputes regarding the role of institutional investors in corporate governance, cumulative voting provides a probable choice for institutional investors to make their voice in governance issues heard whenever they deem it necessary. China may be a good place for putting Gordon's theory into practice, because the institutional investors have increasingly played their role in corporate governance with the reform of shareholdings structure in China. For example, on May 26, 2012, Gree Electric Appliances, Inc. of Zhuhai (000651)[351] issued an announcement of

---

348 See Clark, Gordon L.: "Financial Valuation of the German Model: The Negative Relationship Between Ownership Concentration and Public Market Returns, 1997–2001". *Economic Geography*, Vol. 81, No. 1, 2005, pp. 11–29, 16.

349 See Tosi H.L. / Gomez-Mejia L.R.: "The decoupling of C.E.O. pay and performance: An agency theory perspective". *Administrative Science Quarterly*, Vol. 39, No. 2, 1989, pp. 169–189; Fama, E.F. / Jensen M.C.: "The separation of ownership and control". *Journal of Law and Economics*, Vol. 26, No. 2, 1983, pp. 301–328; Salancik G.R. / Pfeffer J.: "Effects of ownership and performance on executive tenure in U.S. corporations". *Academy of Management Journal*, Vol. 23, No. 4, 1980, pp. 653–664.

350 See Research Center of Corporate Governance of China: *Report of Corporate Governance Index and Evaluation in 2012*, retrieved 12.5.2013, from http://www.022net.com /2012/11-25/471843353297915.html.

351 Gree Electric Appliances, Inc. of Zhuhai was founded in 1991 and it is the largest air conditioner enterprise integrating R&D, manufacturing, marketing and services

resolution, which disclosed a motion declaring the election of ZHOU Shaoqiang sent by State-owned Assets Supervision and Administration Commission of the State Council (SASAC)[352] to be director on the 9th board of the company as denied, while FENG Jiyong – supported by institutional investors – was elected as director of the board. The result of the election has surpassed every expectation of the market and is commented on as a sign of the institutional investors' active involvement in corporate governance.[353] The success of institutions in using cumulative voting would be attributed to the relatively dispersed ownership of GREE in which the shareholdings of the largest shareholder – SASAC of Zhuhai – constitute less than 20% of the entire shares.

While the event of "Gree Electric Appliances" shows the achievements of Chinese corporate governance, it must be acknowledged that the activism of institutional investors and the implement of cumulative voting remains at a preliminary stage in China. The degree of institutional engagement with listed companies remains low[354] and the investors do not value cumulative voting sufficiently to take advantage of it to elect their independent directors and supervisors, while the most

---

globally. It is publicly listed on Shenzhen Stock Exchange in 1996. It has nine production bases in Zhuhai, Chongqing, Hefei, Zhengzhou, Wuhan, Shijiazhuang, Brazil, Pakistan and Vietnam, with an annual production capacity of 60 million residential air conditioners (RAC) and 5.5 million commercial air conditioners (CAC). Gree has topped No.1 in RAC sales volume in the global market since 2005. Retrieved 10.6.2013, from http://www.gree.com.cn/english/aboutgree/companyIntro_jsp_catid _1204.shtml.

352 SASAC is a special commission of the People's Republic of China, directly under the State Council. It was founded in 2003 through the consolidation of various other industry-specific ministries. As part of an economic reform, almost half of state-owned enterprises were sold off in the form of stocks. SASAC is responsible for managing the remaining SOEs, including appointing top executives and approving any mergers or sales of stock or assets, as well as drafting laws related to state-owned enterprises. In particular, authorized by the State Council, in accordance with the Company Law of the People's Republic of China and other administrative regulations, the State-owned Assets Supervision and Administration Commission of the State Council (SASAC) performs investor's responsibilities, supervises and manages the state-owned assets of the enterprises under the supervision of the Central Government (excluding financial enterprises) and enhances the management of the state-owned assets. Other main functions and responsibilities of SASAC can be found at the website http://www.sasac.gov.cn/n2963340/n2963393/2965120.html.

353 See Lu Tong / Yu Baoliang: "GELI DIANQI zhongxiao gudong heyishengchu – jiaqiang jitou touzizhe canyu gongsi zhili de yiyuan he nengli" [How can the medium and small shareholders GELI DIANQI win the election – Enhancement of the motivation and capacity of institutional investors for participation in corporate governance]. *Corporate Governance*, Vol. 7, 2012, pp. 116–119, 117.

354 See Xi, Chao: "Institutional Shareholder Activism in China: Law and Practice". *International Company and Commercial Law Review*, Vol. 17, 2006, p. 35.

common way of expressing their objections is following the "Wall Street Rule" to trade their stocks on the market. By the end of 2011, the average shareholdings of institutional investors only accounted for 15.6%.[355] Cumulative voting does not assure a board seat to all institutions, but rather to those that have more than a certain percentage of shares. This critical percentage depends on – and varies with – the number of directors to be elected at a meeting.[356] According to Article 108 of Company Law – which rules that a joint stock limited company shall set up a board of directors comprising 5–19 persons and the formula for determining the number of shares needed to elect a desired number of directors[357] – if there are 19 directors to be elected, a 6% shareholder is assured of a board seat. However, the average board size of Chinese listed companies is much smaller than 19, with the statistics indicating that it is 11 among the top 100 PLCs.[358] This means that only a minority shareholder or a shareholder consortium with 9% or more of the shares can win a seat on average.

Presumably the election of supervisors by the institutions will be more difficult, mainly because the size of the supervisory board is much smaller than that of the board of directors. Article 117 rules: "The board of supervisors shall include representatives of shareholders and an appropriate percentage of representatives of the company's employees. The percentage of the representatives of employees shall account for not less than 1/3 of all the supervisors, but the concrete percentage shall be specified in the articles of association." Thus, it would further reduce the number of supervisors up for election since normally two-thirds of the supervisors are elected by shareholders, whereas the rest are reserved for workers.

---

355 See Social Security Fund Council: *Weekly on Stocks*, 18.1.2012, retrieved 3.7.2013, from http://news.ihongpan.com/12/0118/seocs083550.html.

356 See Clark, Robert Charles: *Corporate Law*. New York: Aspen Publishers, 1986, pp. 362–365.

357 A rough measure of the minimum number of votes that a stockholder must have to elect a target number of directors by cumulating his votes can be determined by multiplying the total number of voting shares by a number equal to the target number of directors, dividing this by a number equal to the total number of directors to be elected plus one and adding one to the result. X = (Y * N1) / (N + 1) + 1(X = number of shares needed to elect a certain number of directors; Y = total number of voting shares at the election; N1 = desired number of directors to be elected; N = total number of director positions available). See Arthur T. Cole, JR., Legal and Mathematical Aspects of Cumulative Voting, Supreme Court Library Queensland, Vol. 2, No. 3, March 1950, pp. 225–244, 230; Henn, Harry G. / Alexander, John R.: *Laws of Corporations and Other Business Enterprises*. West Publish Corporation: 3rd Edition, 1983, p. 58.

358 See *Evaluation of Corporate Governance in Top 100 PLCs of China in 2012*, retrieved 15.1.2013, from http://wenku.baidu.com/view/74f36a20a5e9856a561260d6.html, p. 23.

II. Adoption of Classified Board

The effect of cumulative voting may be reduced through the adoption of a staggered board of directors. Based upon the formula mentioned above, a rough measure of the minimum number of votes that a stockholder must have to elect a target number of directors by cumulating his votes can be determined by multiplying the total number of voting shares by a number equal to the target number of directors, dividing this by a number equal to the total number of directors to be elected plus one and adding one to the result. Thus, the minority may elect more representatives of themselves by cumulative voting when there are more directors who would be elected and if the number of those directors is less than the minimum number required by the formula, due to the staggered board of directors, the minority cannot elect their own members of the board by cumulative voting. For example, A has 80 shares and B has 20 shares: if there are five seats on the board, cumulative voting assures B of obtaining a seat because – owing to the formula mentioned above – even as few as 17 of the 100 shares would guarantee B a seat on a five-person board. However, if the board is reduced to three seats, B will lose his guaranteed seats. Now, by the same formula, B needs at least (100/4) +1 – or 26 – of the 100 shares to guarantee himself a seat.[359] A particular difficulty was presented by the principal case in that the effect of cumulative voting was entirely negated where only one director was to be elected.

According to Article 108 and 117 of the Company Law, a joint stock limited company shall set up a board of directors comprising 5–19 persons and a board of supervisors, which shall comprise at least 3 persons. Accordingly, the number of directors is not allowed to be less than 5 and the articles can provide any number of directors above 5 and the size of supervisors is not permitted to be less than 3. Articles 46 and 53 provide that the terms of office of the directors and supervisors shall be provided for in the articles of association, although each term of office shall not exceed three years. After the expiry of their terms of office, the directors and supervisors may hold a consecutive term upon re-election. These rules show that the term of directors and supervisors' office is determined by articles if it is less than three years and the law does not regard the same terms of every director and supervisor as a necessity and allows the corporations to adopt a classified board. Therefore, it is a possibility that the controlling shareholders and management would eliminate the effect of cumulative voting by a staggered board.

In terms of the analysis above, there is a possibility that the controlling shareholders and management could take advantage of a staggered board to prevent minority shareholders from successfully electing members of the board by cumulative voting. To resolve this problem, the Chinese corporate law should seek solutions from the legal practice and the court should analyze this problem on a case-by-case basis. In addition, the experience of America may be a reference. For instance, the court in

---

359 See Henn, Harry G. / Alexander, John R.: *Laws of Corporations and Other Business Enterprises.* West Publish Corporation: 3rd Edition, 1983, p. 58.

Humphrys v. Winous Co. – which involved a conflict between a statute that provided for staggered director terms and a statute that permitted cumulative voting[360] – noted that the objective of cumulative voting was to protect minority shareholders, although this protection did not guarantee that minority shareholders would attain representation on the board of directors.[361] The court's decision makes it clear that classified boards are not necessarily precluded by cumulative voting provisions.[362] This attitude presents the notion that both cumulative voting and staggered boards are systems provided by the law for the corporations to choose and the law does not intend to make the realization of minority representation a priority.

III. Remove Minority Representatives with or without Cause

While cumulative voting may be important to the extent that it seeks to measure the power of shareholders in the appointment of directors, it misses the more critical question of the removal of directors. Article 37 (2) of Company Law provides that the shareholders' meeting shall exercise the authorities of electing and replacing the director and supervisors assumed by non-representatives of the employees. Thus, cumulative voting may be circumvented through removing minority-elected directors with or without cause by majority shareholders.[363] If the power of removal by majority vote in a cumulative-voting corporation is to be allowed at all, it might negate the protection of minority interests that cumulative voting is designed to ensure.

In terms of removing the independent directors and supervisors with cause, Article 146 of the Company Law provides the circumstances under which anyone shall not take the post of a director, supervisor or senior manager of a company and in case any director, supervisor or senior manager is under such circumstances during his term of office, the company shall dismiss him from his post. The circumstances include: without or with limited capacity of civil conduct; being sentenced to any criminal penalty due to an offence of corruption, bribery, encroachment of property, misappropriation of property or disrupting the economic order of the socialist market economy and five years not having passed since the completion date of the execution

---

360 See Humphrys v. Winous Co., 133 N.E.2d 780, 782 (Ohio 1956).

361 See Hump hry s v. Winous Co., 133 N.E.2d 780, 785–786 (Ohio 1956). It acknowledged limits of the effectiveness of cumulative voting and this attitude is consistent with the view of Maddock v. Vorclone Corp , in which the court held that cumulative voting did not pretend to guarantee minority representation on the board of directors at all times. "While the right of cumulative voting has for its purpose the affording to a minority of the voting stock an opportunity to elect one or more directors, the scheme does not pretend to assure to a minority a representation in any event. The enjoyment of the right is a thing incident to each share of stock and belongs to no group as such."

362 See Humphrys v. Winous Co., 133 N.E.2d 780, 785–786 (Ohio 1956).

363 See Bowes, Harlowe E. / De Bow, Ledlie A.: "Cumulative Voting at Elections of Directors of Corporations". *Minnesota Law Review*, Vol. 21, No. 4, 1937, pp. 351–370, 367.

of the penalty or having ever been deprived of his political rights due to any crime and three years not having passed since the completion date of the execution of the penalty; being a former director, factory director or manager of a company or enterprise that was bankrupt and liquidated and was personally liable for the bankruptcy of such company or enterprise, with three years not having passed since the date of completion of the bankruptcy and liquidation of the company or enterprise; or being the legal representative of a company or enterprise whereby the business license of this company or enterprise was revoked and this company or enterprise was ordered to close due to violation of the law, being personally liable for the revocation, three years not having passed since the date of the revocation of the business license thereof and having a relatively large amount of debt that is due but uncleared. Consequently, if the independent directors and supervisors elected by minority shareholders through cumulative voting are under the conditions mentioned in the provisions of Article 147, they would be dismissed by companies.

Furthermore, Guiding Opinions on the Establishment of Systems of Independent Directors in Listed Companies (hereinafter "Independent Director Opinion") stipulates extra conditions for removing independent directors. If the directors cannot fulfill the qualifications about independence in Article 3, they could be removed by a shareholders' meeting. Article 3 provides that the following persons may not hold the position of independent director: (1) persons holding a position in the listed company or a subsidiary thereof and their lineal relatives and major social relations (the term "lineal relatives" meaning spouses, parents, children, etc.; and the term "major social relations" meaning siblings, parents-in-law, children-in-law, siblings' spouses, spouse's siblings, etc.); (2) natural person shareholders who directly or indirectly hold not less than 1% of the issued shares of the listed company or who rank in the top ten shareholders of the listed company, and their lineal relatives; (3) persons who hold positions in entities that directly or indirectly hold not less than 5% of the issued shares of the listed company or that rank in the top five shareholders of the listed company, and their lineal relatives; (4) persons who have fallen into one of the three categories listed above at some time in the previous year; (5) persons who provide financial, legal, consultancy or other such services to the listed company or its subsidiaries; (6) other persons specified in the company's articles of association; and (7) other persons determined by the China Securities Regulatory Commission. Furthermore, Article 4 (5) of Independent Director Opinion provides that if an independent director fails to attend three consecutive board meetings in person, the board of directors should invite the shareholders' general meeting to replace him. In addition, Article 32 of the Guidelines for Investor Rights Protection in Small and Medium Board of Enterprise[364] rules that PLCs shall provide

364 Shenzhen Stock Exchange: *Guidelines for Investor Rights Protection in Small and Medium Board of Enterprise*, 13.1.2006, Article 2 rules that the Guidelines apply to small and medium board of enterprise and their controlling shareholders, actual controllers, directors, supervisors, senior managers and sponsors.

in articles that for those directors who have no qualifications of independence and cannot perform duties independently or safeguard the interest of medium and small shareholders and PLCs, shareholders who directly or indirectly hold not less than 1% of the issued shares of the listed company can propose to the board of PLC the motion of questioning or removing such independent directors.

With respect to the right of dismissing independent directors and supervisors without cause, Article 115 in Company Law of 1993 provided that the shareholders' meeting had no right to remove the directors without cause before the expiration of the office's terms, although the Company Law of 2005 eliminated such provision. Furthermore, Article 96 of the Guidelines for Articles of Association of Chinese Listed Companies rules that "before a directors' period of service expires, the shareholders' meeting cannot terminate his duties without a reason". The Guidelines – drafted by CSRC in 2006 – are not law, but set down the basic contents of the articles of association of a listed company. They allow a listed company – according to practical circumstances – to increase the contents of its articles of association to include provisions outside the Guidelines to suit its actual requirements, as long as the law and regulation is not contravened, but requires that if a listed company increases or changes the compulsory Guidelines provisions, according to its needs, it should make a special note in the public announcement by the board of directors of the resolution to amend its articles of association. Therefore, according to the compulsory rule of Article 96, majority shareholders have no right to dismiss directors elected by cumulative voting without cause.

Article 4 (5) of Independent Director Opinion further provides that an independent director may not be removed without cause before the expiration of his term unless the aforementioned circumstance or a circumstance under which a person may not hold the position of director specified in the Company Law arises. If an Independent Director is removed before the expiration of his term, the listed company should disclose the same as a matter for special disclosure. If the dismissed Independent Director holds the opinion that the company's grounds for removing him are inappropriate, he may make a public statement to such effect. This provision is based on the view that independent directors who are supposed to protect minority shareholders shall not be removed without cause and at the will of majority shareholders.

Generally speaking, the Chinese company law has accepted that the removal of directors and supervisors is an inherit right of the shareholders' meeting, although it only permits dismissing directors – especially the independent directors – based on the reasons provided by the law and related regulations and the removal supervisors without cause is allowed. Accordingly, there is a danger that the supervisors elected through cumulative voting would be removed without cause by the shareholders' meeting.

D. Independent Directors and Cumulative Voting

The ability to elect "representative" directors is particularly important in China. For example, Company Law has already recognized the voting right for election as a fundamental power of shareholders' meeting by Article 37 (2), which rules that: "The shareholders' meeting shall exercise the authorities: electing and changing the director and supervisors assumed by non-representatives of the employees, and determining the matters concerning their remuneration." In reality, the voting rights of shareholders for election in China are largely limited because the directors and supervisors are often selected by dominating shareholders.[365]

The term "independent director" first appeared in the "Guiding Opinion for Listed Corporations' Articles of Incorporation" issued by CSRC on December 26, 1997. In Article 112 of this regulation, listed companies were advised to keep an independent director on their board. In terms of defining "independent director", it stipulated that "an independent director cannot be a current employee of the company, an employee of a shareholder, or a relative of an interested person or management." It also encouraged the listed company to stipulate the duty and authority of its independent directors in its own charter.

Furthermore, in 2001, the CSRC formulated the "Independent Directors Opinion", which marked an important move to carry out this new mechanism and stipulated many aspects of independent directors, such as mandating greater independence for directors and defining the board's functions, powers and internal workings, including matters like auditing, setting executive compensation, screening RPTs and disclosure of information. In fact, it marked an important move by the CSRC to carry out this new mechanism. In Independent Director Opinion, a basic framework was adopted for the extensive implementation of the Chinese independent director mechanism, which contained various rules about the qualification and authority of independent directors for all listed companies. In addition, on January 31st , 2004, the State Council of China issued "Several Opinions on Promoting the Reform and Opening-up and Stable Development of Capital Market", which underscores the importance of independent directors in the reform and development of China's capital market.[366]

The definition of "independence" in China focuses on the independence from management and controlling shareholders. Article 1 para.1 of the Independent Directors Opinion stipulates that the term "independent director of a listed company" means a director who does not hold any position in the company other than director and who has no relationship with the listed company engaging him or its principal shareholders that could hinder his making independent and objective judgments. The drafters have considered the independent director as being independent from everyone with a significant interest in the company and as the protector of small shareholders against both management and dominant shareholders.[367] The Independent Directors Opinion not only defines the "independence" generally,

---

365 Pizzo, Michele: "Related party transactions under a contingency perspective". *Journal of Management and Governance*, Vol. 17, No. 2, 2013, pp. 309–330, 322.

366 See China State Council: *Some Opinions of the State Council on Promoting the Reform, Opening and Steady Growth of Capital Markets*, 31.1.2004.

367 Clarke, Donald C.: "The Independent Director in Chinese Corporate Governance". *Delaware Journal of Corporate Law*, Vol. 31, No. 1, 2006, pp. 125–228, 189.

but also provides independence through a negative approach. Article 3 stipulates that the following persons may not serve as independent directors: (1) a person who holds a position in the listed company or its subordinate affiliates as well as the direct relatives of – and those with important social connections[368] to – the former; (2) a person – or the direct relative of a person – who directly or indirectly holds at least 1% of the company's stock or is among the top ten shareholders of the company; (3) a person – or the direct relative of a person – who is employed by an entity that directly or indirectly holds at least 5% of the company's stock or is among the top five non-natural person shareholders of the company; (4) a person about whom any of the above conditions have been met within the last year; (5) a person who supplies accounting, legal, consulting or other similar services to the company or its subordinate affiliates; (6) any other person specified in the company's articles of association; and (7) any other person specified by the CSRC.[369] In addition to lacking

368 "Direct relatives" are defined as a "spouse, mother, father, son, daughter, etc." Independent Directors Opinion, Article 2.

369 Independent Directors Opinion, Article 3. The provisions of independence in the New York Stock Exchange Listed Company Manual 303A.02 Independence Tests (a) provides that no director qualifies as "independent" unless the board of directors affirmatively determines that the director has no material relationship with the listed company (either directly or as a partner, shareholder or officer of an organization that has a relationship with the company) as well as the NASDAQ Marketplace Rule 4200 (a) (15) which rules that "Independent director" means a person other than an executive officer or employee of the company or any other individual having a relationship which, in the opinion of the issuer's board of directors, would interfere with the exercise of independent judgment in carrying out the responsibilities of a director. The Independence Tests (b) of New York Stock Exchange Listed Company Manual 303A.02 rules that a director is not independent if: (i) The director is, or has been within the last three years, an employee of the listed company, or an immediate family member is, or has been within the last three years, an executive officer, of the listed company. (ii) The director has received, or has an immediate family member who has received, during any twelve-month period within the last three years, more than $120,000 in direct compensation from the listed company, other than director and committee fees and pension or other forms of deferred compensation for prior service (provided such compensation is not contingent in any way on continued service). (iii) (A) The director is a current partner or employee of a firm that is the listed company's internal or external auditor; (B) the director has an immediate family member who is a current partner of such a firm; (C) the director has an immediate family member who is a current employee of such a firm and personally works on the listed company's audit; or (D) the director or an immediate family member was within the last three years a partner or employee of such a firm and personally worked on the listed company's audit within that time. (iv) The director or an immediate family member is, or has been with the last three years, employed as an executive officer of another company where any of the listed company's present executive officers at the same time serves or served on that company's compensation

a personal interest in the transaction in question, a director must be independent. "A director is independent if he can base his decision 'on the corporate merits of the subject before the board rather than extraneous considerations or influences.'"[370]

committee. (v) The director is a current employee, or an immediate family member is a current executive officer, of a company that has made payments to, or received payments from, the listed company for property or services in an amount which, in any of the last three fiscal years, exceeds the greater of $1 million, or 2% of such other company's consolidated gross revenues. *New York Stock Exchange Listed Company Manual 303A.02 Independence Tests*, retrieved 17.2.2013, from http://nysemanual.nyse.com/LCMTools/Platform Viewer.asp?selectednode=chp_1_4_3_3&manual=%2Flcm%2Fsections%2Flcm-sections%2F.. NASDAQ Marketplace Rule 4200(a) (15) rules that the following persons shall not be considered independent: A) a director who is, or at any time during the past three years was, employed by the company; B) a director who accepted or who has a family member who accepted any compensation from the company in excess of $100,000 during any period of twelve consecutive months within the three years preceding the determination of independence, other than the following: i) compensation for board or board committee service; ii) compensation paid to a family member who is an employee (other than an executive officer) of the company; or iii) benefits under a tax-qualified retirement plan, or non-discretionary compensation. Provided, however, that in addition to the requirements contained in this paragraph (B), audit committee members are also subject to additional, more stringent requirements under Rule 4350(d).C) a director who is a family member of an individual who is, or at any time during the past three years was, employed by the company as an executive officer; D) a director who is, or has a family member who is, a partner in, or a controlling shareholder or an executive officer of, any organization to which the company made, or from which the company received, payments for property or services in the current or any of the past three fiscal years that exceed 5% of the recipient's consolidated gross revenues for that year, or $200,000, whichever is more, other than the following: i) payments arising solely from investments in the company's securities; or ii) payments under non-discretionary charitable contribution matching programs. E) a director of the issuer who is, or has a family member who is, employed as an executive officer of another entity where at any time during the past three years any of the executive officers of the issuer serve on the compensation committee of such other entity; or F) a director who is, or has a family member who is, a current partner of the company's outside auditor, or was a partner or employee of the company's outside auditor who worked on the company's audit at any time during any of the past three years. G) in the case of an investment company, in lieu of paragraphs (A)-(F), a director who is an "interested person" of the company as defined in Section 2(a)(19) of the Investment Company Act of 1940, other than in his or her capacity as a member of the board of directors or any board committee. *NASDAQ Manual Marketplace Rule 4200(a) (15)* (defining "independent director" for NASDAQ listing purposes), retrieved 27.3.2013, from http://www.sec.gov/rules/other/nasdaqllcf1a4_5/ nasdaqllcamendrules4000.pdf.

370 Seminaris v. Landa, 662 A.2d 1350, 1354 (Del. 1995) (quoting Aronson v. Lewis, 473 A.2d 805, 816 (Del. 1984)).

In particular, a director who is beholden to – or under the influence of – an interested party lacks the requisite independence.[371] "A director is interested if he will be materially affected, either to his benefit or detriment, by a decision of the board, in a manner not shared by the corporation and the shareholders."[372]

Article 2 of Independent Directors Opinion provides that an independent director should have the qualifications required to exercise his functions and powers. Besides the qualifications to hold the position of independent director in a listed company in accordance with laws, administrative regulations and other relevant regulations as well as the company's articles of association and the requirements of being independent. The independent directors must have a basic knowledge of the operation of listed companies and being familiar with related laws, administrative regulations and rules and must have not less than five years' experience in the law or economics or other work experience required for performing the duties and responsibilities of an independent director.

This provision is based upon the view that independence should rest on "the concept of director professionalism," which requires directors to be "expert in their fields," "knowledgeable about critical aspects of the corporation's operations" and "skillful in serving as competent, alert overseers and advisers of management."[373] In China, a recent study based on a random sample of 500 listed companies found that 45% of independent directors were university professors or researchers from institutes. Other (presumably industrial) companies were the source for 28% of the independent directors, while lawyers, accountants and other service industry professionals accounted for 14%. The vast majority of the 5,972 independent directors in PLCs of Shanghai and Shenzhen Stock Exchange have achieved university education.[374] According to the investigation of the Listed Companies Association of

---

371 See In re MAXXAM, Inc., 659 A.2d 760, 773 (Del. Ch. 1995) ("To be considered independent a director must not be 'dominated or otherwise controlled by an individual or entity interested in the transaction.'").

372 See Seminaris v. Landa, 662 A.2d 1350, 1354 (Del. 1995). *See also* In re RJR Nabisco, Inc. Shareholders Litig., 1989 WL 7036 at 14 (Del. Ch. 1989) (a disqualifying interest "is a financial interest in the transaction adverse to that of the corporation or its shareholders").

373 See Koppes, Richard H. / Ganske, Lyle G. / Haag, Charles T.: "Corporate Governance out of Focus: The Debate over Classified Boards". *Business Lawyer*, Vol. 54, No. 3, 5.1999, pp. 1023–1055, 1054–1055; Cox, James D.: "The Paradoxical Corporate and Securities Law Implications of Counsel Serving on the Client's Board". *Washington University Law Quarterly*, Vol. 80, No. 541, 2002, pp. 541–567, 541; Macavoy, Paul W. / Millstein, Iram: *The Recurrent Crisis in Corporate Governance*. Stanford University Press: 2003, pp. 22–23; Gilson, Ronald J. / Kraakman, Reinier: "Reinventing the Outside Director: An Agenda for Institutional Investors". *Stanford Law Review*, Vol. 43, No. 4, 4.1991, pp. 863–906, 884–888.

374 See Research Team of "Guidelines for Performance of Independent Directors in Listed Companies" in the China Association for Public Companies: "The Great Possibility of Enhancing the Role of Independent Directors – Abstract of the

Shanghai, 78% of all listed companies hire independent directors from universities and research institutions, 51% obtain supervisors and directors or senior managers from other enterprises, 46% have experts from accounting firms and law firms and advisory agencies, only 19% have retired government officials and 10% choose employees or retired employees of banks.[375]

Finally, Article 124 in the Company Law of 2013 provides a new legal basis for the independent director in China by stipulating that "a listed corporation shall have independent directors and the concrete measures shall be formulated by the State Council". The empty language in this new article does not mandate a broader application of the independent director mechanism in China in the future, although it officially provides the independent director a better legal basis in the Company Law and elevates it from administrative regulation to the law.

As a global popular corporate governance system developed in the US, independent directors were adopted to mitigate not only the agency problem between shareholders and management, but also the agency problem between controlling shareholders and minority shareholders, whereby the adoption of independent directors was supported by Chinese mainstream scholars such as Zhao Xudong and Zhu Ciyun.[376] With more than ten years having passed, increasingly more Chinese companies have accepted independent directors on their boards. According to the statistics cited by the report of China Association for Public Companies, at the end of 2012 the number of independent directors hired by the PLCs of Shanghai and Shenzhen Stock Exchange had reached 5,972. On average, every company hires 3.3 independent directors. Among the PLCs of China, there are 106 companies (4.2%) with less than two independent directors, 1,785 companies (71.6%) with three and 454 companies (18.2%) with four independent directors, as well as 149 companies (5.9%) with more than five independent directors.[377]

Report on the Performance of Independent Directors". *China Securities Journal*, A14, 16.1.2014.

375 See Research Team of "Guidelines for Performance of Independent Directors in Listed Companies" in the China Association for Public Companies: "The Great Possibility of Enhancing the Role of Independent Directors – Abstract of the Report on the Performance of Independent Directors". *China Securities Journal*, A14, 16.1.2014.

376 See Jiang Ping / Wang Weiguo / Zhao Xudong: *Duli Dongshi Sanren Tan* [Discussions on Independent Directors by Three Scholars], retrieved 20.2.2014, from http://article.chinalawinfo.com/Article_ Detail.asp?ArticleId=28364. Zhu Ciyun / Zhongguo Yinru: "Duli Dongshi Zhidu Yingzhuyi de Ruogan Wenti" [Several Issues about the Adoption of Independent Directors]. In: *Gongsi Zhili yu Ziben Shichang Jianguan-Bijiao yu Jiejian* [Corporate Governance and Regulation of Security Market-Comparison and Reference]. Beijing University Press: 2003, p. 248.

377 See Research Team of "Guidelines for Performance of Independent Directors in Listed Companies" in the China Association for Public Companies: "The Great Possibility of Enhancing the Role of Independent Directors – Abstract of the

The election of independent directors is designed as follows by Independent Director Opinion. 1) Independent directors are to be nominated by any of the following: (a) incumbent members of the board of directors; (b) the board of supervisors; or (c) a shareholder who owns more than 1% equity interest. 2) The listed company must pre-file the nomination information with the CSRC and the CSRC maintains the right to dissent within fifteen days after filing. 3) Approval will be made by the resolution of the shareholders meeting.[378] This means that in the absence of backing from the board and controlling shareholder, the minority shareholders who hold a smaller stake can hardly install their nominees.[379] According to the statistics of the Research Centre of Corporate Governance of Nankai University on independent directors in 2001, 87.36% of the candidates for independent directors were nominated by the board, 15.06% were proposed by controlling shareholders or the actual controller and 1.7% were supported by the commission of board. The remaining candidates were recommended by superior departments or through public recruitment. The statistics in 2011 showed that 90% of the candidates for independent directors were nominated by controlling shareholders.[380] Controlling shareholders and management more often select those with either a personal or financial connection to them, in the hope that such independent directors will side with them in any necessary situation. Independent directors can be either not independent enough in reality or unable to make any effective monitoring.

To deal with these problems, Article 20 of the Code stipulates: "The controlling shareholders shall nominate the candidates for directors and supervisors in strict compliance with the terms and procedures provided for by laws, regulations and the company's articles of association. The nominated candidates shall possess certain relevant professional knowledge and the capability to make decisions or supervise. The resolutions made by the shareholders' meetings for electing personnel or

---

Report on the Performance of Independent Directors". *China Securities Journal*, A14, 16.1.2014.

378 Independent Director Opinion, Article 4.

379 See Shanghai Association of Listed Companies' Board of Director Secretaries & Jinxin Institute of Securities: "Duli Dongshi Zenmoyang le?" [How Are the Independent Directors?]. *Zhengquan Shibao* [Securities Times], 7.8.2003; Liu Qing: "Duli Dongshi Zhidu Shishi zhong de Wenti yu Duice" [Problems and Countermeasures in the Practice of the Independent Director System]. *Zhengquan Shichang Daobao* [Security Market Herald], 10.12. 2003; Li Dongping: "Sanda Wenti Kunrao Dudong Zhidu Shijian" [Three Problems Puzzled the Practice of the Independent Director System]. *Zhengquan Shibao* [Securities Times], 23.3.2003; Clarke, Donald C.: "The Independent Director in Chinese Corporate Governance". *Delaware Journal of Corporate Law*, Vol. 31, No. 1, 2006, pp. 125–228; Liufang, Fang: "Duli Dongshi zai Zhongguo: Jiashe he Xianshi" [Independent Directors in China: Hypothesis and Reality], *Tribune of Political Science and Law*, Vol. 26, No. 5, 2008, pp. 110–115, 110.

380 See Zhu Ciyun: *Gongsifa Yuanlun* [Theories of Corporate Law]. Qinghua University Press: 2011, p. 132.

the board of directors' resolutions appointing personnel shall not be subjected to approval procedures by the controlling shareholders. The controlling shareholders are forbidden to appoint senior management personnel by circumventing the shareholders' meetings or the board of directors." Furthermore, if the minority shareholders can take advantage of cumulative voting to elect independent directors, the control of dominating shareholders to the board would be restricted and the relationship between those representatives on boards and medium and small investors would be enhanced, whereby they would have greater incentives to exercise their rights.[381] On the other hand, the independence of directors may also resolve the problem of partisan representation on the board, which is the most common argument against cumulative voting. Thus, Listing Rules of Growth Enterprise Market (GEM) in Shenzhen Stock Exchange[382] provides that the election of independent directors through cumulative voting by Article 3.1.13. Cumulative voting makes it more likely that a minority of directors is truly independent of management and controlling shareholders.[383]

---

381 See Feinerman, James V.: "New Hope for Corporate Governance in China?". *The China Quarterly*, No. 191, 9.2007, pp. 590–612, 603.

382 See Shenzhen Stock Exchange: *Listing Rules of Growth Enterprise Market (GEM) in Shenzhen Stock Exchange*, 2012, No. 77.

383 See Gilson, Ronald J. / Kraakman, Reinier: "Reinventing the Outside Director: An Agenda for Institutional Investors". *Stanford Law Review*, Vol. 43, No. 4, 4.1991, pp. 863–906, 872–876.

Fourth Chapter: Alternatives to Cumulative Voting – Controlling Related Party Transactions by Independent Directors

From the analysis of the last two chapters, we can observe that cumulative voting has been replaced by independent directors in the US, the EU introduced independent directors rather than cumulative voting and China emphasizes more on the role of cumulative voting in electing independent directors. This chapter focuses on the primary reason for the declining of cumulative voting – the role of independent directors and shareholders' meeting in controlling RPTs. The reason for discussing the control of related-party transactions is that there is a clear concern that such transactions can be abused by insiders such as executives and controlling shareholders. Hence, the control of related-party transactions is an important matter in the respect of minority shareholders' protection. But this task is performed by independent directors and shareholders' meeting rather than representatives on the board elected through cumulative voting, whose role is protecting minority shareholders.

A. Definition of Related Party Transactions

Regarding the definition of RPTs, Article 8.60 of the MBCA provides that (1) "conflicting interest" with respect to a corporation means: the interest a director of the corporation has respecting a transaction effected or proposed to be effected by the corporation (or by a subsidiary of the corporation or any other entity in which the corporation has a controlling interest) if (i) whether or not the transaction is brought before the board of directors of the corporation for action, the director knows at the time of commitment that he or a related person is a party to the transaction or has a beneficial financial interest in or so closely linked to the transaction and of such financial significance to the director or a related person that the interest would reasonably be expected to exert an influence on the director's judgment if he were called upon to vote on the transaction; or (ii) the transaction is brought (or is of such character and significance to the corporation that it would in the normal course be brought) before the board of directors of the corporation for action and the director knows at the time of commitment that any of the following persons is either a party to the transaction or has a beneficial financial interest in or so closely linked to the transaction and of such financial significance to the person that the interest would reasonably be expected to exert an influence on the director's judgment if he were called upon to vote on the transaction: (A) an entity (other than the corporation) of which the director is a director, general partner, agent or employee; (B) a person who controls one or more of the entities specified in sub-clause (A) or an entity that is controlled by – or is under common control with – one or more of the entities specified in sub-clause (A); or (C) an individual who is a general partner, principal or employer of the director.

Furthermore, Article 8.60 (2) provides that "director's conflicting interest transaction" with respect to a corporation means a transaction effected or proposed to be effected by the corporation (or by a subsidiary of the corporation or any other entity in which the corporation has a controlling interest) respecting which a director of the corporation has a conflicting interest. Article 8.60 (3) stipulates that "related person" of a director means (i) the spouse (or a parent or sibling thereof) of the director or a child, grandchild, sibling or parent (or spouse of any thereof) of the director, an individual having the same home as the director or a trust or estate of which an individual specified in this clause is (i) a substantial beneficiary; or (ii) a trust, estate, incompetent, conservatee or minor of which the director is a fiduciary.

According to the EU Action Plan, RPTs – i.e. dealings where the company contracts with its directors or controlling shareholders – may cause prejudice to the company and its minority shareholders, as they give the related party the opportunity to appropriate value belonging to the company. Thus, adequate safeguards for the protection of shareholders' interests hold great importance. In the proposal, RPTs – i.e. transactions between a company and its management, directors, controlling entities or shareholders – create the opportunity to obtain value belonging to the company to the detriment of shareholders and particularly minority shareholders.[384] In terms of the International Accounting Standard 24, "[a] related party transaction is a transfer of resources, services or obligations between a [corporation] and a related party, regardless of whether a price is charged"[385].

In China, Article 10.1.1 of the Rules Governing the Listing of Stocks on Shanghai Stock Exchange (amended in 2014, hereinafter "the Rules") provides that: "A related party transaction of a listed company refers to the transfer of resources or obligations between the listed company or its controlled subsidiary and a related party of the listed company, including the following: (1) transactions enumerated in Section 9.1 hereof; (2) purchasing raw materials, fuels and power; (3) selling products and commodities; (4) providing or accepting labor services; (5) selling by consignment or selling on commission; (6) making deposits at or taking loans from the finance company of a related party; (7) co-investing with a related party; (8) other matters agreed upon that would lead to transfer of resources or obligations." RPTs among controlling shareholders are often detrimental to minority shareholders, who are often regarded as speculators expecting to gain a "free ride" on the firm's performance.[386] In China, according to the annual reports of 1,073 PLCs, there were 332 companies with RPTs

384 The Proposal, p. 6.

385 International Accounting Standard 24 (EC Staff Consolidated version of 20 July 2010).

386 See Lin, Thomas W.: "Corporate Governance in China: Recent Developments, Key Problems, and Solutions". *Journal of Accounting and Corporate Governance*, Vol. 1, No. 1, 6.2004, pp. 1–23.

damaging the interest of corporations by April 25, 2001.[387] Increasingly more Chinese listed companies have been "hollowed" out by controlling shareholders due to unclear RPTs and the expropriation of the interests that belong to minority shareholders.

Thus, in the Code, Article 13 provides that efficient measures shall be adopted by a listed company to prevent its connected parties from interfering with the operation of the company and damaging the company's interests by monopolizing purchase or sales channels. Related party transactions shall observe commercial principles. In principle, the prices of related party transactions shall not deviate from an independent third party's market price or charging standard. The company shall fully disclose the basis for pricing for related party transactions. Article 14 provides that the assets of a listed company belong to the company, which shall adopt efficient measures to prevent its shareholders and their affiliates from misappropriating or transferring the capital, assets or other resources of the company through various means. A listed company shall not provide financial guarantees for its shareholders or their affiliates.

Around the world, the potential to abuse RPTs covering both equity and non-equity RPTs is viewed as an important policy issue owing to some high profile cases that have damaged market integrity through the inequitable treatment of shareholders. Jurisdictions have responded in many different ways and efforts to manage such transactions are ongoing. On the one hand, the policy process or consensus accepts that related party transactions can be economically beneficial, especially in company groups where there are often developmental arguments that they substitute for under-developed markets and institutions.[388] It is true that some are now banned outright, especially loans to executives and directors where abuse in the past has been significant (*e.g.* WorldCom). In some cases, legal and regulatory frameworks around the world implicitly or explicitly acknowledge that RPTs could be productive and serve to increase corporate value. Therefore, they are permitted, although the threat of abuse of minority rights is also acknowledged.[389] On the other hand, there is a clear concern that such transactions can be abused by insiders such as executives and controlling shareholders. Indeed, concern to control corporate self-dealing has been a key aspect of the development of corporate law in many countries over the past century. Searching for a balance is ongoing as institutions and economies change.[390] While a balance has to be struck, this appears difficult in a world increasingly characterized by company groups with – in some cases – fluid boundaries and different shareholders.[391]

387 See Li Jianwei: *Duli Dongshi Zhidu Yanjiu – Cong Faxue he Guanlixue de Shuangchong Jiaodu* [Study on Independent Directors – From the Perspective of Law and Management]. China Renmin University Press: 2004, p. 34.
388 OECD, RPTs and MSR, Assessment and Recommendations, p. 11.
389 OECD, RPTs and MSR, Assessment and Recommendations, p. 11.
390 OECD, RPTs and MSR, Assessment and Recommendations, p. 11.
391 OECD, RPTs and MSR, p. 20.

B. Approval of Related Party Transactions by Independent Directors in the US

In the US, some of the most important aspects in the development of corporate law over the past 20 years have been the emphasis on bringing more independent directors onto boards and the creation of more board committees including independent directors.[392] In the wake of US scandals, both the Sarbanes-Oxley Act of 2002 and the new listing rules of the major US securities markets – which are premised upon a belief that director independence is essential for good corporate governance – require that a majority of directors is independent and that companies have adequate internal control mechanisms.[393] It is indisputable that the American mode of corporate governance depends on disinterested directors as independent decision-makers.[394] In terms of the minority shareholders' protection, the most important function of independent directors is the approval of RPTs, which constitutes a specific group of conflicts of interest and represents the most significant measures taken by controlling shareholders and directors for tunneling the companies. In almost all economies, the board is charged with making decisions about RPTs primarily in the interests of all shareholders. Within the decision-making process of the board, independent board members, the audit committee and internal/external auditors are required to perform a significant role in monitoring and approving RPTs to prevent abuse in all jurisdictions.[395]

392 See Leech, Nuyes E. / Mundheim, Robert H.: "The Outside Director of the Publicly held Corporation". *The Business Lawyer*, Vol. 31, No. 4, 7.1976, pp. 1799–1838, 1800.

393 The New York Stock Exchange listing standards require that two board committees (in addition to the audit committee) – the compensation and nominating-governance committees – entirely comprise independent directors and audit and compensation committees solely comprise independent directors. *New York Stock Exchange Listed Company Manual 303A.02 Independence Tests*, retrieved 17.2.2013, from http://nysemanual.nyse.com/LCMTools/PlatformViewer.asp?selectednode=chp_1_4_3_3&manual=%2Flcm%2Fsections%2Flcm-sections%2F. Corporate Governance Rule Proposals Reflecting Recommendations from the NYSE Corporate Accountability and Listing Standards Committee as Approved by the NYSE Board of Directors, August 1, 2002; Bainbridge, Stephen M.: *A Critique of the NYSE's Director Independence Listing Standards*. UCLA School of Law, Research Paper No. 02–15, 2002, retrieved 15.7.2014, from http://www.ssrn.com/abstract_id=317121; The NASD requires conflict transactions to be approved by committees consisting solely of independent directors. *NASDAQ Manual Marketplace Rule 4350(c)-(d)* (2006), retrieved 27.3.2013, from http://www.sec.gov/rules/other/nasdaqllcf1a4_5/nasdaqllcamendrules4000.pdf.; Sarbanes-Oxley Act of 2002 requires public companies to have an audit committee consisted solely of independent directors. See Sarbanes-Oxley Act of 2002 § 301, 15 USC, § 78j-l(m)(5)-(6) (2007); Bainbridge, Stephen M.: *Corporate Governance after the Financial Crisis*. Oxford University Press: 5.2012, p. 78.

394 See Haas, Steven M.: "Toward a Controlling Shareholder Safe Harbor". *Virginia Law Review*, Vol. 90, No. 8, 12.2004, pp. 2245–2304, 2283.

395 OECD, RPTs and MSR, p. 30.

I. Independent Directors and Related Party Transactions

According to both corporate statutes and the case law, it has long been the case that approval of conflicted interest transactions between controlling shareholders and the company by vote of a majority of the disinterested directors effectively immunizes such transactions from judicial review by invoking the defendant-friendly business judgment rule as the standard of review.[396] First, Delaware General Corporation Law section 144 provides that no contract or transaction between a corporation and one or more of its directors or officers, or between a corporation and any other corporation, partnership, association or other organization in which one or more of its directors or officers are directors or officers, or have a financial interest shall be void or voidable solely for this reason, or solely because the director or officer is present at or participates in the meeting of the board or committee that authorizes the contract or transaction, or solely because any such director's or officer's votes are counted for such purpose, if the material facts, as to the director's or officer's relationship or interest and as to the contract or transaction, are disclosed or are known to the board of directors or the committee and the board or committee, in good faith, authorizes the contract or transaction by the affirmative votes of a majority of the disinterested directors, even though the disinterested directors are less than a quorum.[397]

---

396 Delaware General Corporation Law Section 144; MBCA, Third Edition, Revised through 2002, adopted by the Committee on Corporate Laws of the Section of Business Law with the support of the American Bar Foundation, Article 41 states that a conflict of interest transaction is not void if the conflict is disclosed to the board of directors and approved by a sufficient number of disinterested directors' votes; Rosenblatt v. Getty Oil Co., 493 A.2d 929, 937 (Del. 1985) (stating the fact that directors were independent was a crucial factor in concluding that trans- action was fair); Aronson v. Lewis, 473 A.2d 805, 812 (Del. 1984) (stating that in a derivative action, the transaction must be approved by a majority consisting of independent directors for the business judgment rule to be applicable); Weinberger v. UOP, Inc., 457 A.2d 701, 709 n.7 (Del. 1983) (suggesting that a parent corporation might have been able to prove the fairness of the merger with its subsidiary if independent committee of outside directors had been appointed to negotiate on behalf of the subsidiary); Auerbach v. Bennett, 47 N.Y.2d 619, 632, 393 N.E.2d 994, 1001, 419 N.Y.S.2d 920, 927 (1979) (noting that as independent directors made up special litigation committee, presumption was they could recommend dismissal of derivative action). Marciano v. Nakash, 535 A.2d 400, 405 (Del. 1987).

397 Delaware General Corporation Law section 144 provides in pertinent part: (a) No contract or transaction between a corporation and 1 or more of its directors or officers, or between a corporation and any other corporation, partnership, association, or other organization in which 1 or more of its directors or officers, are directors or officers, or have a financial interest, shall be void or voidable solely for this reason, or solely because the director or officer is present at or participates in the meeting of the board or committee which authorizes the contract or transaction, or solely because any such director's or officer's votes are counted for such

Second, in MBCA, Article 8.61 (b) (1) provides that a director's conflicting interest transaction may not be enjoined, set aside or give rise to an award of damages or other sanctions in a proceeding by a shareholder, or by or in the right of the corporation, because the director – or any person with whom or which he has a personal, economic or other association – has an interest in the transaction if directors' action respecting the transaction was at any time taken in compliance with section 8.62. Article 8.62 (d) provides that with respect to a director's conflicting interest transaction, "qualified director" means any director who does not have either (1) a conflicting interest respecting the transaction or (2) a familial, financial, professional or employment relationship with a second director who has a conflicting interest respecting the transaction, whereby this relationship would – under the circumstances – reasonably be expected to exert an influence on the first director's judgment when voting on the transaction.

Third, Puma v. Marriott applies, which involved a transaction between the corporation and its controlling shareholders, establishing the rule that business judgment rule shall apply to a controlling shareholder's going-concern transaction with its corporation in the non-final period where the interests of shareholders are aligned in the market[398] if the transaction has been approved by independent directors. Thus, independent ratification in such transactions precludes the court "from substituting its uninformed opinion for that of the experienced, independent board members"[399].

Fourth, in Weinberger v. UOP, Inc., the Delaware Supreme Court suggested that a corporation utilize its independent directors to alleviate the conflict of interest inherent in parent-subsidiary merger negotiations. The court, in dicta, stated:

> *Although perfection is not possible, or expected, the result here could have been entirely different if UOP had appointed an independent negotiating committee of its outside directors to deal with Signal at arm's length. Since fairness in this context can be equated to conduct*

---

purpose, if: (1) The material facts as to the director's or officer's relationship or interest and as to the contract or transaction are disclosed or are known to the board of directors or the committee, and the board or committee in good faith authorizes the contract or transaction by the affirmative votes of a majority of the disinterested directors, even though the disinterested directors be less than a quorum; or (2) The material facts as to the director's or officer's relationship or interest and as to the contract or transaction are disclosed or are known to the shareholders entitled to vote thereon, and the contract or transaction is specifically approved in good faith by vote of the shareholders; or (3) The contract or transaction is fair as to the corporation as of the time it is authorized, approved or ratified, by the board of directors, a commit-tee or the shareholders.

398 "So long as the interests of controlling and minority shareholders are aligned, independent approval and market checks together provide sufficient constraints to obviate the need for the current entire fairness review." Haas, Steven M.: "Toward a Controlling Shareholder Safe Harbor". *Virginia Law Review*, Vol. 90, No. 8, 12.2004, pp. 2245–2304, 2249.

399 See Puma v. Marriott, 283 A.2d 693, 696 (Del. 1971).

by a theoretical, wholly independent, board of directors acting upon the matter before them, it is unfortunate that this course apparently was neither considered nor pursued.[400]

It is particularly significant that the court believed that the minority shareholders needed the protection afforded by independent directors, even though the merger had been conditioned upon securing the approval of a majority of UOP's minority shareholders.[401] As Chief Justice Veasey suggested:

I would urge boards of directors to demonstrate their independence, not only as a guard against the intrusion of the federal government but as a guard against anything that might happen to them in court from a properly presented complaint. We didn't fall off of the turnip truck, you know. We can tell whether somebody is acting independently or not. Directors who are supposed to be independent should have the guts to be a pain in the neck and act independently.

As stated in Aronson:

The requirement of director independence inheres in the conception and rationale of the business judgment rule. The presumption of propriety that flows from an exercise of business judgment is based in part on this unyielding precept. Independence means that a director's decision is based on the corporate merits of the subject before the board rather than extraneous considerations or influences. While directors may confer, debate, and resolve their differences through compromise, or by reasonable reliance on the expertise of their colleagues and other qualified persons, the end result, nonetheless, must be that each director has brought his or her own informed business judgment to bear with specificity upon the corporate merits of the issues without regard for or succumbing to influences which convert an otherwise valid business decision into a faithless act.[402]

II. Independent Directors and Business Judgment Rule

In Delaware, business judgment rule is described as a "presumption that in making a business decision the directors of a corporation acted on an informed basis, in good faith and in the honest belief that the action taken was in the best interests of the company".[403] According to Principles of Corporate Governance: Analysis and Recommendations Article4.01(c), a director or officer who makes a business judgment in good faith fulfills his duty under this Section if: (1) he is not interested ... in the subject of his business judgment; (2) he is informed with respect to the subject of his business judgment to the extent he reasonably believes to be appropriate under the circumstances; and (3) he rationally believes that his business judgment is in

400 Weinberger v. UOP, Inc., 457 A.2d 701, 709–710 (Del. 1983).
401 See Weinberger v. UOP, Inc., 457 A.2d 701, 712 (Del. 1983).
402 Aronson v. Lewis, 473 A.2d 805, 816 (Del. 1984).
403 Aronson v. Lewis, 473 A.2d 805, 812 (Del. 1984), overruled on other grounds, Brehm v. Eisner, 746 A.2d 244 (Del. 2000).

the best interests of the corporation.[404] An often-quoted statement describing the business judgment rule can be found in Warshaw v. Calhoun:

> *In the absence of a showing of bad faith on the part of the directors or of a gross abuse of discretion, the business judgment of the directors will not be interfered with by the courts. … The acts of the directors are presumptively acts taken in good faith and inspired for the best interests of the corporation, and a minority shareholder who challenges their bona fides of purpose has the burden of proof.*[405]

The case of Panter v. Marshall Field & Co. rules that:

> *Directors of corporations discharge their fiduciary duties when in good faith they exercise business judgment in making decisions regarding the corporation. When they act in good faith, they enjoy a presumption of sound business judgment, reposed in them as directors, which courts will not disturb if any rational business purpose can be attributed to their decision. In the absence of fraud, bad faith, gross overreaching or abuse of discretion, courts will not interfere with the exercise of business judgment by corporate directors.*[406]

In the landmark case of Aronson v. Lewis, the Supreme Court of Delaware – in some of the most quoted words of the past decade of corporation law jurisprudence – declared that:

> *The business judgment rule is a presumption that in making a business decision the directors of a corporation acted on an informed basis, in good faith and in the honest belief that the action taken was in the best interests of the company. Absent an abuse of discretion, that judgment will be respected by the courts. The burden is on the party challenging the decision to establish facts rebutting the presumption.*[407]

An important illustration of the business judgment rule is the often-cited Sinclair Oil Corp. v. Levien: "a board of directors enjoys a presumption of sound business judgment and its decisions will not be disturbed if they can be attributed to any rational business purpose."[408] A statement appears in Bodell v. General Gas & Electric Corp.:

> *[The controlling principle is that the substance of a business decision or transaction will not be reviewed or scrutinized by a court as long as the acts of the directors] … were performed in good faith, in the exercise of their best judgment, and for what they believe to be the advantage of the corporation and all its stockholders.*[409]

---

404 *Principles of Corporate Governance: Analysis and Recommendations*, Tentative Draft No. 4, 1985, Note on Proposed Revisions in Part III of Tentative Draft No. 2, Part IV Duty of Care and the Business Judgment Rule, Article 4.01.

405 Warshaw v. Calhoun, 221 A.2d 487, 493 (Del. 1966).

406 Panter v. Marshall Field & Co., 646 F.2d 271, 293 (7th Gir. 1981).

407 Aronson v. Lewis, 473 A.2d805, 812 (Del. 1984).

408 Sinclair Oil Corp. v. Levien, 280 A.2d 717 (Del. 1971), at 720.

409 Bodell v. General Gas & Electric Corp., 140 A. 264, 268 (Del. 1927).

Fundamentally speaking, the business judgment rule that makes it difficult to hold directors personally liable for improvident decisions "encourages competent individuals to become directors who otherwise might decline for fear of personal liability"[410]. "Delaware courts implement this philosophy by refusing to assess the substantive soundness of director judgments and by holding directors only to a gross negligence standard of care."[411] The foundation stone of the American law of corporate governance is that there must be a minimum of interference by the courts in internal corporate affairs. A statement in the ALI Corporate Governance Project reads:

> *Except in the egregious case of bad judgment or when there is evidence of bad faith, courts have made no attempt to second-guess directors on the substantive soundness of decisions reached. Similarly, in so-called conflict transactions, while mandating that all such transactions be subject to scrutiny, the courts have held that not all such transactions deserve judicial scrutiny. Thus, to avoid unnecessary interference, the courts have solicited non-judicial mechanisms developed within the corporation for reviewing conflict transactions, namely, approval by disinterested directors or shareholders following the disclosure of all material facts. The courts have assiduously sought to keep hands off the powerful yet delicate mechanism of corporate wealth production at the core of our economic well-being.*[412]

A more modest expression of this judicial deference to director decisions – as embodied in the business judgment rule – is as follows: "Where money damages or equitable relief is sought, the business judgment rule is a judicial policy of not reviewing the substantive merits of a board of directors' business decision for the purpose of determining whether directors breached or fulfilled their duty of care."[413]

Several arguments support the business judgment rule. On the one hand, most frequently invoked as bases for the business judgment rule are courts' lack of experience and expertise in business decision-making and the risk of permitting or requiring the courts to become – in effect – appellate boards of directors.[414]

---

410 Stuart R. Cohn, Cohn, Stuart R.: "Demise of the Director's Duty of Care: Judicial Avoidance of Standards and Sanctions through the Business Judgment Rule". *Texas Law Review*, Vol. 62, No. 4, 1983, pp. 591–638, 599–600.

411 Johnson, Lyman P.Q.: "Corporate Officers and the Business Judgment Rule". *The Business Lawyer*, Vol. 60, No. 2, 2.2005, pp. 439–469, 456.

412 Hansen, Charles: "The ALI Corporate Governance Project: Of the Duty of Due Care and the Business Judgment Rule, a Commentary". *The Business Lawyer*, Vol. 41, No. 4, 8.1986, pp. 1237–1253, 1239–1240.

413 Johnson, Lyman: "The Modest Business Judgment Rule". *The Business Lawyer*, Vol. 55, No. 2, 2.2000, pp. 625–652, 631.

414 See Gevurtz, Franklin A.: "The Business Judgment Rule: Meaningless Verbiage or Misguided Notion?". *Southern California Law Review*, Vol. 67, No. 2, 1994, pp. 287–338, 304–321; Block, Dennis J. / Maimone, Michael J. / Ross, Steven B.: "Duty of Loyalty and the Evolution of the Scope of Judicial Review, The Scope of Judicial Review". *Brooklyn Law Review*, Vol. 59, No. 1, 1993–1994, pp. 65–106, 70; Rome v.

Judges are public officials rather than business people: "courts ... do not possess the experience, expertise, or information necessary to make complicated business decisions"[415]. Courts are quick to adopt this rationale, asserting that they are not business experts,[416] they are ill-equipped to second-guess business judgments[417] and lack an intangible "sense" of the specific circumstances confronting a business[418]. Courts worry about "hindsight bias," namely the tendency to "assign an erroneously high probability of occurrence to a probabilistic event simply because it ended up occurring"[419]. The deference of the business judgment rule properly quells the temptation to overlook the fact that the "entrepreneur's function is to encounter risks and to confront uncertainty and a reasoned decision at the time made may seem a wild hunch viewed years later against a background of perfect knowledge"[420]. Furthermore, based on the viewpoints of behavioral economics, Professor Bainbridge argues that like all decision-makers with their own cognitive limitations and information asymmetries, "judges sensibly respond to these challenges by choosing – as their decision making strategy – a policy of deferring to director judgments"[421]. However, despite being helpful, this justification is not entirely satisfactory, because it does not explain why the same judges who readily plunge into many areas (for example, construction, ecology, and accounting – where they have only limited or no experience and where their expertise – if any – is not obvious) are unable to decide whether a business decision was made negligently.[422]

Archer, 197 A.2d 49, 53 (Del. 1964) (to judge whether a settlement of a derivative action should be approved); Zapata Corp. v. Maldonado, 430 A.2d 779, 789 (Del. 1981) (to determine if a derivative action should be dismissed); Veasey, E. Norman: "Seeking a Safe Harbor from Judicial Scrutiny of Directors' Business Decisions – An Analytical Framework for Litigation Strategy and Counseling Directors". *The Business Lawyer*, Vol. 37, No. 3, April 1982, pp. 1247–1274, 1265–1266.

415 Fischel, Daniel R.: "The Corporate Governance Movement". *Vanderbilt Law Review*, Vol. 35, No. 6, 1982, pp. 1259–1292, 1288.

416 See Dodge v. Ford Motor Co., 170 N.W 668, 684 (Mich. 1919) (stating "judges are not business experts").

417 Auerbach v. Bennett, 393 N.E.2d 994, 1000 (N.Y. 1979) (noting that the business judgment rule is grounded, in part, on the "prudent recognition that courts are ill equipped and infrequently called on to evaluate what are and must be essentially business judgments.").

418 Branson, Douglas M.: "The Rule That Isn't a Rule – The Business Judgment Rule". *Valparaiso University Law Review*, Vol. 36, No. 3, 2002, pp. 631–651, 637.

419 Bainbridge, Stephen M.: "The Business Judgment Rule as Abstention Doctrine". *Vanderbilt Law Review*, Vol. 57, No. 1, 2004, pp. 83–134, 114–115.

420 Joy v. North, 692 E2d 880, 886 (2d Cir. 1982), cert denied, 460 U.S. 1051 (1983).

421 See Johnson, Lyman P.Q.: "Corporate Officers and the Business Judgment Rule". *The Business Lawyer*, Vol. 60, No. 2, 2.2005, pp. 439–469, 457.

422 For a discussion of the honest-error-of-judgment rule, see Eisenberg, Melvin A.: "The Duty of Care of Corporate Directors and Officers". *University of Pittsburgh Law Review*, Vol. 51, No. 4, 1990, pp. 945–972, 959–963.

On the other hand, directors who made faulty decisions already face the risk of sanction from both stockholders who may vote them out of office[423] and the corrective, competitive pressure of product, labor and capital markets;[424] by contrast, judges do not face these sanctions for faulty decisions.[425] There are legal and market mechanisms that hold directors – but not judges – to account; thus, courts defer to director decisions.

In essence, the business judgment rule reflects an inherent tension between two competing values: the need to preserve the board of directors' decision-making discretion and the need to hold the board accountable for its decisions. On the one hand, "because the power to review differs only in degree and not in kind from the power to decide, the discretionary authority of the board of directors must be insulated from shareholder and judicial oversight in order to promote efficient corporate decision making". The separation of ownership and control in modern public corporations admittedly implicates that accountability alone is an inadequate normative account of corporate law. A fully-specified account of corporate law must incorporate the value of authority, i.e. the need to develop a set of rules and procedures that provides the most efficient decision-making system.[426] As it turns out, corporate decision-making efficiency can only be ensured by preserving the board's decision-making authority from being trumped by courts under the guise of judicial review.[427] On the other hand, "because directors are obligated to maximize shareholder wealth, there must be mechanisms to ensure director accountability"[428]. As we have seen, there is an inevitable tension between authority and accountability. "The more you try to hold decision makers to account, the more you interfere with their decision-making processes. The more discretion you give decision makers, the less accountable they become. For an independent board to effectively guard against agency costs, it must actively promote a culture of responsiveness to shareholder concerns."[429]

423 See, Hilton Hotels Corp. v. ITT Corp., 978 F. Supp. 1342, 1351 (D. Nev. 1997) (noting that "unhappy shareholders can always vote the directors out of office.").

424 See Kumpf v. Steinhaus, 779 F.2d 1323, 1325 (7th Cir. 1985) (stating that "[t]he press of market forces ... will more effectively serve the interests of all participants than will an error-prone judicial process."); Fischel, Daniel R.: "The Business Judgment Rule and the Trans Union Case". *The Business Lawyer*, Vol. 40, No. 4, 8.1985, pp. 1437–1455, 1439–1443.

425 See Kamen v. Kemper Fin. Servs., Inc., 908 F.2d 1338, 1343 (7th Cir. 1990) (no market "mechanism 'selects out' judges who try to make business decisions."), rev'd on other grounds, 500 U.S. 90 (1991).

426 See Dooley, Michael P.: "Two Models of Corporate Governance". *The Business Lawyer*, Vol. 47, No. 2, 2.1992, pp. 461–527, 463.

427 See Bainbridge, Stephen M.: *The New Corporate Governance in Theory and Practice.* Oxford University Press: 7.2008, p. 108.

428 Bainbridge, Stephen M.: *The New Corporate Governance in Theory and Practice.* Oxford University Press: 7.2008, p. 108.

429 See Veasey, E. Norman: "Policy and Legal Overview of Best Corporate Governance Principles". *SMU Law Review*, Vol. 56, No. 4, 2003, pp. 2135–2150, 2147.

In this respect, the task for corporate law makers is to find a happy medium that carefully balances these competing values.[430] The business judgment rule preserves the statutory scheme of centralizing authority in the independent directors by limiting judicial review,[431] as well as encouraging independent directors to review corporate decision-making with an eye on promoting shareholder interests and reducing managerial misbehavior.[432] This safe harbor not only provides substantial incentives for both boards and managers to favor director independence, but also promotes board-level monitoring as a substitute for shareholder monitoring such as the liability rules enforced by shareholder litigation, which is regarded as playing a relatively minor role in aligning the interests of managers with those of shareholders.[433] The independent director is regarded as the mechanism to avoid the substance by focusing on the procedure,[434] because no substantive rationale is available to determine how much should go to stockholders and how much should yield to other constituencies, while it is impossible to formulate a coherent and rational system of substantive directives to management that serves the interests of both stockholders and the public.[435] In other

---

430 See Bainbridge, Stephen M.: *The New Corporate Governance in Theory and Practice*. Oxford University Press: 7.2008, p. 130.

431 See Dooley, Michael / Veasey, E. Norman: "The Role of the Board in Derivative Litigation: Delaware Law and the Current ALI Proposals Compared". *Business Lawyer*, Vol. 44, No. 2, 1989, pp. 503–542, 522.

432 See Hillman, Amy J. / Dalziel, Thomas: "Beyond "Independent" Directors: A Functional Approach to Board Independence". *Harvard Law Review*, Vol. 119, No. 5, 3.2006, pp. 1553–1575, 1561; Johnson, Jennifer J. / Siegel, Mary: "Corporate Mergers: Redefining the Role of Target Directors". *University of Pennsylvania Law Review*, Vol. 136, No. 2, 12.1987, pp. 315–416, 386; Elson, Charles M. / Gyves, Christopher J.: "The Enron Failure and Corporate Governance Reform". *Wake Forest Law Review*, Vol. 38, No. 3, 2003, pp. 855–884, 875–878.

433 See Pease, Donald E.: "Outside Directors: Their Importance to the Corporation and Protection from Liability". *Delaware Journal of Corporate Law*, Vol. 12, No. 1, 1987, pp. 25–106, 35–40.

434 See Brudney, Victor: "The Independent Director: Heavenly City or Potemkin Village?". *Harvard Law Review*, Vol. 95, No. 3, 1982, pp. 597–659, 607.

435 See Haas, Steven M.: "Toward a Controlling Shareholder Safe Harbor". *Virginia Law Review*, Vol. 90, No. 8, 12.2004, pp. 2245–2304, 2283; Some courts of the US, in examining the directors' duty of care, have been concerned particularly with whether the directors had obtained independent, carefully-prepared advice on the critical elements necessary to make an informed decision. Hanson Trust PLC v. ML SCM Acquisition, Inc., 781 F.2d 264, 276 (2d Cir. 1986) ("proper exercise of due care by a director in informing himself of material information and in overseeing the outside advice on which he might appropriately rely is ... a pre-condition to performing his ultimate duty of acting in good faith"); Samjens Partners I v. Burlington Indus., Inc., 663 F. Supp. 614, 625 (S.D.N.Y. 1987) (finding relevant to determination that board's decisions were justifiable and made in good faith fact that board reached decision after consultation with financial and legal advisors); Coffee, John C. / Schwartz, Donald E.: "The Survival of the Derivative Suit: An

words, the dominance of independent directors by business judgment rule is "the result of a fundamental, unarticulated judicial concern with the ambiguity of standards and the significant gap between the reality of directors' roles and the theoretical construct embedded in statutory obligations"[436].

III. Enhanced Judicial Review

Despite the US corporate law having established independent directors to provide sufficient safeguards for shareholders, the capacity of independent directors to act as an effective check on management has been the subject of academic debate. Linking independence to improved firm performance has proved challenging, whereby the

---

Evaluation and a Proposal for Legislative Reform". *Columbia Law Review*, Vol. 81, No. 2, 3.1981, pp. 261–336, 323 (requiring independent counsel to advise the board on merits of derivative action); Kahn v. United States Sugar Corp., Court of Chancery of the State of Delaware, New Castle, December 10, 1985, 11 Del. J. Corp. L. 908, 7–9, 31–33 (Del. Ch. Dec. 10, 1985) (finding directors' use of independent investment banking firms to value the company insufficient to ward off liability for breach of fiduciary duty); Stout, Lynn A.: "In Praise of Procedure: An Economic and Behavioral Defense of Smith v. Van Gorkom and the Business Judgment Rule". *Northwestern University Law Review*, Vol. 96, No. 2, 2002, pp. 675–693, 678.

436 Cohn, Stuart R.: "Demise of the Director's Duty of Care: Judicial Avoidance of Standards and Sanctions through the Business Judgment Rule". *Texas Law Review*, Vol. 62, No. 4, 1983, pp. 591–638. See also Haas, Steven M.: "Toward a Controlling Shareholder Safe Harbor". *Virginia Law Review*, Vol. 90, No. 8, 12.2004, pp. 2245–2304, 2283; In examining the directors' duty of care, some courts in the US have been particularly concerned with whether the directors had obtained independent, carefully-prepared advice on the critical elements necessary to make an informed decision. Hanson Trust PLC v. ML SCM Acquisition, Inc., 781 F.2d 264, 276 (2d Cir. 1986) ("proper exercise of due care by a director in informing himself of material information and in overseeing the outside advice on which he might appropriately rely is ... a pre-condition to performing his ultimate duty of acting in good faith"); Samjens Partners I v. Burlington Indus., Inc., 663 F. Supp. 614, 625 (S.D.N.Y. 1987) (finding relevant to a determination that the board's decisions were justifiable and made in good faith and that the board reached the decision after consultation with financial and legal advisors); Coffee, John C. / Schwartz, Donald E.: "The Survival of the Derivative Suit: An Evaluation and a Proposal for Legislative Reform". *Columbia Law Review*, Vol. 81, No. 2, 3.1981, pp. 261–336, 323 (requiring independent counsel to advise the board on the merits of derivative action); Kahn v. United States Sugar Corp., Court of Chancery of the State of Delaware, New Castle, December 10, 1985, 11 Del. J. Corp. L. 908, 7–9, 31–33 (Del. Ch. Dec. 10, 1985) (finding directors' use of independent investment banking firms to value the company insufficient to ward off liability for breach of fiduciary duty); Stout, Lynn A.: "In Praise of Procedure: An Economic and Behavioral Defense of Smith v. Van Gorkom and the Business Judgment Rule". *Northwestern University Law Review*, Vol. 96, No. 2, 2002, pp. 675–693, 678.

empirical data on this issue is decidedly mixed: on the one hand, there is broad support for the view that independent directors are custodians of shareholder interests, whose presence on the board helps reduce agency problems and improve firm performance;[437] however, on the other hand, some empirical studies have even found a negative correlation between board independence and corporate performance.[438] Thus, the courts

---

437 From an agency perspective, independent directors are expected to play a more active and effective monitoring role than executive (inside) directors. Fama, E.F. / Jensen M.C.: "The separation of ownership and control". *Journal of Law and Economics*, Vol. 26, No. 2, 1983, pp. 301–328, 319; Johnson J.L. / Daily, C.M. / Ellstrand, A.E.: "Board of directors: A review and research agenda". *Journal of Management*, Vol. 22, No. 3, 1996, pp. 409–438, 416; Millstein, Ira M. / MacAvoy, Paul W.: "The Active Board of Directors and Performance of the Large Publicly Traded Corporation". *Columbia Law Review*, Vol. 98, No. 5, 1998, pp. 1283–1322, 1292–1299; Borowski, Irwin: "Corporate Accountability: The Role of the Independent Director". *Journal of Corporation Law*, Vol. 9, No. 3, 1984, pp. 455–472, 455–456 (describing the important, albeit "limited," role that independent directors play in improving corporate accountability); Hill, Charles W. L. / Snell, Scott A.: "External Control, Corporate Strategy, and Board Performance in Research Intensive Industries". *Strategic Management Journal*, Vol. 9, No. 6, 1988, pp. 577–590, 588; Chhaochharia, Vidhi / Grinstein, Yaniv: "CEO Compensation and Board Structure". *The Journal of Finance*, Vol. 64, No. 1, 2.2009, pp. 231–261.

438 As this is not the place to review the literature comprehensively, see generally Dalton, Dan R. / Daily, Catherine M. / Ellstrand, Alan E. / Johnson, Jonathan L.: "Meta-Analytic Reviews of Board Composition, Leadership Structure, and Financial Performance". *Strategic Management Journal*, Vol. 19, No. 3, 1998, pp. 269–290. (Meta-analyses by Dalton, Daily, Ellstrand, and Johnson and others have not found convincing evidence to suggest that a greater number of independent directors necessarily results in better firm performance); Fisch, Jill E.: "The New Federal Regulation of Corporate Governance". *Harvard Journal of Law & Public Policy*, Vol. 28, 2004, pp. 39–50; Hermalin, Benjamin E. / Weisbach, Michael S.: "Boards of Directors as an Endogenously Determined Institution: A Survey of the Economic Literature, Federal Reserve Bank of New York". *Economic Policy Review* 4.2003, pp. 7–26; Lin, Laura: "The Effectiveness of Outside Directors as a Corporate Governance Mechanism: Theories and Evidence". *Northwestern University Law Review*, Vol. 90, No. 3, 1996, pp. 898–976; Bainbridge, Stephen M.: *A Critique of the NYSE's Director Independence Listing Standards*. UCLA School of Law, Research Paper No. 02–15, 2002, retrieved 15.7.2014, from http://www.ssrn.com/abstract_id=317121; One study suggesting that outside directors do add value is Borokhovich, Kenneth A. / Parrino, Robert / Trapani, Teresa: "Outside Directors and CEO Selection". *Journal of Financial and Quantitative Analysis*, Vol. 31, No. 3, 9.1996, pp. 337–355 (A study of CEO successions at 588 large public firms between 1970 and 1988); Larry E Ribstein, Larry E.: "Market vs. Regulatory Responses to Corporate Fraud: A Critique of the Sarbanes-Oxley Act of 2002". *Journal of Corporation Law*, Vol. 28, No. 1, Fall 2002, pp. 1–74. (Board independence has done little to prevent past mismanagement and fraud); Healy, Paul M. / Palepu, Krishna G.: "Governance and Intermediation Problems in Capital Markets: Evidence from

recognize the risks and carefully scrutinize the board's conduct by the entire fairness standard to ensure that the board did not merely rubber-stamp incumbent management's wishes. At the same time, courts also recognize that this is merely a risk: although there is no guarantee that independent directors will act in the shareholders' interests, there equally is no certainty that they will rubber-stamp management's proposals. When this factor is coupled with the courts' further recognition of the importance of preserving the board's decision-making authority,[439] courts are likely to proceed to treat such issues on a case-by-case basis in which the critical question is whether the conduct of the independent board members is worthy of deference.[440]

1. *Criticism against Independent Directors*

Some early studies found correlations between independent directors and improved firm performance. For example, Stuart Rosenstein and Jeffrey Wyatt found that shareholder wealth increased when independent directors were appointed.[441] Michael Weisbach studied board decisions to remove a CEO, finding that boards mainly comprising independent directors were more likely to base the removal decision on poor performance, as well as being more likely to remove an under-performing

---

the Fall of Enron". *Journal of Economic Perspectives*, Vol. 17, No. 2, Spring 2003, pp. 3–26; Agrawal, Anup / Knoeber, Charles R.: "Firm Performance and Mechanisms to Control Agency Problems Between Managers and Shareholders". *Journal of Financial and Quantitative Analysis*, Vol. 31, No. 3, 9.1996, pp. 377–397; Daily, Catherine M. / Dalton, Dan R.: *Board of Directors Leadership and Structure: Control and Performance Implications*. Max M. Fisher College of Business: Ohio State University, 1994; The most comprehensive study is that of Bhagat and Black, who hold that there is no evidence that greater board independence leads to better firm performance. In describing efforts to show correlation between firm performance and board independence, they report that "most studies find little correlation, but a number of recent studies report evidence of a negative correlation between the proportion of independent directors and firm performance – the exact opposite of conventional wisdom." Bhagat, Sanjai / Black, Bernard: "The Uncertain Relationship Between Board Composition and Firm Performance". *The Business Lawyer*, Vol. 54, No. 3, 5.1999, pp. 921–963, 945; Bhagat, Sanjai / Black, Bernard: "The Non-Correlation Between Board Independence and Long-Term Firm Performance". *Journal of Corporation Law*, Vol. 27, No. 2, Winter 2002, pp. 231–273, 266.

439 See Bainbridge, Stephen M.: "Independent Directors and the ALI Corporate Governance Project". *George Washington Law Review*, No. 61, Vol. 4, 1992–1993, pp. 1034–1083, 1082.

440 See Bainbridge, Stephen M.: "Independent Directors and the ALI Corporate Governance Project". *George Washington Law Review*, No. 61, Vol. 4, 1992–1993, pp. 1034–1083, 1083.

441 See Rosenstein, Stuart / Wyatt, Jeffrey G.: "Outside Directors, Board Independence, and Shareholder Wealth". *Journal of Financial Economics*, Vol. 26, No. 2, 8.1990, pp. 175–191.

CEO, compared with insider-dominated boards.[442] He also found that CEO removals by outsider-dominated boards added to firm value, unlike CEO removals by insider-dominated boards.[443] Barry Baysinger and Henry Butler found that corporate financial performance tended to increase (up to a point) as the percentage of independent directors increased.[444] James Cotter found that boards dominated by outsiders generated higher shareholder gains from tender offers.[445]

However, other studies present arguments to the contrary. For example, a well-known report by Paul MacAvoy found that board composition had no effect on profitability.[446] April Klein likewise found little evidence of a general association between firm performance and board composition, although she found a positive correlation between the presence of insiders on board finance and investment committees and firm performance.[447] A meta-analysis of numerous studies in this area concluded that there was no convincing evidence that firms with a majority of independent directors outperformed other firms.[448] It further concluded that there were some evidences that a "moderate number" of insiders correlated with higher performance. Another meta-analysis reported at about the same time likewise found no evidence that board composition affected financial performance.[449] Finally, a 2007 literature review concluded that "the econometric research on whether independent directors enhance

---

442 See Weisbach, Michael S.: "Outside Directors and CEO Turnover". *Journal of Financial Economics*, Vol. 20, 1988, pp. 431–460.

443 See Bainbridge, Stephen M.: *The New Corporate Governance in Theory and Practice.* Oxford University Press: 7.2008, p. 191.

444 See Baysinger Barry D. / Butler Henry N.: "Revolution Versus Evolution in Corporation Law: The ALI's Project and the Independent Director". *George Washington Law Review*, Vol. 52, No. 4&5, 1984, pp. 557–581, 572.

445 See Cotter, James F. / Shhdasani, Anil / Zenner, Marc: "Do Independent Directors Enhance Target Shareholder Wealth During Tender Offers?". *Journal of Financial Economics*, Vol. 43, No. 2, 1997, pp. 195–218; Black, Bernard S.: "The Value of Institutional Investor Monitoring: The Empirical Evidence". *UCLA Law Review*, Vol. 39, No. 4, 1992, pp. 895–940, 900 (asserting that boards with a majority of independent directors make better acquisition decisions, citing an unpublished study by John Byrd and Kent Hickman).

446 See Mallette, Paul / Fowler, Karen L.: "Effects of Board Composition and Stock Ownership on the Adoption of "Poison Pills"". *The Academy of Management Journal*, Vol. 35, No. 5, 12.1992, pp. 1010–1035.

447 See Klein, April: "Firm Performance and Board Committee Structure". *Journal of Law and Economics*, Vol. 41, No. 1, 4.1998, pp. 275–304.

448 See Bhagat, Sanjai / Black, Bernard: "The Uncertain Relationship Between Board Composition and Firm Performance". *The Business Lawyer*, Vol. 54, No. 3, 5.1999, pp. 921–963, 922.

449 See Dalton, Dan R. / Daily, Catherine M. / Ellstrand, Alan E. / Johnson, Jonathan L.: "Meta-Analytic Reviews of Board Composition, Leadership Structure, and Financial Performance". *Strategic Management Journal*, Vol. 19, No. 3, 1998, pp. 269–290.

financial performance for the shareholders is, at best, inconclusive"[450]. The authors of that survey also conducted their own study of 254 public companies in 50 industry sectors, finding no evidence that "it makes any difference at all to shareholders' financial return whether a board has a higher or lower percentage of independent directors"[451]. However, Jeffrey Gordon has capped an exhaustive review of the literature by advancing a plausible explanation for the ambiguous nature of the evidence:

> *The strongest explanation is the diminishing marginal returns hypothesis: most of the empirical evidence assesses incremental changes in board independence in firms where there is already substantial independence and after the cultural entrenchment of norms of independent director behavior. But ... the most important effects of the move to independent directors, particularly over the long term, are systematic rather than firm specific and thus are unlikely to show up in cross-sectional studies. One systematic effect, the lock-in of shareholder value as virtually the exclusive corporate objective, could have benefits for early adopters, but other effects, such as the facilitation of accurate financial disclosure and corporate law compliance, have principally external effects.*[452]

The conventional justification for director independence is grounded in agency cost economics.[453] The high expectations of independent directors have been only partially fulfilled.[454] Independent directors seem to have had an impact on replacing executive

---

450 Fogel, Eric M. / Geier, Andrew M.: "Strangers in the House: Rethinking Sarbanes-Oxley and the Independent Board of Directors". *Delaware Journal of Corporate Law*, Vol. 32, No. 1, 2007, pp. 33–72, 35.

451 Fogel, Eric M. / Geier, Andrew M.: "Strangers in the House: Rethinking Sarbanes-Oxley and the Independent Board of Directors". *Delaware Journal of Corporate Law*, Vol. 32, No. 1, 2007, pp. 33–72, 52.

452 Gordon, Jeffrey N.: "The Rise of Independent Directors in the United States, 1950–2005: Of Shareholder Value and Stock Market Prices". *Stanford Law Review*, Vol. 59, No. 6, 2007, pp. 1465–1568, 1505–1506.

453 See Bainbridge, Stephen M.: *The New Corporate Governance in Theory and Practice.* Oxford University Press: 7.2008, p. 191.

454 See Gordon, Jeffrey N.: "The Rise of Independent Directors in the United States, 1950–2005: Of Shareholder Value and Stock Market Prices". *Stanford Law Review*, Vol. 59, No. 6, 2007, pp. 1465–1568; Gower & Davies: *Principles of modern company law.* Davies, Paul L. / Worthington, Sarah (eds.). Sweet & Maxwell: 9th Edition, London 2012, pp. 14–76, pp. 383–686; Kraakman, Reinier / Armour, John / Davies, Paul / Enriques, Luca / Hansmann, Henry B. / Hertig, Gérard / Hopt, Klaus J. / Kanda, Hideki / Rock, Edward B.: *The anatomy of corporate law – A Comparative and Functional Approach.* Oxford University Press: 2nd Edition, 2009, p. 66: Independent directors are "a wide-spectrum prophylactic,""potentially valuable for treating all agency problems, but not exclusively dedicated to treating any." Lin, Laura: "The Effectiveness of Outside Directors as a Corporate Governance Mechanism: Theories and Evidence". *Northwestern University Law Review*, Vol. 90, No. 3, 1996, pp. 898–976; Gillette, Ann B. / Noe, Thomas H. / Rebello, Michael J.: "Board Structures around the World: An Experimental Investigation". *Review of*

directors, albeit often mainly due to pressures from institutional investors. Undeniably, independent directors have been unable to prevent huge scandals.[455] One reason for this is that they are usually nominated or selected by the CEO or executive directors who have professional or personal relationships with them. Peter Drucker – a leading scholar of business management – asserts that boards of directors are "an important ceremonial and legal fiction" that "do not function."[456] Professor Brudney contends that outside directors – as part-time overseers – have neither time nor critical information necessary to oversee the management's performance.[457] In the well-known Panter dissent, Judge Cudahy charged that "the very idea that, if we cannot trace with precision a mighty flow of dollars into the pockets of each of the outside directors, these directors are necessarily disinterested arbiters of the stockholders' destiny, is appallingly naive."[458] In Bass v. Evans, Vice Chancellor Jacobs found the functioning of a special committee of directors to be "little more than a charade,"[459] while the Delaware Supreme Court later characterized the outside members of the board of this same company as "torpid, if not supine."[460]

In particular, commentators have expressed doubts about the true "independence" of non-management directors in light of the directors' informational dependence on management and the psychology of group decision-making.[461] An important – and

---

Finance, Vol. 12, No. 1, 2008, pp. 93–140; Duchin, Ran / Matsusaka, John G. / Ozbas, Oguzhan: "When are Outside Directors Effective?". *Journal of Financial Economics*, Vol. 96, No. 2, 5.2010, pp. 195–214; Fahlenbrach, Rüdiger / Low, Angie / Stulz, René M.: "Why do Firms Appoint CEOs as Outside Directors?". *Journal of Financial Economics*, Vol. 97, No. 1, 7.2010, pp. 12–32.

455 E.g. Enron, where the board was composed of a majority of qualified independent directors. As to Enron see Milhaupt, Curtis J. / Pistor, Katharina: *Law and Capitalism: What Corporate Crises Reveal about Legal Systems and Economic Development around the World.* University of Chicago Press: 2008, p. 47.

456 Drucker, Peter F.: *Management: Tasks, Responsibilities, Practices.* Harper & Row Management Library, 1974, p. 644.

457 Brudney, Victor: "The Independent Director: Heavenly City or Potemkin Village?". *Harvard Law Review*, Vol. 95, No. 3, 1982, pp. 597–659, 610–611; Gilson, Ronald J. / Kraakman, Reinier: "Reinventing the Outside Director: An Agenda for Institutional Investors". *Stanford Law Review*, Vol. 43, No. 4, 4.1991, pp. 863–906, 884.

458 Panter v. Marshall Field & Co., 646 F.2d 271, 293 (7th Gir. 1981); Allen, William T.: "Independent Directors in MBO Transactions: Are They Fact or Fantasy?" *The Business Lawyer*, Vol. 45, No. 4, 8.1990, pp. 2055–2063, 2056.

459 Robert M. Bass Group, Inc. v. Evans, 552 A.2d 1227 (Del. Ch. 1988).

460 Mills Acquisition Co. v. Macmillan, Inc., 559 A.2d 1261, 1280 (Del. 1989).

461 Brudney, Victor: "The Independent Director: Heavenly City or Potemkin Village?". *Harvard Law Review*, Vol. 95, No. 3, 1982, pp. 597–659, 610; Werner, Walter: "Corporation Law in Search of Its Future". *Columbia Law Review*, Vol. 81, No. 1981, 1611–1666, 1656–1658 (the "intimate relationship" between management and the non-management directors in the boardroom environment creates "a structural bias against action by outside directors that appears contrary to the interests of their inside colleagues").

necessary – condition for directors to be effective is the amount and nature of the information that they have. If directors only have access to publicly available information, it is difficult to imagine that they will be able to evaluate management better than an outside shareholder. In addition, the mere fact that directors do not have superior information would in itself likely be the result of a strained relationship with management, since presumably no information of value would have been transmitted during board meetings. The informational advantage of directors over outsiders presumably provides a measure of the potential for these directors to add value.[462] Financial economists should not generally assume that independent directors seek to maximize shareholder value; rather, the decisions of independent directors – like those of other economic agents – might well be influenced by their incentives, in turn reflecting a product of various features of the environment in which they operate. The information that independent directors have should be similarly recognized as being endogenously determined by corporate structures and processes rather than being exogenously given.[463]

Professor Brudney warned that the concept of independence "does not carry a clear meaning for many of its proponents or the same meaning for all its proponents"[464] and "no definition of independence yet offered precludes an independent director from being a social friend of, or a member of the same clubs, associations, or charitable efforts as, the persons whose compensation or self-dealing transaction he is asked to assess"[465]. In essence, the proponents of a structural bias theory believe that directors cannot be independent because all directors are "economically or psychologically dependent upon or tied to the corporation's executives, particularly chief executive"[466] in a variety of ways, whereby it is

---

462 See Bebchuk, Lucian A. / Weisbach, Michael S.: "The State of Corporate Governance Research". *The Review of Financial Studies*, Vol. 23, No. 3, Corporate Governance, 3.2010, pp. 939–961, 944.

463 See Bebchuk, Lucian A. / Weisbach, Michael S.: "The State of Corporate Governance Research". *The Review of Financial Studies*, Vol. 23, No. 3, Corporate Governance, 3.2010, pp. 939–961, 945.

464 Brudney, Victor: "The Independent Director: Heavenly City or Potemkin Village?". *Harvard Law Review*, Vol. 95, No. 3, 1982, pp. 597–659, 610.

465 Brudney, Victor: "The Independent Director: Heavenly City or Potemkin Village?". *Harvard Law Review*, Vol. 95, No. 3, 1982, pp. 597–659, 613.

466 Cox, James D. / Munsinger, Harry L.: "Bias in the Boardroom: Psychological Foundations and Legal Implications of Corporate Cohesion". *Law and Contemporary Problems*, Vol. 48, No. 3, Summer 1985, pp. 83–135, 99–100 (noting that both economic and psychological factors affect director independence); Brudney, Victor: "The Independent Director: Heavenly City or Potemkin Village?". *Harvard Law Review*, Vol. 95, No. 3, 1982, pp. 597–659, 622; Wade, Cheryl L.: "What Independent Directors Should Expect from Inside Directors: Smith v. Van Gorkom as a Guide to Intra-Firm Governance". *Washburn Law Journal*, Vol. 45, No. 6, 2006, pp. 367–387.

a delusion or pretense to expect them to represent shareholder views when a conflict transaction arises.[467]

2. Entire Fairness Review

Those considerations mentioned above have persuaded some observers that independent directors offer little hope as a source of expert, disinterested judgment when management is interested, even when functioning in good faith.[468] The duty of loyalty – which primarily addresses situations involving conflict of interest and self-dealing, where the duty of loyalty is rigorously enforced by requiring the directors to justify as intrinsically fair any transaction in which they had a financial interest[469] – requires

---

467 See Brudney, Victor: "The Independent Director: Heavenly City or Potemkin Village?". *Harvard Law Review*, Vol. 95, No. 3, 1982, pp. 597–659, 610–611; Alan Palmiter, Alan R.: "Reshaping the Corporate Fiduciary Model: A Director's Duty of Independence". *Texas Law Review*, Vol. 67, No. 7, 1989, pp. 1351–1464, 1395–1412. "Financial and business ties are not the only sources of conflicts of interest and soft ties to management can jeopardize shareholder primacy just as easily as can pecuniary conflicts. In terms of the relation between CEO and independent directors, feelings of cordiality and friendliness will have developed over the years of service, as the perquisites-annual pay, insurance and retirement benefits originated by the CEO may be generous. When the independent director is asked to serve on a special committee to preside over a sale of the company, he may receive some modest special remuneration for this service." Allen, William T.: "Independent Directors in MBO Transactions: Are They Fact or Fantasy?" *The Business Lawyer*, Vol. 45, No. 4, 8.1990, pp. 2055–2063, 2057, 2060.

468 See Deborah DeMott, Deborah A.: "Reweaving the Corporate Veil: Management Structure and the Control of Corporate Information". *Law and Contemporary Problems*, Vol. 41, No. 3, 1980, pp. 183–221, 217; Eisenberg, Melvin Aron: "Legal Models of Management Structure in the Modern Corporation: Officers, Directors, and Accountants". *California Law Review*, Vol. 63, No. 2, 1975, pp. 375–439, 380; Cox, James D. / Munsinger, Harry L.: "Bias in the Boardroom: Psychological Foundations and Legal Implications of Corporate Cohesion". *Law and Contemporary Problems*, Vol. 48, No. 3, Summer 1985, pp. 83–135, 85.

469 A comprehensive statement of duty of loyalty appears in Guth v. Loft, Inc.: "Corporate officers and directors are not permitted to use their position of trust and confidence to further their private interests. While technically not trustees, they stand in a fiduciary relation to the corporation and its stockholders. A public policy, existing through the years, and derived from a profound knowledge of human characteristics and motives, has established a rule that demands of a corporate officer or director, peremptorily and inexorably, the most scrupulous observance of his duty, not only affirmatively to protect the interests of the corporation committed to his charge, but also to refrain from doing anything that would work injury to the corporation, or to deprive it of profit or advantage which his skill and ability might properly bring to it, or to enable it to make in the reasonable and lawful exercise of its powers. The rule that requires an undivided and unselfish

independent directors to act in good faith and in the best interest of shareholders and imposes a norm of selfless conduct on corporate actors.[470]

First, in the context of hostile takeover, independent directors may not be so independent in passing on such matters, given that they effectively serve at the pleasure of the managers whose jobs are at stake. These managers provide the information on which the outside directors will act.[471] Information from the inside directors concerning either the dire or beneficial consequences they perceive arising from the proposed merger – coupled with an active role in the merger negotiations – might strongly predispose the independent directors to simply follow management's recommendation.[472] In Dynamics Corp. of Am. v. CTS Corp., the court held:

> *When managers are busy erecting obstacles to the takeover of the corporation by an investor who is likely to fire them if the takeover attempt succeeds, they have a clear conflict of interest, and it is not cured by vesting the power of decision in a board of directors in which insiders are a minority (five of CTS's eight directors are outsiders). No one likes to be fired, whether he is just a director or also an officer. The so-called outsiders moreover are often friends of the insiders. And since they spend only part of their time on the affairs of the corporation, their knowledge of those affairs is much less than that of the insiders, to whom they are likely therefore to defer.*[473]

This perspective has been reflected in judicial opinions. Delaware Courts made the revolutionary 1985 and 1986 decisions of Unocal Corp. v. Mesa Petroleum Co. and

---

loyalty to the corporation demands that there shall be no conflict between duty and self-interest." Guth v. Loft, Inc., 5 A.2d 503, 510 (Del. 1939); Lyman Johnson, Lyman: "After Enron: Remembering Loyalty Discourse in Corporate Law". *Delaware Journal of Corporate Law*, Vol. 28, No. 1, 2003, pp. 27–73, 28; Allen, William T. / Jacobs, Jack B. / Strine, Leo E. Jr.: "Function over Form: A Reassessment of Standards of Review in Delaware Corporation Law". *The Business Lawyer*, Vol. 56, No. 4, 8.2001, pp. 1287–1321, 1289.

470 See Bratton, William W.: "Self-Regulation, Normative Choice, and the Structure of Corporate Fiduciary Law". *The George Washington Law Review*, Vol. 61, No. 4, 1993, pp. 1084–1129, 1089.

471 See Galef v. Alexander, 615 F.2d 51 (US Court of Appeals, 2d Cir. 1980); Lewis v. Anderson, 615 F.2d 778 (9th Cir. 1980) (good faith exercise of business judgment by special litigation committee is immune from judicial scrutiny); Auerbach v. Bennett, 47 N.Y.2d 619, 393 N.E.2d 994, 419 N.Y.S.2d 920 (1979) (no judicial inquiry into actions of special litigation committee appointed by board of directors).

472 Shnell, James H.: "A Procedural Treatment of Derivative Suit Dismissals by Minority Directors". *California Law Review*, Vol. 69, No. 3, 1981, pp. 885–910, 899 (discussing the problem that while outside directors may not have sufficient information about the corporation to decide whether a derivative suit should proceed, corporate managers give the outside directors biased information).

473 Dynamics Corp. of Am. v. CTS Corp., 794 F.2d 250 (7th Cir. 1986), rev'd on other grounds, 107 S. Ct. 1637 (1987).

Revlon, Inc. v. MacAndrews & Forbes Holdings, Inc.[474] to impose high requirements of duty of care to independent directors. Under Unocal, where a target company board adopts antitakeover defensive measures, the board has the burden to establish that (i) it reasonably perceived that the unsolicited takeover bid was a threat to corporate effectiveness and policy and (ii) the defensive measure adopted was reasonable in response to the threat.[475] The second step of the Unocal analysis – as elaborated ten years later in Unitrin, Inc. v. American Gen. Corp.[476] – provides that a defensive measure will be found disproportionate (i.e. an unreasonable response in relation to the threat) if it is either draconian (coercive or preclusive) or falls outside a range of reasonable responses.[477] Those cases hold that if the board satisfies the Unocal reasonableness standard, its defensive actions are subsequently subject to review under the business judgment standard, while if the board's actions fail to pass muster under Unocal, the defensive measures will be invalidated unless the board can demonstrate that its actions were entirely fair.[478]

Second, in Kahn v. Lynch Communications Systems, Inc.[479] – which involves Alcatel U.S.A. Corporation's freeze-out of non-controlling shareholders in Lynch Communication Systems, Inc. – the Delaware Supreme Court held that the stringent entire fairness form of review would govern the freeze-out transaction even though the target board comprised a majority of independent directors, a special committee of the target's independent directors was empowered to negotiate and veto the merger and the merger was made subject to approval by a majority of

474 See Revlon, Inc. v. MacAndrews & Forbes Holdings, Inc., 506 A.2d 173 (Del. 1986).

475 See Unocal Corp. v. Mesa Petroleum Co., 493 A.2d 946 (Del. 1985), at 954–955.

476 See Unitrin, Inc. v. American Gen. Corp., 651 A.2d 1361 (Del. 1995).

477 Unitrin, Inc. v. American Gen. Corp., 651 A.2d 1361 (Del. 1995).

478 See Unitrin, 651 A.2d at 1377 n. 18 & 1390; see also Unocal, 493 A.2d at 958.

479 In Kahn v. Lynch Communications Systems, Inc., Alcatel Corporation owned 43.3% of Lynch Communication's common shares, enjoyed certain supermajority voting privileges and appointed five of the firm's eleven board members. The litigation was set in motion when Lynch proposed merging with a third-party, a plan promptly rejected by Alcatel through its dominant veto power. Alcatel instead countered with a proposal that Lynch should merge into one of Alcatel's other subsidiaries. Lynch formed a special committee of independent directors, which rejected the proposal. Alcatel responded with a series of other offers, although all hovered around the same price. In all, the Lynch special committee rejected four Alcatel proposals, including one share exchange and three cash offers. The decisive moment arrived when Alcatel played its trump card: third-party proposal veto power combined with a bear hug. In other words, Alcatel warned the Lynch special committee that it would launch a hostile tender offer if the committee rejected its final offer. Because the special committee knew that Alcatel would veto any third-party option, it conceded and approved the deal. The remaining independent directors on Lynch's board then ratified the terms of the acquisition. See Kahn v. Lynch Communications Systems, Inc., 638 A. 2d 1113, 1119.

the disinterested target stockholders,[480] because merger transactions involving a controlling shareholder contain an "inherent coercion" of the interests of minority shareholders and the independent directors were dominated by the controlling shareholders and not truly "independent".[481] If the parent corporation adopts an arm's-length negotiating structure, including an independent negotiating committee with a right to say "no" and receives the approval of a majority of the minority shareholders, the standard of review shifts to business judgment.[482]

The Delaware Supreme Court held that a controlling or dominating shareholder standing on both sides of a transaction – as in a parent-subsidiary context – bore the burden of proving its entire fairness. The demonstration of fairness required was set forth by this Court in Weinberger v. UOP, Inc.:

> *"The concept of fairness has two basic aspects: fair dealing and fair price. The former embraces questions of when the transaction was timed, how it was initiated, structured, negotiated, disclosed to the directors, and how the approvals of the directors and stockholders were obtained. The latter aspect of fairness relates to the economic and financial considerations of the proposed merger, including all relevant factors: assets, market value, earnings, future prospects, and any other elements that affect the intrinsic or inherent value of a company's stock. However, the test for fairness is not a bifurcated one as between fair dealing and price. All aspects of this issue must be examined as a whole since the question is one of entire fairness."*[483]

Kahn v. Lynch Communications Systems, Inc. has explicitly stated that entire fairness is the only standard of review for controlling shareholder transactions and has been understood as representative of a strong protectionist theory of minority shareholders' interests in public corporations, because an entire fairness standard of review provides a greater level of protection to minority shareholders in the final period when interests diverge and market rewards and punishments fail to constrain the risk of cheating by the controlling shareholder.[484] The rationale for subjecting

480 Kahn v. Lynch Communications Systems, Inc., 669 A. 2d 79, 86.

481 Steven Haas, Steven M.: "Toward a Controlling Shareholder Safe Harbor". *Virginia Law Review*, Vol. 90, No. 8, 12.2004, pp. 2245–2304, 2266.

482 Gilson, Ronald J. / Gordon, Jeffrey N.: "Controlling Shareholders". *University of Pennsylvania Law Review*, Vol. 152, No. 2, 12.2003, pp. 785–843, 799. This holding is supported by Kahn v. Tremont, which rules that the entire fairness standard applies to the deal because of dominating shareholders' controlling interest in the entities, although when a special transactional committee is truly independent in its conduct and not merely appear to be independent because of the pedigree of its members and is designed to be a surrogate for minority stockholder bargaining with a controlling stockholder, it may shift to the stockholders the burden of proof in an entire fairness context. Kahn v. Tremont Corp., 694 A.2d 422 (Del. 1997).

483 Kahn v. Lynch Communications Systems, Inc, 638 A.2d 1110, 1115 (Del. 1994) (citing Weinberger v. UOP, Inc., 457 A.2d 701, 711 (Del. 1983)).

484 See Haas, Steven M.: "Toward a Controlling Shareholder Safe Harbor". *Virginia Law Review*, Vol. 90, No. 8, 12.2004, pp. 2245–2304, 2249.

controlling shareholder transactions to the entire fairness review reflects a distrust of the mechanisms of independent director for protecting minority shareholder.[485] However, because the dangers are limited to certain transactions and comparing with the entire fairness standard, a controlling shareholder safe harbor based on the independent director provisions found in Puma v. Marriott would lead to a more economically efficient result,[486] the Delaware Supreme Court failed to justify an over-inclusive application of entire fairness.[487]

In the case of In re Pure Resources Inc., Shareholders Litigation, the court's conclusion is that a fully empowered special committee of independent directors – including the Pure anti-coercion litany[488] and the right to say "no" – affords sufficient process whereby entire fairness review in a freeze-out merger can be eliminated, because the robust engagement by a special committee of independent directors as a bargaining agent for the minority shareholders is necessary to avoid coercion.[489] As demonstrated in Solomon v. Pathe Communications Corp., Delaware courts do not apply the "entire fairness" standard to tender-offer transactions involving a controlling shareholder if the tender offer is not coercive.[490] The decisions in In

---

485 For a discussion of director independence, see generally Cox, James D.: "Searching for the Corporation's Voice in Derivative Suit Litigation: A Critique of Zapata and the ALI Project". *Duke Law Journal*, Vol. 1982, No.6, pp. 959–1011.

486 See Haas, Steven M.: "Toward a Controlling Shareholder Safe Harbor". *Virginia Law Review*, Vol. 90, No. 8, 12.2004, pp. 2245–2304, 2271.

487 See Haas, Steven M.: "Toward a Controlling Shareholder Safe Harbor". *Virginia Law Review*, Vol. 90, No. 8, 12.2004, pp. 2245–2304, 2269.

488 Pure's broad interpretation of "coercion" is consistent with Delaware jurisprudence in the hostile-bid area, where "substantive coercion" – bid pressure that might induce target shareholders to mistakenly accept a low-ball offer – constitutes a "threat" that in turn justifies a target board response much like "structural coercion" – bid pressure that arises from a structure exploiting shareholder collective-action problems. In re Pure Resources Inc., Shareholders Litigation, 808 A.2d 421, 438–440 (Del.Ch. 2002).

489 See In re Pure Resources Inc., Shareholders Litigation, 808 A.2d 421, 445–447 (Del. Ch. 2002).

490 The Delaware Supreme Court held that a shareholder with voting control over 89.5% of a corporation's outstanding stock owed no obligation with respect to the fairness of the price offered in a tender offer for the stock of the controlled corporation, unless the offer was structurally coercive or disclosure concerning the offer was inadequate. Solomon v. Pathe Communications Corp., 672 A.2d 35, 40 (Del. 1996). With respect to the ultimate determination of whether the transactional procedure satisfies the fair-dealing component, the inquiry shifts to whether the inherent coercion and the form of the transaction actually influence the non-controlling shareholders' votes. Gilson, Ronald J. / Gordon, Jeffrey N.: "Controlling Shareholders". *University of Pennsylvania Law Review*, Vol. 152, No. 2, 12.2003, pp. 785–843, 802.

re Aquila[491] and In re Siliconix Inc. Shareholders Litigation have also followed this doctrine by finding that "unless coercion or disclosure violations can be shown, no defendant has the duty to demonstrate the entire fairness of ... a proposed tender offer"[492]. Accordingly, it makes perfect sense in a freeze-out tender offer both to place certain limits on the controller's behavior and to require the independent directors to act as genuine bargaining agents, including forming an opinion about the desirability of the controller's offer.[493]

Third, according to the provisions of MBCA Article 8.61 (b) (3), the RPTs shall be approved by independent directors or qualified shareholders, otherwise these transactions shall be reviewed by the court through the fairness standard: "A director's conflicting interest transaction may not be enjoined, set aside, or give rise to an award of damages or other sanctions, in a proceeding by a shareholder or by or in the right of the corporation, because the director, or any person with whom or which he has a personal, economic, or other association, has an interest in the transaction, if the transaction, judged according to the circumstances at the time of commitment, is established to have been fair to the corporation". "The principal-agent and the principal-principal conflicts in such transactions are particularly striking because the director and controlling shareholder acts on both sides, thereby putting them in a position in which they have an incentive to shape the price and the contractual conditions in his own interest to the detriment of the shareholders, such as the unfair transfer pricing, transfer of the assets from the controlled corporation to the controlling shareholders and the use of the controlled corporation's assets as collateral for a controlling shareholder's debt."[494]

Therefore, despite the well-known conflict of interest, Delaware corporate law definitively allocates decision-making authority to the board, as well as provides both substantive and procedural mechanisms ensuring a substantial degree of

491 See In re: Aquila Inc. Shareholders Litigation, 2002 WL 27815 (Del. Ch. Jan. 3, 2002).

492 The tender offers in Siliconix and Aquila contained a majority of the minority tender conditions and agreements to consummate DGCL Â§253 mergers at the same price as the tender offers. While the Chancery Court in those cases determined that the tender offers were not coercive, they did not specify factors for determining whether a tender offer was coercive. See In re Siliconix Inc. Shareholders Litigation, 2001 WL 716787 (Del. Ch. June, 2001).

493 See Gilson, Ronald J. / Gordon, Jeffrey N.: "Controlling Shareholders". *University of Pennsylvania Law Review*, Vol. 152, No. 2, 12.2003, pp. 785–843, 829.

494 Davies, Paul L. / Hopt, Klaus J.: "Corporate Boards in Europe – Accountability and Convergence". *American Journal Comparative Law*, Vol. 61, No. 2, 2013, pp. 301–375, 352; See also Gilson, Ronald J. / Gordon, Jeffrey N.: "Controlling Shareholders". *University of Pennsylvania Law Review*, Vol. 152, No. 2, 12.2003, pp. 785–843, 790; Macavoy, Paul W. / Millstein, Iram: *The Recurrent Crisis in Corporate Governance*. Stanford University Press: 2003, pp. 22–23; Eisenberg, Melvin Aron: "Legal Models of Management Structure in the Modern Corporation: Officers, Directors, and Accountants". *California Law Review*, Vol. 63, No. 2, 1975, pp. 375–439, 398–402.

judicial deference to the board. The role of independent directors in approving transactions that are closely related to the benefits of minority shareholders was not denied by the Delaware Courts, although it imposed more requirements such as they should have the power to say "no" to the controlling shareholders and established the standard of entire fairness applied to review these decisions made by independent directors, because there were valid reasons for a protectionist view of minority shareholders, especially when collective shareholder interests diverged in the so-called "final period".[495] The target's board possesses broad authority to determine whether to merge the firm and select a merger partner. The initial decision to enter into a negotiated merger[496] transaction is thus reserved to the board's collective business judgment, with shareholders having no statutory power to initiate merger negotiations[497]. The board also has the sole power to negotiate the terms on which the merger will take place and arrive at a definitive merger agreement embodying its decisions concerning these matters.[498]

Although it is seldom possible to challenge the independent directors' decision-making in the US in terms of the controlling shareholders' transactions – aside from when they are completely manipulated by dominating shareholders – independent directors must naturally select appropriate procedures and execute them in good faith to qualify the duty of care and their decisions for protection under the business judgment rule. Independent directors have come to be viewed as a species of fiduciary, certainly not as constrained as trustees or executors, but nonetheless subject to a pervasive duty of loyalty when exercising their broad powers over corporate property and processes.[499] The US corporate law admits that the use of independent directors to make decisions is not the perfect solution to the problem of the inside directors' unavoidable conflict of interest, while maintaining that it is the optimal solution.[500]

---

495 Steven Haas, Steven M.: "Toward a Controlling Shareholder Safe Harbor". *Virginia Law Review*, Vol. 90, No. 8, 12.2004, pp. 2245–2304, 2248.

496 Bainbridge, Stephen M.: *The New Corporate Governance in Theory and Practice.* Oxford University Press: 7.2008, p. 134.

497 Smith v. Van Gorkom, 488 A.2d 858, 873 (Del. 1985).

498 *See* Veasey, E. Norman: "The Defining Tension in Corporate Governance in America". *The Business Lawyer*, Vol. 52, No. 2, 2.1997, pp. 393–406, 394 (drawing a distinction between "enterprise" and "ownership" decisions with respect to judicial review of board actions).

499 See Cede & Co. v. Technicolor, Inc., 634 A.2d 345, 367 (Del. 1993) ("Duty of care and duty of loyalty are the traditional hallmarks of a fiduciary who endeavors to act in the service of a corporation and its stockholders. Each of these duties is of equal and independent significance."); Brudney, Victor: "Contract and Fiduciary Duty in Corporate Law". *Boston College Law Review*, Vol. 38, No. 4, 1997, pp. 595–665, 599 ("Legal conventions divide fiduciary obligations into obligations of loyalty and obligations of care.").

500 "The conclusion that use of only independent directors is the optimal solution is reflected in the fact that they currently serve a variety of purposes. Outside or

C. Independent Advisors and Shareholder Approval

The control of RPTs by the approval of independent directors may not work under all conditions, meaning that it appears to be important to provide the checks and balances with direct resort to shareholder approval under some conditions. According to the view of Sofie Cools, shareholder power should comprise matters in which directors face an inherent conflict of interest. "The problems of shareholder passivity, short-termism and empty voting and the concern about stakeholder interests do not call for a further reduction of shareholder power beyond this limitation."[501] Shareholder approval for RPTs can be regarded as an alternative or complement to the board approval procedure, although the practice is not widespread and often only applies to large transactions or those not on market terms.[502] Therefore, in China and the EU, the measures for controlling RPTs are shareholders' approval and independent directors as advisors for shareholders.

I. China

Generally speaking, the powers provided by Articles 5 and 6 in the Independent Directors Opinion mainly focus on key areas where the potential for conflict of interest is particularly high, such as the approval of major connected transactions and the provision of advice to the board of directors or the shareholders' meeting on the important matters such as the nomination, appointment and removal as well as remuneration of directors and senior management personnel. First, Articles 5 para.1 of Independent Directors Opinion provides that major related party transactions have to obtain ratification from the independent directors before being submitted to the board of directors for discussion[503] and independent directors make decisions

---

independent directors serve numerous functions in a corporation, ranging from ensuring compliance with the corporate statutes to monitoring management's performance." See generally Brudney, Victor: "The Independent Director: Heavenly City or Potemkin Village?". *Harvard Law Review*, Vol. 95, No. 3, 1982, pp. 597–659, 610–611. "Whatever else regulators, courts, or commentators may say on the subject, it remains the independent board that stands the best chance, and bears the heaviest responsibility, of assuring investor confidence in the corporation." Hillman, Amy J. / Dalziel, Thomas: "Beyond "Independent" Directors: A Functional Approach to Board Independence". *Harvard Law Review*, Vol. 119, No. 5, 3.2006, pp. 1553–1575, 1575.

501 Cools, Sofie: "The Dividing Line Between Shareholder Democracy and Board Autonomy: Inherent Conflicts of Interest as Normative Criterion". *European Company and Financial Law Review*, Vol. 11, No. 2, 2014, pp. 258–296, 258.

502 OECD, RPTs and MSR, p. 34.

503 In addition, Article 10.2.1 of the Rules provides that: "When the board of directors of a listed company considers a related party transaction, the related director shall withdraw from voting and shall not exercise any voting rights as a proxy of other directors. Such board meeting may be held if over half of the non-related directors

based on the reports of independent financial advisors,[504] while the shareholders' meeting still holds the major power of controlling the RPTs. This applies because in the Company Law, Article 148 (3) and (4) rule that no director or senior manager may have any of the following acts: breaching the provisions of the articles, shareholders' assembly or board of directors, loaning the company's fund to others or providing any guaranty to any other person by using the company's property as in violation of the articles of association,[505] signing a contract or trading with this company by violating the articles of association or without the consent of the shareholders' meeting or shareholders' assembly.[506]

Second, Article 5 para.4 of the Independent Directors Opinion provides that if a listed company establishes a remuneration committee, audit committee, nomination committee or other such committees under the board of directors, independent directors should account for at least half of the members thereof. Moreover, Article 6 provides that independent directors should express independent opinions

---

are present and the resolution of such board meeting requires the approval of over half of the non-related directors. If fewer than three non-related directors are present at the board meeting, the listed company shall submit the transaction to the shareholders' general meeting for consideration. The related director as mentioned in the preceding paragraph refers to the following directors or a director that meets any of the following conditions: (1) the counterparty to the transaction; (2) having direct or indirect controlling power over the counterparty to the transaction; (3) holding a position in the counterparty to the transaction, or in any legal person or other organization that either directly or indirectly controls the counterparty to the transaction, or in any legal person or other organization under the direct or indirect control of the counterparty to the transaction; (4) he is a close family member (as defined in (4) of Section 10.1.5 hereof) of the counterparty to the transaction, or of the direct or indirect controller of the counterparty to the transaction; (5) he is a close family member (as defined in (4) of Section 10.1.5 hereof) of a director, supervisor or senior officer of the counterparty to the transaction, or of a director, supervisor or senior officer of the direct or indirect controller of the counterparty to the transaction; or (6) other directors whose independent business judgment may be affected as determined by the CSRC, the Exchange or the listed company in accordance with the principle that essence is more important than form."

504 Independent Directors Opinion, Articles 5 para.1 (1) before rendering their judgment, independent directors may engage an intermediary organization to issue an independent financial consultant report for use as a basis for rendering their judgment; (2) proposing the engagement or dismissal of an accounting firm to the board of directors; (3) proposing to the board of directors the convening of an extraordinary shareholders' general meeting; (4) proposing the convening of a meeting of the board of directors; (5) independently engaging external auditing institutions and consultancies; and (6) openly soliciting shareholders' voting rights before the holding of a shareholders' general meeting.

505 Company Law, Article 148 (3).

506 Company Law, Article 148 (4).

on material matters of the listed company. In addition to performing the duties and responsibilities mentioned above, an independent director should express his independent opinion to the board of directors or the shareholders' general meeting on the following matters: 1) the nomination, appointment and removal of directors; 2) the engagement or dismissal of senior management personnel; 3) the remuneration of the company's directors and senior management personnel; 4) existing or new loans totaling more than Rmb3 million or more than 5% of the listed company's most recently audited net asset value extended to the listed company by its shareholders, persons in actual control or affiliates or other transactions involving funds amounting to more than Rmb3 million or more than 5% of the listed company's most recently audited net asset value between the listed company and its shareholders, persons in actual control or affiliates and whether the company has taken effective measures to recover the money owed; 5) matters that may – in an Independent Director's opinion – prejudice the rights and interests of small and medium shareholders; and 6) other matters specified in the company's articles of association.[507] Article 55 of the Code provides the main duties of the nomination committee: (1) to formulate standards and procedures for the election of directors and make recommendations; (2) to extensively seek qualified candidates for directorship and management; and (3) to review the candidates for directorship and management and make recommendations. Article 37 para.2 of Company Law provided the right of shareholders to elect directors and supervisors by ruling that "the shareholders' meeting shall exercise the authorities of electing and changing the director and supervisors assumed by non-representatives of the employees, and determining the matters concerning their remuneration". Thus, we can observe that regarding the problem of election and remuneration of directors and supervisors, the shareholders' meeting is the decision-maker and the responsibility of independent directors lies in conducting research and making recommendations for shareholders' meeting.

Furthermore, Article 51 of Measures for the Administration of the Takeover of Listed Companies (hereinafter "Measures for Administration of the Takeover") prescribes that in the case of a management buyout, the company should have no less than half of its directors as independent directors. In terms of the resolution, first the takeover plan shall be carried out upon the resolution of the non-affiliated directors only. The resolution has to obtain approval from two-thirds or more of the independent directors and subsequently it must be submitted to the shareholders' meeting for majority consent.[508]

507 Independent Directors Opinion, Article 6 para.1 (4).

508 CSRC, *Measures for the Administration of the Takeover of Listed Companies* (hereinafter "Measures for Administration of the Takeover"), effective on 15.3.2012, Article 51.

Finally, the conflicts of interest may be greatly exacerbated when the target company's board of directors receives an unsolicited takeover bid;[509] thus, according to Article 32 of Measures for Administration of the Takeover, the independent directors have the power of providing suggestions to shareholders about whether they shall accept the tender offer. It stipulates that the board of directors of the target company shall submit the report of the target company's board of directors together with the independent financial consultant's professional opinions to the CSRC, submit duplicates thereof to the CSRC agency of the place where the listed company is located and the stock exchange and announce the same within ten days of the issuance of the takeover offer by the purchaser. The report by the board of directors of the target company shall provide advice to the shareholders concerning whether to accept the takeover offer, whereby the independent directors of the target company shall express their views separately and both the advice and the opinions shall be announced together. If the purchaser makes major amendments to the terms of the takeover offer, the board of directors of the target company shall submit a supplementary report on the amendments, while the independent directors shall express supplementary opinions and both the report and the opinions shall be announced together.[510] In the Company Law, Article 37 para.9 stipulates that the power endowed to shareholders' meetings includes making other important decisions such as mergers, divestiture, liquidation, dissolution or other structural changes.

We can see that the supervisory functions of independent directors – provided by the Independent Directors Opinion – focus on providing suggestions for the board rather than making decisions on major issues of corporate management, which is their role in the US.[511] The independent directors as advisors are actually decided by the whole insider corporate governance system of China. In light of the insider corporate governance structure designed by the Company Law of 1993, installing shareholders' meeting as the organ of super power and the board of directors serving as the executive organ of the general meeting, the power of independent directors is legally restricted under the corporate governance model of being shareholders' meeting-centered. Article 4 primarily lays the foundation for corporate governance structure by stating that "the shareholders of a company shall be entitled to enjoy the capital proceeds, participate in making important decisions, choose managers, and so

509 There are many cases involving hostile takeover. See Unocal Corp. v. Mesa Petroleum Co., 493 A.2d 946, 955 (Del. 1985); Unitrin v. American General Corp., 651 A.2d 1361, 1376 (Del. 1995); Dynamics Corp. of Am. v. CTS Corp., 794 F.2d 250, 256 (7th Cir. 1986), rev'd on other grounds, 481 U.S. 69 (1987); Bennett v. Propp, 187 A.2d 405, 409 (Del. 1962).

510 Measures for Administration of the Takeover, Article 32.

511 Wu Xiaoping: "Huiqian Goutong: Duli Dongshi Zhize bentuhua Tanyi" [Discussions before the Board's Meeting: Study on the Localization of Independent Directors' Functions], *Law Research*, Vol. 4, 2014, pp. 97–104, 99.

on". Furthermore, in Article 37 and 99,[512] the powers endowed to shareholders' meetings mainly include: (1) deciding management policy and the investment plan, company elections, and the removal of directors and supervisors (Article 37 paras. 1–2.); (2) amending corporate charters (Article 37 para.10); (3) approving the annual budget (Article 37 para.5), the directors' and supervisors' reports (Article 37, paras. 3–4), and the plan of profit distribution (Article 37 para.6); and (4) making other important decisions such as mergers, divestiture, liquidation, dissolution or other structural changes (Article 37 para.9), increasing or decreasing corporate legal capital (Article 37 para.7), and issuing corporate bonds (Article 37 para.8). In addition, Article 16 rules that where a company intends to invest in any other enterprise or provide a guarantee for others, according to the provisions of its articles of association this shall be decided at the meeting of the board of directors or shareholders' meeting.

In Article 46, the Company Law stipulates that "the board of directors shall be responsible to the shareholders' meeting". The authority of the board of directors includes the abilities to "carry out the resolution made by shareholders' meeting" (Article 46, para.2), to make decisions on the business management and investment plan (Article 46, para.3), as well as to select managers (Article 46, para.9) and to prepare proposals for the shareholders during the meeting.[513] Such an arrangement may be influenced by the Constitution of People's Republic of China (hereinafter "Constitution"): the National People's Congress of the People's Republic of China is the highest organ of state power based on Article 57 and the State Council is responsible for and reports on its work to the National People's Congress or – when the National People's Congress is not in session – to its Standing Committee according to Article 92.[514]

The idea behind such design is that shareholders are the owners of companies and the directors and supervisors should be responsible for them. In such a system, the shareholders can directly perform their rights to manage the corporation and monitor the management board through making decisions on major issues in the general meeting. Most jurisdictions around the world indeed require a shareholder vote for fundamental changes like mergers, dissolutions and takeover defenses that

---

512 Company Law, Article 99 provides that "the provisions regarding the authorities of the shareholders' meeting of a limited liability company as prescribed in the first paragraph of Article 37 of this Law shall apply to the shareholders' assembly of a joint stock limited company".

513 The proposal subjects include the company's annual budget (Article 46, para.4), profit distribution (Article 46, para.9), and increase or decrease in the company's capital (Article 46, para.6), issuance of corporate bonds (Article 46, para.6), setting up internal departments (Article 46, para.8) and the company's internal management systems and regulations (Article 46, para.10), as well as other major structural changes including mergers, divestitures and the company's dissolution (Article 46, para.7).

514 See Constitution of People's Republic of China, adopted at the Fifth Session of the Fifth National People's Congress and promulgated for implementation by the Proclamation of the National People's Congress on December 4, 1982.

are large and may create conflicts of interest for directors.[515] Although directors and managers derive benefits from pursuing value-generating projects, they also face inherent conflicts of interest obliquely when a merger or dissolution is on the table or when the company is the target of a takeover bid.[516] Comparing with the rights of a shareholders' meeting provided by the AktG – which rules that the shareholders' meeting may only decide on matters concerning the management of the company if required by the management board by Article 119 (2)[517] – the shareholders' meeting in China enjoys more rights in corporate management and monitor such as making decisions in management policy and the investment plan, company elections and the removal of directors and supervisors.

On the other hand, the fact that independent directors generally serve as "expert or counsel" for the corporate governance to assist other directors and managers in making more rational decisions on the corporate business is also a result of legal localization. In 2011, in Shanghai Stock Exchanges, there were 38 independent directors from 26 companies delivering dissenting opinions about corporate issues. This number accounts for only 1.23% of all independent directors and 2.77% of all listed companies in Shanghai Stock Exchanges.[518] Therefore, there is a view that independent directors are powerless to protect small and medium shareholders from the depredations of large shareholders and management, serving as the "vases" in the governance of their company, according to the investigation and research of some scholars.[519] However, in the mind of the Chinese businessmen, independent

515 See Kraakman, Reinier / Armour, John / Davies, Paul / Enriques, Luca / Hansmann, Henry B. / Hertig, Gérard / Hopt, Klaus J. / Kanda, Hideki / Rock, Edward B.: *The anatomy of corporate law – A Comparative and Functional Approach.* Oxford University Press: 2nd Edition, 2009, pp.183–224, 184; Melvin Eisenberg, Melvin A.: "The Legal Roles of Shareholders and Managers in Corporate Decision-making". *California Law Review,* Vol. 57, No. 1, 1969, pp. 1–181, 27–30.

516 See Castanias, Richard P. / Helfat, Constance E.: "Managerial and Windfall Rents in the Market for Corporate Control". *Journal of Economic Behavior & Organization,* Vol. 18, No. 2, 7.1992, pp. 153–184.

517 AktG, Article 119 (1) rules that the shareholders' meeting shall resolve on matters with respect to the ratification of the acts of the members of the management board and the supervisory board. Article 120 (1) and (4) rule that the shareholders' meeting shall annually, during the first eight months of the fiscal year, resolve on ratification of the acts of the members of the management board and the supervisory board and the approval of the compensation scheme.

518 See Zhao Xiaohui / Tao Junjie: "Duli Dongshi Zhidu yi Jiji Kewei" [Independent Directors betweenthebeetleandtheblock], *ChinaBusinessTimes,* 9.10.2010, Front Page.

519 See Research Team of "Guidelines for Performance of Independent Directors in Listed Companies" in the China Association for Public Companies: "The Great Possibility of Enhancing the Role of Independent Directors – Abstract of the Report on the Performance of Independent Directors". *China Securities Journal,* A14, 16.1.2014; Li Jianwei: "Lun Woguo Duli Dongshi Chansheng Jigou de Chongjian"

directors do not necessarily play their role by the dissenting vote, which is regarded as affecting the efficiency of corporate governance. The consultation between independent directors and other directors before the meeting of the board is regarded as an appropriate system to promote the supervisory role of independent directors and increase the efficiency of decision-making of the board.[520] For example, an independent director said that they received the motion that would be proposed to the board meeting two weeks before the consultation meeting, thus affording them plenty of time to understand the motion, whereby the CEO would discuss the motion with them in the consultation meeting and amend it based on the advice of independent directors. If the motion cannot be passed at the consultation meeting, it will not be proposed at the board meeting. Accordingly, there is no need for dissenting voting on the board.[521] The consultation meeting between independent directors and other directors and the influence of political system on corporate governance – such as the central position of shareholders' meeting – as well as the emphasis on electing independent directors though cumulative voting display the innovation and localization of US corporate governance measures.[522]

II. European Union

According to the analysis above, I conclude that in the US the power of approving the RPTs is the most significant one for the role of independent directors in protecting minority shareholders,[523] although these arrangements have not yet been

---

[Discussions on the Reconstruction of the Election of Independent Directors]. *Law Science* (Journal of Northwest University of Politics and Law), No. 2, 2004, pp. 67–74, 67; Liufang, Fang: "Duli Dongshi zai Zhongguo: Jiashe he Xianshi" [Independent Directors in China: Hypothesis and Reality], *Tribune of Political Science and Law,* Vol. 26, No. 5, 2008, pp. 110–115, 110; Ni Shoubin: "Zhongguo Shangshi Gongsi Dongshihui Zhili yu Zhidu Wanshan" [Improvement of the Governance and Institution of the Board in Listed Companies of China]. *Hebei Law Science,* Vol. 24, No. 9, 2006, pp. 22–27, 23; Yi Rentao / Lv Xinzhi: "Duli Dongshi Zhidu Qushe Lun" [On The Transplantation Of Independent Director], *Law Science Magazine,* No. 8, 2011, pp. 121–123, 122.

520 See Yang Hua: *Gonsi Zaizao: Zhongguo Shangshi Gongsi Zhili Jiegou de Xinlujing* [Restructure of Corporations: New Path for the Listed Corporations of China], Zhongxin Press: 2011, p. 26; Jie, Chen / Zhongke, Zhonglian: „Yingzao Dudong Zhize de "Duli" Fenwei". *Board,* Vol. 1, 2014.

521 See Yan Xuefeng / Zhu Linchu: "Fahui Zhuanchang Zuohao Dongshi" [Be a Good Director Based on Professional Knowledge]. *Board,* Vol. 10, 2013.

522 China Securities Regulatory Commission: *Report on the Development of Chinese listed corporate governance,* 2010, Introduction.

523 The vetting of related party transactions is regarded as a crucial function for independent directors in controlled companies. See Kraakman, Reinier / Armour, John / Davies, Paul / Enriques, Luca / Hansmann, Henry B. / Hertig, Gérard / Hopt, Klaus J. / Kanda, Hideki / Rock, Edward B.: *The anatomy of corporate law –*

adopted in the Commission Recommendation, where Article 5 only provides that boards should be organized in such a way that a sufficient number of independent non-executive or supervisory directors play an effective role in key areas where the potential for conflict of interest is particularly high. For this purpose – but subject to point 7 – nomination,[524] remuneration[525] and audit committees[526] should be created within the (supervisory) board, where that board plays a role in the areas of

---

A Comparative and Functional Approach. Oxford University Press: 2nd Edition, 2009, pp. 153–181.

524 Commission Recommendation (12) provides that given the different approaches in the Member States with respect to the bodies responsible for appointing and removing directors, the role of a nomination committee created within the (supervisory) board should essentially be to ensure that where the (supervisory) board plays a role in the appointment and removal process (either through a power to table proposals or to make decisions, as defined by national law), this role is performed in as objective and professional a way as possible. The nomination committee should thus essentially make recommendations to the (supervisory) board with respect to the appointment and removal of directors by the body competent under national company law.

525 Commission Recommendation (13) provides that in the area of remuneration, corporate governance codes adopted in Member States tend to primarily focus on the remuneration of executive or managing directors, since the potential for abuse and conflicts of interest is essentially located there. Many codes also recognize that some consideration should be given at the board level to the remuneration policy for senior management. Finally, the issue of stock options is granted special attention. Given the different approaches in the Member States with respect to the bodies responsible for setting the remuneration of directors, the role of a remuneration committee created within the (supervisory) board should essentially be to ensure that where the (supervisory) board plays a role in the remuneration setting process (either through a power to table proposals or to make decisions, as defined by national law), this role is performed in as objective and professional a way as possible. The remuneration committee should thus essentially make recommendations to the (supervisory) board with respect to those remuneration issues for decision by the body competent under national company law.

526 Commission Recommendation (14) provides that two key responsibilities of the (supervisory) board seem to ensure that the financial reports and other related information disseminated by the company present an accurate and complete picture of the company's position and monitor the procedures established for the evaluation and management of risks. In this context, most corporate governance codes assign to the audit committee an essential role in assisting the (supervisory) board to fulfil these duties. In some Member States, such responsibilities are attributed – wholly or partly – to corporate bodies external to the (supervisory) board. It is therefore appropriate to provide that an audit committee created within the (supervisory) board should as a general rule make recommendations to the (supervisory) board with respect to those audit issues and that such functions may be performed by other structures – external to the (supervisory) board – which would be equally effective.

nomination, remuneration and audit under national law, taking into account Annex I. Article 6.1 which stipulates that the primary purpose of the committees should be to increase the efficiency of the (supervisory) board by ensuring that decisions are based on due consideration, as well as helping to organize its work with a view to ensuring that the decisions that it takes are free from material conflicts of interest. The creation of the committees is not intended – in principle – to remove the matters considered from the purview of the (supervisory) board itself, which remains fully responsible for the decisions taken in its field of competence. In addition, the duty of loyalty is highly developed in Anglo-American countries, while in continental European countries it has only received more hesitant attention.[527]

In the EU, the practical involvement of independent directors in the assessment of related party transactions significantly varies across the European jurisdictions, some of which foresee a role for independent directors in this area, while others do not.[528] In Belgium, Article 524 of the Companies Code requires related party transactions to be reviewed by a special committee consisting of three independent directors and at least one independent expert. The committee's opinion is not binding on the board, which has the final say on the relevant transaction. However, if the committee's opinion is not followed, the board should publicly disclose the reasons for it. As reported by scholars, this information duty has been effective in deterring deviations from the committee's view.[529] Italian Exchange Commission increases the involvement of the independents in the approval of related party transactions.[530] In particular, in the event of transactions holding greater importance (which are defined under quantitative parameters), the board has the power to authorize the transaction after the favorable report of the committee of independent directors; otherwise, the approval of the transaction falls to the shareholders' meeting.[531]

527 See Hopt, Klaus J.: "Conflict of Interest, Secrecy and Insider Information of Directors, A Comparative Analysis". *European Company and Financial Law Review*, 2013, pp. 167–193, 192.

528 See Ferrarini, Guido / Filippelli, Marilena: "Independent directors and controlling shareholders around the world". *ECGI Working Paper* N. 258/2014, 5.2014, p. 28.

529 See Geens, Koen: "Corporate boards in Belgium". In: Davies, Paul / Hopt, Klaus / Nowak, Richard / van Solinge, Gerard (eds.): *Corporate Boards in Law and Practice.* Oxford University Press: 2013, pp. 119–174.

530 In March 2010, the Italian exchange commission issued a regulation to control related party transaction, Consob Resolution no. 17221 of 12 March 2010, later amended by Resolution no. 17389 of 23 June 2010.

531 "Procedure rules might not be enough if a substantial part of the board is "captured" by the controlling shareholder. Provided that the independents in the board have significant voting power vis a vis the controlling shareholder (for example, if they hold a majority of the seats), they can stop the transaction at board level. However, the opposition at board level does not block the suspected transaction, because the block-holder can still pass the decisions using his voting power at the shareholders general meeting." OECD, RPTs and MSR, Assessment and Recommendations, p. 18.

The French law requires both the ex-ante authorization of the board of directors and the ex-post ratification by the general meeting (in both cases with the abstention of the interested party). Nonetheless, here the devil is in the detail: the French rules do not apply to current transactions entered into under normal conditions or shareholders with less than 10 percent of the voting power.[532] In the GCGC, Article 4.3.4 states: "All members of the management board shall disclose conflicts of interest to the supervisory board without delay and inform the other members of the management board thereof. All transactions between the enterprise and the members of the management board as well as persons they are close to or companies they have a personal association with must comply with standards customary in the sector. Important transactions shall require the approval of the supervisory board." While the GCGC merely addresses RPTs involving members of the board of management and supervisory board, AktG has primarily focused on conflicts between controlling shareholders and minority shareholders and the disclosure of transactions between the company and its affiliated companies in an annual report that must be controlled and verified by an independent auditor through Article 312 (1): in the absence of a control agreement, the management board of a controlled company shall render a report on the company's relations with affiliated enterprises within the first three months of each fiscal year. Such a report shall specify all transactions entered into by the company during the previous fiscal year with the controlling enterprise or any enterprise affiliated with such controlling enterprise or at the instruction or in the interest of any such enterprise and all other acts that the controlled company has undertaken or refrained from undertaking at the instruction or in the interest of any such enterprise. Regarding transactions, such a report shall specify any consideration given or received and – in terms of acts undertaken – state the reasons for such acts and the advantages and disadvantages for the controlled company. If compensation for disadvantages was given, such report shall specify the manner in which it was actually given during the fiscal year and for which measures the company has been granted an entitlement.

Overall, there seems to be a tendency toward more strictness vis-à-vis RPTs and self-dealing in Europe.[533] Rules on disclosure and procedures to solve conflicts of interest (like the obligation to abstain from voting on the issues when the director is a related party) are probably the main course of reforms taken in some

---

532 OECD, RPTs and MSR, Assessment and Recommendations, p. 18.

533 See Gilson, Ronald J. / Schwartz, Alan: "Constraints on Private Benefits of Control: Ex Ante Control Mechanisms versus Ex Post Transaction Review". *Journal of Institutional and Theoretical Economics*, Vol. 169, No.1, 3.2013, pp. 160–183; Gelter M.: "Why Do Shareholder Derivative Suits Remain Rare in Continental Europe?". *Brooklyn Journal of International Law*, Vol. 37, No. 3, 2012, pp. 843–892; Gower & Davies: *Principles of modern company law*. Davies, Paul L. / Worthington, Sarah (eds.). Sweet & Maxwell: 9th Edition, London 2012, pp. 17–18.

jurisdictions of Continental Europe regarding self-dealing regulation.[534] In most cases, anti-self-dealing provisions are addressed to curb expropriation by directors and – to a lesser degree – expropriation by dominant shareholders.[535] Current EU rules require companies to include in their annual accounts a note on transactions entered into with related parties, stating the amount and nature of the transaction and other necessary information.[536] All EU consolidated listed companies have to disclose annually any transactions with directors, senior executives and controlling shareholders in accordance with IAS 24, IFRS adopted in September 2002.[537] As in the US, the procedural bias of the European reforms may also reflect a traditional reluctance to give such tasks to courts and thus the failure of courts that have an expertise in this activity to emerge.[538]

However, since this requirement tends to be regarded as insufficient, the European Corporate Governance Forum issued a statement on related party transactions recommending the introduction of common principles across Europe in 2011. According to the EU Action Plan, the Forum proposed in particular that transactions above a certain threshold should be subject to evaluation by an independent advisor and that the most substantial transactions should be approved by shareholders. The EU Green Paper 2011 raised the question of providing more protection against related party transactions. A considerable proportion of respondents called for stronger safeguards. Regarding this response and the guidelines contained in the statement of the European Corporate Governance Forum, the Commission considers that shareholders' control over RPTs should be strengthened.[539]

Thus, in April 2014, the European Commission proposed a new regime to provide safeguards for the protection of shareholders' interests when listed companies entered into transactions with related parties.[540] Transactions with related parties is one of the five main issues identified by the Commission:[541] "Currently, shareholders

---

534 See Conac, Pierre-Henri / Enriques, Luca / Gelter, Martin: "Constraining Dominant shareholders' self-dealing: The legal framework in France, Germany and Italy". *European Company and Financial Law Review*, Vol. 4, No. 4, 2007, pp. 491–528; Enriques, Luca: "The law on company Directors' self-dealing: A comparative analysis". *International and Comparative Corporate Law Journal*, Vol. 2, No. 3, 2000, pp. 297–333.

535 OECD, RPTs and MSR, Assessment and Recommendations, p. 17.

536 See Article 43(1) (7b) of Directive 78/660/EEC and Article 34(7b) of Directive 83/349/EEC.

537 OECD, RPTs and MSR, p. 30.

538 See Gilson, Ronald J. / Schwartz, Alan: "Constraints on Private Benefits of Control: Ex Ante Control Mechanisms versus Ex Post Transaction Review". *Journal of Institutional and Theoretical Economics*, Vol. 169, No. 1, 3.2013, pp. 160–183; Gelter M.: "Why Do Shareholder Derivative Suits Remain Rare in Continental Europe?". *Brooklyn Journal of International Law*, Vol. 37, No. 3, 2012, pp. 843–892.

539 EU Action Plan, p. 10.

540 The Proposal, p. 2.

541 The Proposal, p. 4. 1) Insufficient engagement of institutional investors and asset managers; 2) Insufficient link between pay and performance of directors; 3) Lack

do not have access to sufficient information ahead of the planned transaction and do not have adequate tools to oppose to abusive transactions. As institutional investors and asset managers are in most cases minority shareholders, more control rights over RPTs would improve their ability to protect their investments."[542] "On the objectives to ensure shareholder oversight on directors' remuneration and related party transactions, the existing Member State rules in these areas are very different and as a result, they provide an uneven level of transparency and protection for investors. In both cases, the result of the divergence of rules is that investors are, in particular in case of cross-border investments, subject to difficulties and costs when they want to monitor companies and engage with them, and have no effective tools to protect their investments."[543] The proposal realized that transactions with related parties might cause prejudice to companies and their shareholders as they might give the related party the opportunity to appropriate value belonging to the company.[544]

As a result, the new article 9c will require listed companies that related party transactions representing more than 5% of the companies' assets or transactions that can have a significant impact on profits or turnover to submit these transactions to the approval of shareholders and may not unconditionally conclude it without their approval. For smaller related party transactions that represent more than 1% of their assets, listed companies shall publicly announce such transactions at the time of the conclusion of the transaction, accompanying the announcement with a report from an independent third party assessing whether the transaction is on market terms and confirming whether it is fair and reasonable from the perspective of the shareholders. In order to target only transactions that could be the most disadvantageous for minority shareholders and to keep the administrative burden limited, member states should be allowed to exclude transactions entered into between the company and members of its group that are fully owned by the listed company. For the same reason, Member States should also be able to allow companies to request the advance approval by shareholders for certain clearly defined types of recurring transactions above 5 percent of the assets and request from shareholders an advance exemption from the obligation to produce an independent third party report for recurrent transactions above 1 percent of the assets, under certain conditions.[545]

---

of shareholder oversight on related party transactions and 4) Inadequate transparency of proxy advisors; 5) Difficult and costly exercise of rights flowing from securities for investors.

542 The Proposal, p. 6.

543 The Proposal, p. 6.

544 The Proposal, p. 6.

545 Article 9c Right to vote on related party transactions:

1. Member States shall ensure that companies, in case of transactions with related parties that represent more than 1% of their assets, publicly announce such transactions at the time of the conclusion of the transaction, and accompany the announcement by a report from an independent third party assessing whether or not it is on market terms and confirming that the transaction is fair

The next stage in the European legislative process will be for the Council of the EU and the European Parliament to discuss the proposal internally and prepare their respective positions for the informal negotiations in trilogues at a later stage. In the European Parliament, the rapporteur on the file will be appointed in the coming days and will lead the discussions in the Legal Committee from October onwards. Within the Council of the EU, the discussions among the 28 Member States are currently facilitated by the Italian Presidency. The ambition of the Italian Presidency is to finalize an agreement on the file among the Member States by December 2014. If the European Parliament and the Council are ready with their respective

---

and reasonable from the perspective of the shareholders, including minority shareholders. The announcement shall contain information on the nature of the related party relationship, the name of the related party, the amount of the transaction and any other information necessary to assess the transaction. Member States may provide that companies can request their shareholders to exempt them from the requirement of subparagraph 1 to accompany the announcement of the transaction with a related party by a report from an independent third party in case of clearly defined types of recurrent transactions with an identified related party in a period of not longer than 12 months after granting the exemption. Where the related party transactions involve a shareholder, this shareholder shall be excluded from the vote on the advance exemption.

2. Member States shall ensure that transactions with related parties representing more than 5% of the companies' assets or transactions which can have a significant impact on profits or turnover are submitted to a vote by the shareholders in a general meeting. Where the related party transaction involves a shareholder, this shareholder shall be excluded from that vote. The company shall not conclude the transaction before the shareholders' approval of the transaction. The company may however conclude the transaction under the condition of shareholder approval.
   Member States may provide that companies can request the advance approval by shareholders of the transactions referred to in subparagraph 1 in case of clearly defined types of recurrent transactions with an identified related party in a period of not longer than 12 months after the advance approval of the transactions. Where the related party transactions involve a shareholder, this shareholder shall be excluded from the vote on the advance approval.
3. Transactions with the same related party that have been concluded during the previous 12 months period and have not been approved by shareholders shall be aggregated for the purposes of application of paragraph 2. If the value of these aggregated transactions exceeds 5% of the assets, the transaction by which this threshold is exceeded and any subsequent transactions with the same related party shall be submitted to a shareholder vote and may only be unconditionally concluded after shareholder approval.
4. Member States may exclude transactions entered into between the company and one or more members of its group from the requirements in paragraphs 1, 2 and 3, provided that those members of the group are wholly owned by the company.

positions by the end of the year, the informal trilogues among the Council, the European Parliament and the European Commission may start in 2015. The Directive is expected to be adopted not earlier than in the second half of 2015. Once the Directive is adopted, Member States will have 18 months in which to implement it into national law.[546]

In sum, transactions will require shareholder approval if they represent more than 5% of the companies' assets or can have a significant effect on profits or turnover rather than approval of independent directors and adopting cumulative voting. In the case of smaller transactions representing more than 1% of assets, companies will instead need to make a disclosure and obtain an opinion from an independent third party that the transaction is fair and reasonable from the perspective of the shareholders, including minority shareholders. In the EU, shareholder franchise has been at the forefront of corporate governance reform and debates for a few decades now. Nonetheless, how the scope of their franchise should be demarcated remains unclear. Shareholder say should comprise – as well as being limited to – those matters in which directors face conflicting interests purely owing to their position of a director (in some cases only when the decision is material for the company). Assigning shareholders more powers causes unnecessary costs of organizing shareholder meetings and threatens to lead to poor decision-making and avoidable influence of special interest shareholders. By contrast, giving shareholders fewer powers may engender unacceptably high agency costs within the board of directors.[547]

---

546 UK Corporate Update: *European related party transaction rules: the impact on listed companies*, 11.9.2014.

547 Cools, Sofie: "The Dividing Line Between Shareholder Democracy and Board Autonomy: Inherent Conflicts of Interest as Normative Criterion". *European Company and Financial Law Review*, Vol. 11, No. 2, 2014, pp. 258–296, 296.

Fifth Chapter: Conflicts between Cumulative Voting and Long Governance

This Chapter demonstrates the conflicts between cumulative voting and long governance, which is the third road followed by three Economy Giants. The first part analyzes the weakness of cumulative voting – representing shareholder primacy theory and pursuing private and short-term profits. The claim that the shareholder primacy norm benefits us all in the long run by ensuring the maximization of aggregate social wealth is questionable.[548] After all, the "corporation" consists of a variety of constituencies, including stockholders, and even stockholders certainly are not a unified group with identical interests.[549] Further, the second part demonstrates several disadvantages of the shareholder primacy so as to point out the limited influence of a shareholder-centered model which is discussed in the First Chapter as the reason for adopting cumulative voting and independent directors in China and EU. The following three parts demonstrate the long governance adopted by US, EU and China to cover the weakness of the shareholder primacy theory. In terms of the corporate governance value in the US, EU and China, there is a trend towards long governance, which has conflicts with the system of minority representatives and aspires, rather than supporting one approach over another in the fundamental debate on corporate governance, i.e. the shareholder value vs. stakeholder value

---

548 "Hansmann and Kraakman believe that enterprises should be organized and operated to serve the interests of society as a whole, and that the interests of shareholders deserve no greater weight in this social calculus than do the interests of any other members of society. Berle's argument is that corporations ought to be run for the benefit of shareholders, not because they "own" the corporation, or because of some contract or agency relation, but because all other constituencies can be better off as a result through maintaining the corporation as a private sector institution with a strong profit-maximizing imperative." Boatright, John R.: "Fiduciary Duties and the Shareholder-Management Relation: Or, What's so special about Shareholders?". *Business Ethics Quarterly*, Vol. 4, No. 4, 10.1994, pp. 393–407, 401–402.

549 Unocal Corp. v. Mesa Petroleum Co., 493 A.2d 946, 955 (Del. 1985) ("Our analysis begins with the basic principle that corporate directors have a fiduciary duty to act in the best interests of the corporation and stockholders."); Malone v. Brincat, 722 A.2d 5, 10 (Del. 1998) ("The directors of Delaware corporations stand in a fiduciary relationship not only to the stockholders but also to the corporations upon whose boards they serve. Although the fiduciary duty of a Delaware director is unremitting, the exact course of conduct that must be charted to properly discharge that responsibility will change in the specific context of the action the director is taking with regard to either the corporation or its shareholders.").

debate, to represent an intermediate "third way".[550] It means the interests of different stakeholders should be subject to the whole benefit of corporations and deserve reasonable balance among them. Although the shareholders obtain more attention from the management, it is different from the shareholder-centered model that their benefit cannot be regarded as the priority for corporate governance. The boundaries between the shareholder value and stakeholder approaches are often blurred, to the extent that the same corporate actions may, in the long run, maximize both shareholder wealth and enterprise value.[551] In one word, this Chapter tries to propose that the profound reasons for the limited adoption of cumulative voting in China and the negative attitude towards it in the EU are the conflicts between cumulative voting and the long governance – the corporate governance value adopted by the EU and China.

A. Weaknesses of Cumulative Voting

In essence, cumulative voting is a powerful tool designed to give some control to minority shareholders who may attain representation on the board of directors roughly proportional to the number of shares that they own by distributing votes properly. However, cumulative voting may not be able to solve the problems with the nomination of the independent directors, although it creates a new type of director that is accountable to significant parties other than the controlling insiders. This reflects the inherent problems for solving the trade-off between independence and accountability for independent directors. The Spanish case is interesting in this respect, because the appointment of an independent director is in theory possible through the regulation of cumulative voting, although the judges have clearly stated that an independent nominated by a significant shareholder is always an inside director. Furthermore, if the controller is successful in convincing the judge that the significant investor is a raider, the director appointed by him could be removed, even in the case of an independent director. Nonetheless, it could be a promising reform to combine the institutions of cumulative voting and electing independent

550 Masouros, Pavlos E.: *Corporate Law and Economic Stagnation: How Shareholder Value and Short-Termism Contribute to the Decline of the Western Economies.* Eleven International Publishing: 28.1.2013, p. 271.

551 "Connecting supervisors and directors to the interests of enterprises represents the compromise between shareholder-centered and stakeholder-centered model." Davies, Paul L. / Hopt, Klaus J.: "Corporate Boards in Europe – Accountability and Convergence". *American Journal Comparative Law*, Vol. 61, No. 2, 2013, pp. 301–375; See also Tuschke A. / Luber M.: "Corporate Governance in Germany: Converging Towards Shareholder Value-Orientation or Not So Much?". In: Rasheed A. / Yoshikawa, T. (eds.): *The convergence of corporate governance: promise and prospects.* Palgrave Macmillan: 2012, pp. 75–92; Freeman, R. Edward: "Stockholders and Stakeholders: A New Perspective on Corporate Governance". *California Management Review (pre-1986)*, Vol. 25, No. 3, p. 88.

directors. It is important to distinguish between raiders and monitors: a minority of professional directors would not threaten a replacement of operating management, a major shift in corporate strategy or spying a competitor.[552]

On the one hand, the presence on the board of one or more directors representing such a constituency could trigger disharmony on the board, disrupt and impair the efficient management of the corporation, as well as could lead to an atmosphere of uncertainty at the top level. There is a fear that both strategic behavior by minority shareholders and higher decision-making costs arising from the risk of conflict and possible deadlock on the board and minority shareholders will be unable to make decisions due to conflicts among their various interests or that they will seek to benefit themselves at the expense of other groups and the firm as a whole.[553] As Frank H. Easterbrook and Daniel R. Fischel pointed out in "Voting in Corporate Law", cumulative voting gives disproportionate weight to certain "minority" shares and the lack of proportion once more creates a needless agency cost of management that would arise without an equal voting right carried by each element of the residual interest because voting flows with the residual interest in the firm.[554] "Because cumulative voting permits representation of 'minority' interests in the firm's governance, it increases the chance that there will be multi-peaked preferences among the members of the board. Thus cumulative voting and other minority representation schemes expose the firm to an uncompensated risk of making inconsistent or illogical decisions."[555] There is a risk that a shareholder affiliated with the controlling group might try to "disguise" themselves as an independent investor, with the result that the alleged "minority" director(s) would – in truth – be expressed by the controlling group "*en travesti*". Avoiding this risk is not easy, although a combination of disclosure obligations imposed on the proposing

552 Gutiérrez, María / Sáez, Maribel: "Deconstructing Independent Directors". *Journal of Corporate Law Studies*, Vol. 13, No. 1, 4.2013, pp. 63–94, 85.

553 See American Bar Association Section of Business Law, the Committee on Corporate Laws, Guidelines for the Unaffiliated Director of the Controlled Corporation, *The Business Lawyer*, Vol. 45, No. 1, November 1989, pp. 429–440, 430 (evaluating the roles of "affiliated" as compared with "unaffiliated" directors of a controlled corporation and stating that all directors have the same duties to the corporation and to all of its shareholders"); Kraakman, Reinier / Armour, John / Davies, Paul / Enriques, Luca / Hansmann, Henry B. / Hertig, Gérard / Hopt, Klaus J. / Kanda, Hideki / Rock, Edward B.: *The anatomy of corporate law – A Comparative and Functional Approach.* Oxford University Press: 2nd Edition, 2009, p. 56.

554 Easterbrook, Frank / Fischel, Daniel: "Voting in Corporate Law". *Journal of Law and Economics*, Vol. 26, No. 2, 1983, pp. 395–427, 409.

555 "To be more specific, cumulative voting makes realignments of control blocs very difficult by distributing a form of hold up power widely; although every share has the same holdup potential, the aggregate holdup value exceeds the value of the firm and thus makes negotiation very difficult." Easterbrook, Frank / Fischel, Daniel: "Voting in Corporate Law". *Journal of Law and Economics*, Vol. 26, No. 2, 1983, pp. 395–427, 410.

shareholder and her nominees – with a requirement that minority directors are proposed by shareholders independently from the management of the other shareholders that support the managers – could achieve this goal.[556]

Fundamentally speaking, cumulative voting is a system focusing on shareholder primacy theory that does not account for the fact that shareholders' interests diverge.[557] First, commentators have said that shareholder primacy fails to allow for the fact that many investors will follow modern portfolio techniques and diversify their risks, which can be achieved by investing across all capital assets in the financial markets. These techniques advocate investors having a portfolio that is constituted by various securities.[558] This kind of diversified approach will mean that investors are likely to be both shareholders and bondholders in corporations.[559] Some shareholders might – either directly or indirectly – actually hold shares of competing corporations, whereby their interests will probably diverge from other shareholders.[560] Second, shareholders will have different approaches to risk and views concerning what they want to gain from their shareholding.[561] There is the distinction between those who are seeking long-term interests and those with short-term interests. Some shareholders are focused on achieving capital appreciation from an increase in share value, while others are looking for dividend income.[562] Third, the shareholder group of any large corporation will not be a homogeneous group; rather, they come in all shapes and sizes. Large shareholders – and particularly institutional investors – have interests that can diverge from those of minority shareholders[563] and it might be the case

556 See Ventoruzzo, Marco: "Empowering Shareholders in Directors' Elections: A Revolution in the Making". *European Company and Financial Law Review*, Vol. 8, No. 2, 6.2011, pp. 105–144, 137.

557 See Bainbridge, Stephen M.: *The New Corporate Governance in Theory and Practice*. Oxford University Press: 7.2008, pp. 56.

558 See Kaufman, Allen / Englander, Ernie: "A team production model of corporate governance". *Academy of Management Executive*, Vol. 19, No. 3, 2005, pp. 9–22, 16.

559 See Smith, Thomas A.: "The Efficient Norm for Corporate Law: A Neo-traditional Interpretation of Fiduciary Duty". *Michigan Law Review*, Vol. 98, No.1, 1999, pp. 214–269, 214; Blair, Margaret M.: *Ownership and Control: Rethinking Corporate Governance for the Twenty-first Century*. Washington, D.C.: Brookings Institution: 1995, p. 229.

560 See Hu H. / Black B.: "Hedge Funds, Insiders, and the Decoupling of Economic and Voting Ownership: Empty Voting and Hidden (Morphable) Ownership". *Journal of Corporate Finance*, Vol. 13, No. 2–3, 2007, pp. 343–367.

561 See LoPucki L.: "The Myth of the Residual Owner: An Empirical Study". *Washington University Law Quarterly*, Vol. 82, No. 4, 2004, pp. 1341–1378, 1351–1352.

562 See Keay, Andrew: "Shareholder Primacy in Corporate Law: Can it Survive? Should it Survive?". *European Company and Financial Law Review*, Vol. 7, No. 3, 2010, pp. 369–413, 406.

563 See Miller R.: "Ethical Challenges in Corporate-Shareholder and Investor Relations: Using the Value Exchange Model to Analyze and Respond". *Journal of Business Ethics*, Vol. 7, No. 1–2, 1988, pp. 117–132, 125.

that managers will prefer the interests of the former over the latter as the former have more power and can possibly remove them.

On the other hand, cumulative voting can be used by a minority stockholder who is motivated by narrow, selfish interests rather than the broader interests of all stockholders and the stockholder pursuing private and short-term profits might use board access and the threat of disruption to hold up the corporation for greenmail.[564] The fact is that the vast majority non-controlling shareholders of listed corporations are currently short-termist.[565] According to several finance academics, shareholder primacy produces a short-term focus and short-term earnings performance overshadows all else, which fails to maximize social wealth.[566] Short-termism has "substantial corporate and societal costs,"[567] has "created a national problem that needs to be fixed,"[568] represents "a disease that infects American business and distorts management and boardroom judgment"[569] and has "eroded faith in corporations continuing to be the foundation of the American free enterprise system"[570]. Some writings about short-termism have even suggested that shareholder pressure was a

564 Greenmail is the practice of purchasing enough shares in a firm to threaten a takeover, thereby forcing the target firm to buy those shares back at a premium in order to suspend the takeover. Axley, Ralph E.: "The Case Against Cumulative Voting". *Wisconsin Law Review*, Vol. 1950, No. 2, 1950, pp. 278–287, 283.

565 See Masouros, Pavlos E.: *Corporate Law and Economic Stagnation: How Shareholder Value and Short-Termism Contribute to the Decline of the Western Economies.* Eleven International Publishing: 28.1.2013, p. 281.

566 See Lipton, Martin / Rosenblum, Steven A.: "A New System of Corporate Governance: The Quinquennial Election of Directors". *The University of Chicago Law Review*, Vol. 58, No. 1, Winter 1991, pp. 187–253, 205–215; Wallman S.: "The Proper Interpretation of Corporate Constituency Statutes and Formulation of Director Duties". *Stetson Law Review*, Vol. 21, No. 1, 1991, pp. 163–196, 176–177; van der Weide M.: "Against Fiduciary Duties to Corporate Stakeholders". *Delaware Journal of Corporate Law*, Vol. 21, No. 1, 1996, pp. 27–86, 61; Loderer C. / Roth L. / Waelchli U. / Joerg P.: "Shareholder Value: Principles, Declarations, and Actions". *Financial Management*, Vol. 39, No. 1, Spring 2010, pp. 5–32.

567 See Lipton, Martin / Rosenblum, Steven A.: "A New System of Corporate Governance: The Quinquennial Election of Directors". *The University of Chicago Law Review*, Vol. 58, No. 1, Winter 1991, pp. 187–253, 203, 210–212.

568 See Jacobs, Jack B.: "Patient Capital: Can Delaware Corporate Law Help Revive It?". *Washington and Lee Law Review*, Vol. 68, No. 4, 2011, pp. 1645–1664, 1657.

569 See Lipton, Martin / Wachtell / Lipton / Rosen & Katz: "The Proposed "Shareholder Bill of Rights Act of 2009"". *Wall Street Journal*, Tue. 12.5.2009, retrieved 15.5.2014, from http://blogs.law.harvard.edu/corpgov/2009/05/12/the-proposed-"shareholder-bill-of-rights-act-of-2009"/.

570 See Aspen Institute: *Overcoming Short-Termism: A Call for a More Responsible Approach to Investment and Business Management*, 2009, retrieved 15.05.2014, from http://www.aspeninstitute.org/sites/default/ files/content/docs/business%20and%20society%20program/overcome_short_state0909, p. 2.

cause of the Enron and WorldCom scandals,[571] the crash of 1987[572] and the excessive risk-taking by financial firms in the run-up to the 2008–2009 financial crisis.[573] The financial crisis has revealed that shareholders in many cases supported managers' excessive short-term risk-taking. Chancellor Leo Strine and Justice Jack Jacobs – prominent figures in the Delaware judiciary – have expressed strong short-termism concerns.[574] When William Donaldson was Chairman of the SEC, he accepted that short-termism is a "fundamental problem"[575]. When adopting a 2010 rule to provide shareholders with access to the company's proxy card, the SEC was responsive to short-termism arguments by limiting the provided access to shareholders who have held their shares for more than three years.[576]

In details, shareholder primacy means that managers are under pressure from the financial markets to engage in perverse behavior that reduces the prospect of

---

571 See Strine, Leo E. Jr.: "Response, Toward a True Corporate Republic: A Traditionalist Response to Bebchuk's Solution for Improving Corporate America". *Harvard Law Review*, Vol. 119, No. , 2006, pp. 1759–1783, 1764 (noting that the "increasing sway of institutional investors over corporations, and the institutions' laser-beam focus on quarter-to-quarter earnings, helped create managerial incentives that contributed to the debacles at corporations like Enron, WorldCom, HealthSouth, and Adelphia").

572 See Lipton, Martin: "Corporate Governance in the Age of Finance Corporatism". *University of Pennsylvania Law Review*, Vol. 136, No. 1, 1987, pp. 1–72, 72. ("The overleveraged takeover and the short-term oriented speculative activity associated with the takeover frenzy of the eighties were, predictably, significant factors leading to the [1987] crash.").

573 See Lipton, Martin / Wachtell / Lipton / Rosen & Katz: "The Proposed "Shareholder Bill of Rights Act of 2009"". *Wall Street Journal*, Tue. 12.5.2009, retrieved 15.5.2014, from http://blogs.law.harvard.edu/corpgov/2009/05/12/the-proposed-"shareholder-bill -of-rights-act-of-2009"/. (Identifying "coincidence of increased stockholder pressure for high returns and weakened prudential regulation" as "key contributors to the current crises").

574 See Jacobs, Jack B.: "Patient Capital: Can Delaware Corporate Law Help Revive It?". *Washington and Lee Law Review*, Vol. 68, No. 4, 2011, pp. 1645–1664, 1657–1663 (expressing concern about the short-term mindset of institutional investors and legal developments empowering shareholders); Strine, Leo E. Jr.: "One Fundamental Corporate Governance Question We Face: Can Corporations Be Managed for the Long Term Unless Their Powerful Electorates Also Act and Think Long Term?". *Business Lawyer*, Vol. 66, No. 1, 11.2010, pp. 1–32, 26 (expressing concern about shareholders' increasing focus on short-term results and suggesting limits on the ability of activist shareholders to make proposals motivated by short-term interests).

575 See Donaldson, William H.: *Speech by SEC Chairman: 2005 CFA Institute Annual Conference*, 8.5.2005, retrieved 15.6.2014, from http://www.sec.gov/news/speech/spch050805whd.htm.

576 See Securities and Exchange Commission: *Facilitating Shareholder Director Nominations*, 17 CFR PARTS 200, 232, 240 and 249, 16.9.2010, p. 25.

long-term benefits,[577] on the basis that the markets take the view that "the price of a share today reflects the best estimate of the value of future profits and growth that will accrue to that corporation"[578] or are convinced that if they do not do so the shareholders will have them removed through either pressure or a resolution at a shareholders' meeting, or as a result of a takeover. However, the stock market is not an appropriate gauge of a corporation's performance, given that it is unable to deal with uncertainty and it frequently fails to price assets correctly,[579] thereby not reflecting the intrinsic value of the corporation. For instance, the market undervalues plans where there will be long-term benefits.[580] They also may have some self-interest as they will benefit if they have any shares in the corporation and may receive bonuses for improving the corporation's position in the short term.[581] If short-termism is practiced, then it causes serious under-investment in capital expenditure, which jeopardizes the corporation's viability in the long term.[582] The short-term approach harms the development of the corporation and sacrifices long-term value.[583]

B. Criticism against Shareholder Primary

Although the US corporate governance model has exerted great global influence, the shareholder primacy theory has been subjected to a number of concerted challenges and there is little doubt that it has shown substantial resilience.[584] The US company, accounting and securities law has come under criticism after the recent crises. Capital markets often have a short-term perspective and can be volatile and create

577 See Blair, Margaret M.: *Ownership and Control: Rethinking Corporate Governance for the Twenty-first Century*. Washington, D.C.: Brookings Institution: 1995, p. 122.

578 See Blair, Margaret M.: *Ownership and Control: Rethinking Corporate Governance for the Twenty-first Century*. Washington, D.C.: Brookings Institution: 1995, p. 202.

579 See Bagley, Constance E. / Page, Karen L.: "The Devil Made Me Do It: Replacing Corporate Directors' Veil of Secrecy with the Mantle of Stewardship". *San Diego Law Review*, Vol. 36, No. 4, 1999, pp. 897–946, 920.

580 See Parkinson J.E.: *Corporate Power and Responsibility*. Oxford University Press: 1993, p. 92.

581 See Letza, Steve / Sun, Xiuping / Kirkbride, James: "Shareholding Versus Stakeholding: a critical review of corporate governance". *Corporate Governance: An International Review*, Vol. 12, No. 3, 2004, pp. 242–263, 249.

582 See Sheehy, Benedict: "The Importance of Corporate Models, Economic and Jurisprudential Values and the Future of Corporate Law". *De Paul Business and Commercial Law Journal*, Vol. 2, No. 3, 2004, pp. 463–513, 502.

583 See Letza, Steve / Sun, Xiuping / Kirkbride, James: "Shareholding Versus Stakeholding: a critical review of corporate governance". *Corporate Governance: An International Review*, Vol. 12, No. 3, 2004, pp. 242–263, 249.

584 See Keay, Andrew R.: "Moving Towards Stakeholderism? Constituency Statutes, Enlightened Shareholder Value and All That: Much A do about Little?" *Business Law Review*, Vol. 22, No. 1, 2011, pp. 1–49.

speculative bubbles. The high tech boom of the 1990s in the US and subsequent market crash is an example. For instance, Michael Porter argued that during this time the pressure coming from shareholders with short horizons discouraged US companies from making the long-term investments necessary to compete with German and Japanese companies.[585] Martin Lipton and Steven Rosenblum also warned that unless the corporate governance system of the US could provide companies with the same insulation from short-term shareholder pressure enjoyed by German and Japanese companies, "the relative health of American ... corporations, and the relative wealth of their stockholders, will inevitably erode"[586].

While one may argue one-sided Americanization in the field of corporate governance,[587] it would seem that in the past 20 years the stakeholder theory – the other leading theory that addresses the objective of the corporation and remains applicable in many Continental European countries, most notably Germany – has become increasingly popular in many Anglo-American jurisdictions.[588] Under the stakeholder-centered model,[589] the firm is an integral component of the social fabric

---

585 Porter, Michael E.: "Capital Choices: Changing the Way America Invests in Industry". *Journal of Applied Corporate Finance*, Vol. 5, No. 2, Summer 1992, pp. 4–16, 4–11. (arguing pressure coming from shareholders with short horizons discourages long-term investments).

586 Lipton, Martin / Rosenblum, Steven A.: "A New System of Corporate Governance: The Quinquennial Election of Directors". *The University of Chicago Law Review*, Vol. 58, No. 1, Winter 1991, pp. 187–253, 218 (arguing institutional stockholders and takeover activity produce short-term bias, making it desirable to insulate management from pressure by short-term shareholders).

587 Von Werder, Axel: „Ökonomische Grundfragen der Corporate Governance". In: Hommelhoff, Peter / Hopt, Klaus J. / von Werder, Axel (eds.): *Handbuch Corporate Governance*. Otto Schmidt Vertrag: 2nd Edition, Köln 2009, p. 8; Janssen E.: "The Stakeholder Model: The Influence of the Ownership and Governance Structures". *Journal of Business Ethics*, Vol. 56, No. 4, 2005, pp. 1–13, 4; "Corporate governance defines relationships between a company's management, its board, its shareholders and its other stakeholders." OECD Principles, p. 11.

588 See Keay, Andrew: "Shareholder Primacy in Corporate Law: Can it Survive? Should it Survive?". *European Company and Financial Law Review*, Vol. 7, No. 3, 2010, pp. 369–413, 370.

589 See Schneper, William D. / Guillén, Mauro F.: "Stakeholder Rights and Corporate Governance: A Cross-National Study of Hostile Takeovers". *Administrative Science Quarterly*, Vol. 49, No. 2, 2004, pp. 263–295, 263. The stakeholder-centered view of the firm has been defined as the belief that "each group of stakeholders merits consideration for its own sake and not merely because of its ability to further the interests of some other group, such as shareowners"; Donaldson, T., Preston L.E.: "The stakeholder theory of the corporation Concepts, evidence and implications". *Academy of Management Review*, Vol. 20, No. 1, 1995, pp. 65–91, 69; Blair argued that only stakeholders with a significant firm-specific investment should enjoy influence in discussions about corporate control. Blair, Margaret M.: *Ownership and Control: Rethinking Corporate Governance for the Twenty-first*

and is characterized by the intersecting interests of various stakeholders, including not only shareholders and managers, but also employees, banks and the surrounding community, as well as discipline managers.[590] The enactment in over 40 states in the US of what are generally known as constituency statutes that either require or permit directors to consider the interests of stakeholders – other than the shareholders – might lead to a similar conclusion.[591] Moreover, it has recently been noted

---

Century. Washington, D.C.: Brookings Institution: 1995, p. 372; For the stakeholders model for corporate governance, see also Mitchell R.K. / Agle B.R. / Wood D.J.: "Toward a theory of stakeholder identification and salience Defining the principle of who and what really counts". *Academy of Management Review*, Vol. 22, No. 4, 1997, pp. 853–886; Aguilera R. / Jackson G.: "The cross-national diversity of corporate governance Dimensions and determinants". *Academy of Management Review*, Vol. 28, No. 3, 2003, pp. 447–465; Roe, Mark J.: "Political preconditions to separating ownership from corporate control". *Stanford Law Review*, Vol. 53, No. 3, 2000, pp. 539–606.

590 Du Plessis, Hargovan and Bagaric define corporate governance as:

> The system of regulating and overseeing corporate conduct and of balancing the interests of all internal stakeholders and other parties (external stakeholders, governments and local communities) who can be affected by the corporation's conduct in order to ensure responsible behavior by corporations and to achieve the maximum level of efficiency and profitability for a corporation.

Du Plessis, Jean J. / Hargovan, Anil / Bagaric, Mirko: *Principles of Contemporary Corporate Governance*. Cambridge University Press: 2nd Edition, 2011, p. 10. This approach is well exemplified by the German rule that the corporation should be run in the "interest of the enterprise", which is defined as a combination of shareholders, employees, and other stakeholders' interests. Medill, Joseph: "The floor speech". *Columbia Law Review*, Vol. 94, No.1, 1.1994.

Merkt, Hanno: "Germany – Internal and External Corporate Governance". In: Fleckner, Andreas M. / Hopt, Klaus J. (eds.): *Comparative Corporate Governance: A Functional and International Analysis*. Cambridge University Press: 2013, pp. 521–571. A similar approach is followed in the Netherlands and the Nordic countries, where maximizing "enterprise value", as a combination of shareholder and stakeholder value, is seen as the main corporate purpose. Hopt, Klaus J.: "Comparative Corporate Governance: The State of the Art and International Regulation". *American Journal of Comparative Law*, Vol. 59, No. 1, 2011, pp. 1–83, 30; Schneper, William D. / Guillén, Mauro F.: "Stakeholder Rights and Corporate Governance: A Cross-National Study of Hostile Takeovers". *Administrative Science Quarterly*, Vol. 49, No. 2, 2004, pp. 263–295, 268; Marcoux, Alexei M.: "A Fiduciary Argument against Stakeholder Theory". *Business Ethics Quarterly*, Vol. 13, No. 1, 1.2003, pp. 1–24, 15.

591 There is a significant amount of legal literature on the topic. For examples, see Mitchell, Lawrence E.: "A Theoretical and Practical Framework for Enforcing Corporate Constituency Statutes". *Texas Law Review*, Vol. 70, No. 3, 1992, pp. 579–643; Wallman S.: "The Proper Interpretation of Corporate Constituency Statutes and Formulation of Director Duties". *Stetson Law Review*, Vol. 21, No. 1, 1991, pp. 163–196; Hanks J. Jr.: "Playing With Fire: Nonshareholder Constituency Statues in the 1990s". *Stetson Law Review*, Vol. 21, No. 1, 1991, pp. 97–120; Orts E.: "Beyond

that financial innovation in the commercial world means that shareholder primacy is problematic[592] and it has been pointed out that contracts drafted by creditors of the corporation frequently restrict the implementation of shareholder primacy.[593] One commentator has noted that it is possible to observe a shift in the greater employment of stakeholder rhetoric in the documents and communications of large US companies.[594] There is even case in the US specifically holding that no duty is imposed on directors to maximize shareholder wealth.[595]

According to the shareholder primacy, all it does is merely benefit shareholders and only – perhaps – some of the shareholders at that. In any event, the shareholder primacy approach might move managers to transfer value to shareholders away from other stakeholders to ensure that the former gains benefits rather than increasing overall value and making the wealth of the entity greater.[596] It is more efficient for the managers to run the business to benefit the shareholders because the directors can work more efficiently if they are focused only on one objective and the interests of one type of stakeholder and shareholders have the greatest incentive to monitor the directors' managing role, which will lead to increased benefits for all.[597]

Shareholders: Interpreting Corporate Constituency Statutes". *George Washington Law Review*, Vol. 61, No. 1, 1993, pp. 14–135; Springer J.: "Corporate Constituency Statutes: Hollow Hopes and False Fears" *Annual Survey of American Law*, Vol. 1999, No. 1, 1999, pp. 85–128; Hale K.: "Corporate Law and Stakeholders: Moving Beyond Stakeholder Statutes". *Arizona Law Review*, Vol. 45, No. 3, 2003, pp. 823–856; Bisconti A.: "The Double Bottom Line: Can Constituency Statutes Protect Socially Responsible Corporations Stuck in Revlon Land?". *Loyola of Los Angeles Law Review*, Vol. 42, No. 3, 2009, pp. 765–806.

592 See Baird, Douglas G. / Henderson, M. Todd: "Other People's Money". *Stanford Law Review*, Vol. 60, No. 5, 2008, pp. 1309–1343; Partnoy F.: "Financial Innovation in Corporate Law". *Iowa Journal of Corporation Law*, Vol. 31, 2006, pp. 799–828.

593 See Tung F.: "The New Death of Contract: Creeping Corporate Fiduciary Duties for Creditors". *Emory Law Journal*, Vol. 57, 2008, pp. 809–871, 853.

594 See Fairfax L.: "The Rhetoric of Corporate Law: The Impact of Rhetoric on Corporate Norms". *Journal of Corporation Law*, Vol. 31, No. 3, 2006, pp. 875–718; Fairfax L.: "Easier Said Than Done? A Corporate Law Theory for Actualizing Social Responsibility Rhetoric". *Florida Law Review*, Vol. 59, No. 4, 9.2007, pp. 771–828, 771.

595 For example, see Paramount Communications Inc v Time Inc 571 A. 2d 1140, 1150 (Del, 1989).

596 While it is often said that all constituencies benefit from the directors being focused on maximizing shareholder wealth, it is difficult to see all constituencies benefiting and one commentator actually restricts himself to saying "many constituents" benefit. See MacIntosh, Jeffrey G.: "Designing an Efficient Fiduciary Law". *The University of Toronto Law Journal*, Vol. 43, No. 3, Special Issue on Corporate Stakeholder Debate: The Classical Theory and Its Critics, Summer 1993, pp. 425–473, 456.

597 See Smith, Thomas A.: "The Efficient Norm for Corporate Law: A Neo-traditional Interpretation of Fiduciary Duty". *Michigan Law Review*, Vol. 98, No.1, 1999, pp. 214–269, 215.

If directors and managers owed duties to various constituencies, then it would be impossible for directors to balance all of the divergent interests and managers would make poor decisions.[598] However, Claudio F. Loderer, Lukas Roth, Urs Waelchli and Petra Joerg demonstrate that economic theory – upon which shareholder primacy prides itself – does not show that shareholder primacy is best for society as a whole.[599] In fact, shareholder primacy can lead to costs to society as a whole owing to the increased costs of corporations in doing business with constituencies who assume that the corporation's managers might be forced to violate their trust and good faith by engaging in activity that maximizes shareholder wealth.[600] If managers have shareholder value as their aim, this could lead to the corporation failing to pay its creditors and employees, because managers may have adopted excessive risk in trying to pursue big deals. Embracing some of the risky opportunities provided by capital markets will increase the expected value of shares, although it will reduce the value of other claims, "thus decreasing the expected value of the sum of financial claims against the firm"[601]. An obvious example is the closing down of a factory and/or making some employees redundant to save on outgoings that can be transferred in the form of dividends to shareholders and the boosting of the share price.[602]

Given that the shareholders are merely one group among many who are affected by the corporation's actions, why should they benefit in priority to others? The preference for shareholder primacy is often said to be a consequence of a concern that the business should be run for the benefit of the residual claimants and while the corporation is solvent the claimants are the shareholders.[603] Shareholders' claim not only comes last, but necessarily in no fixed amount: their contract with the corporation is highly incomplete, specifying neither a date for repayment of their investment nor a rate of dividend return. This would seem to leave them highly

598 See Committee on Corporate Law, Other Constituency Statutes: "Potential for Confusion". *The Business Lawyer*, Vol. 45, No. 4, 1990, pp. 2253–2271, 2269.

599 See Loderer C. / Roth L. / Waelchli U. / Joerg P.: "Shareholder Value: Principles, Declarations, and Actions". *Financial Management*, Vol. 39, No. 1, Spring 2010, pp. 5–32.

600 See Wallman S.: "The Proper Interpretation of Corporate Constituency Statutes and Formulation of Director Duties". *Stetson Law Review*, Vol. 21, No. 1, 1991, pp. 163–196.

601 See Smith, Thomas A.: "The Efficient Norm for Corporate Law: A Neo-traditional Interpretation of Fiduciary Duty". *Michigan Law Review*, Vol. 98, No.1, 1999, pp. 214–269, 220.

602 This situation occurred when two mammoth corporations – Royal Dutch Shell and Anglo-American – made a large number of workers redundant. See, Robertson D.: "Shell cuts jobs as profits plunge 70%". *The Times*, 30.7.2009; Keay A.: "Ascertaining the Corporate Objective: An Entity Maximization and Sustainability Model". *Modern Law Review*, Vol. 71, No. 5, 9.2008, pp. 663–698, 677–681.

603 See Easterbrook, Frank H. / Fischel, Daniel R.: *The Economic Structure of Corporation Law*. Harvard University Press: Cambridge, Mass, 1991, pp. 36–39.

vulnerable to exploitation by those in control of the corporation.[604] Furthermore, shareholders do not have a right to possess and use corporate assets as they would their own; instead, they create a fictitious person to conduct business, with the shareholders as the beneficiaries. Thus, there is a problem of ensuring that the hired managers run the corporation in the interests of the shareholders,[605] who exhibit information vulnerability because managers have access to information about the day-to-day operations, the successes and failures as well as the financial inflows and outflows of the firm.[606]

There are a significant number of persons – other than shareholders – who can be said to be residual claimants. This is especially the case if one accepts that the corporation is a nexus of contracts whereby there are many persons constituting the nexus that can be said to be residual claimants. The nexus of contracts means that the corporation is to be seen as nothing more than a number of complex, private, consensual transactions or contract-based relations – either express or implied – and they comprise many different kinds of relations that are worked out by those voluntarily associating in a corporation.[607] Many stakeholders such as creditors, managers, employees, suppliers, customers and communities make firm-specific

---

604 See Baums, Theodor / Scott, Kenneth E.: "Taking Shareholder Protection Seriously? Corporate Governance in the United States and Germany". *The American Journal of Comparative Law*, Vol. 53, No. 1, 2005, pp. 31–75, 34. "Equity investors are paid last, after debt investors, employees, and other investors with (relatively) "fixed" claims. These equity investors have the "residual" claim in the sense that they get only what is left over-but they get all of what is left over." Easterbrook, Frank H. / Fischel, Daniel R.: *The Economic Structure of Corporation Law*. Harvard University Press: Cambridge, Mass, 1991, p. 18; Cronqvist, Henrik / Nilsson, Mattias: "Agency Costs of Controlling Minority Shareholders". *The Journal of Financial and Quantitative Analysis*, Vol. 38, No. 4, 12.2003, pp. 695–719; Jensen M.C. / Mecklin W.H.: "Theory of the firm Managerial behavior, agency costs and ownership structure". *Journal of Financial Economics*, Vol. 3, No. 4, 1976, pp. 305–360; Schneper, William D. / Guillén, Mauro F.: "Stakeholder Rights and Corporate Governance: A Cross-National Study of Hostile Takeovers". *Administrative Science Quarterly*, Vol. 49, No. 2, 2004, pp. 263–295.

605 Boatright, John R.: "Fiduciary Duties and the Shareholder-Management Relation: Or, What's so special about Shareholders?". *Business Ethics Quarterly*, Vol. 4, No. 4, 10.1994, pp. 393–407, 394.

606 See Marcoux, Alexei M.: "A Fiduciary Argument against Stakeholder Theory". *Business Ethics Quarterly*, Vol. 13, No. 1, 1.2003, pp. 1–24, 12, 13; Easterbrook, Frank H. / Fischel, Daniel R.: *The Economic Structure of Corporation Law*. Harvard University Press: Cambridge, Mass, 1991, p. 93.

607 Easterbrook, Frank H. / Fischel, Daniel R.: "The Corporate Contract". *Columbia Law Review*, Vol. 89, No. 7, Contractual Freedom in Corporate Law, November, 1989, pp. 1416–1448, 1426.

investments that tie their economic fortunes to the firm's fate.[608] The effect of invoking a shareholder primacy approach is, arguably, to damage the incentives of non-shareholding stakeholders to make firm-specific investments in corporations as they are aware that their investments will be subordinated to shareholder interests at all times.[609]

For example, employees invest firm-specific human capital in the corporation, which places them in a position where they are vulnerable to management caprice:[610] if the corporation is liquidated they will lose their jobs, which are based on their particular skills. Furthermore, the managers and other employees might be entitled to compensation based on performance rather than – or in addition to – a fixed salary, whereby if the corporation fails they will not receive these benefits. Professor Luigi Zingales has posited that human capital has become the most important asset in today's firm.[611] This certainly means that we need to reconsider the idea that the shareholders are special or at least more special than people such as the providers of critical human capital. Both shareholders and employees bear some of the risk of the enterprise, although shareholders bear the preponderance and provide insurance for employees.[612] The survival of the firm is often much more important for its employees than for its shareholders, who can always diversify their risk by investing in different companies.[613] In fact, shareholders are rarely called upon to make decisions about significant issues. Their control over a firm lies more on the governance structures that they have accepted, including the delegation of the most power to a board of directors. Similarly, the control exercised by employees lies less in making specific decisions and more in their contribution to establishing the general features of the employment relation that prevails in most firms. Furthermore, insofar as there are marked differences among the employment relations in

608 Blair, Margaret M. / Stout L.: "Director Accountability and the Mediating Role of the Corporate Board". *Washington University Law Quarterly*, Vol. 79, No. 2, 2001, pp. 403–448, 418.

609 Kelly G. / Parkinson J.: "The Conceptual Foundations of the Corporation: a Pluralist Approach". In: Parkinson J. / Gamble A. / Kelly G. (eds.): *The Political Economy of the Corporation*. Hart Publishing: 2000, p. 131.

610 See O'Connor, Marleen A.: "The Human Capital Era: Re-conceptualizing Corporate Law to Facilitate Labor-Management Cooperation". *Cornell Law Review*, Vol. 78, No. 5, 1993, pp. 899–965, 905–917.

611 See Zingales L.: "In Search of New Foundations". *Journal of Finance*, Vol. 55, No. 4, 2000, pp. 1623–1653, 1643.

612 See Boatright, John R.: "Employee Governance and the Ownership of the Firm". *Business Ethics Quarterly*, Vol. 14, No. 1, 1.2004, pp. 1–21, 13.

613 See Boatright, John R.: "Fiduciary Duties and the Shareholder-Management Relation: Or, What's so special about Shareholders?". *Business Ethics Quarterly*, Vol. 4, No. 4, 10.1994, pp. 393–407, 396.

different countries, these can be attributed to the different choices made during a long history of development.[614]

First, shareholder rights do not constitute the whole of ownership shared by other corporate constituencies including the labor. In Bligh v Brent, the court pointed out that: "The notion that the shareholders of the corporation own the corporation goes back to the days of the early joint stock companies when they were, whether incorporated or not, perceived by the law as partnerships, and, of course, partners can be said to own partnership assets. In these joint stock companies the shareholders had equitable ownership of the assets and they controlled the directors. But things changed with the development of the corporation as we know it today, and the shareholders were regarded as having no direct interest in corporation assets. They were not entitled to the corporation's earnings, and they merely had the right to dividends and to transfer their shares."[615] Accordingly, ownership should not be conceived as a specific set of rights such as the rights to residual revenues and to ultimate control but, rather, as a set of rights that secures a claim on revenues of whatever kind. If this definition is adopted, other groups besides shareholders are owners of a firm.[616] Given that this is not the case in large corporations, whereby there are other stakeholders like creditors and employees who also bear the risk, the residual should also go to these stakeholders. One solution is that stakeholders should share in the capital of the firm in proportion to their specific "investment" in the firm.[617] "More subtly – and perhaps more importantly – long-term employees make significant investments in firm-specific human capital. Any employee who advances to senior management levels necessarily invests considerable time and effort in learning how to do his job more effectively. Much of this knowledge will be specific to the firm for which he works. Moreover, the longer he works for the firm, the more firm-specific his human capital becomes. Such an employee is likely to make better decisions for the firm than an outsider, even assuming equal levels of information relating to the decision at hand. The insider can put the decision in a broader context, seeing the relationships and connections that it has to the firm as whole."[618]

Second, employee governance needs not be in conflict with shareholder governance, given a full understanding of ownership,[619] rather than conflicting, the two

614 Boatright, John R.: "Employee Governance and the Ownership of the Firm". *Business Ethics Quarterly*, Vol. 14, No. 1, 1.2004, pp. 1–21, 15.

615 Bligh v Brent, 2 Y & C Ex 268(1837).

616 See Boatright, John R.: "Employee Governance and the Ownership of the Firm". *Business Ethics Quarterly*, Vol. 14, No. 1, 1.2004, pp. 1–21, 12.

617 See Janssen E.: "The Stakeholder Model: The Influence of the Ownership and Governance Structures". *Journal of Business Ethics*, Vol. 56, No. 4, 2005, pp. 1–13, 4

618 Bainbridge, Stephen M.: *The New Corporate Governance in Theory and Practice.* Oxford University Press: 7.2008, p. 190.

619 "On such a view, every asset provided to a firm is accompanied by an ownership structure that entails some set of rights. These rights include a claim on a firm's revenues and control of certain assets. The major factors that determine

forms of governance are complementary and mutually beneficial. In particular, decision making is shared in such a way that the two groups make decisions on matters where they have superior information and an incentive to increase the value of the firm.[620] The presence of employee representatives on the board may improve the information available to the board because the information that the (supervisory) board receives from the company is filtered by the management. The employee representatives are usually members of the works council and as such they have thorough information about what is going on at the grassroots level of the company. Some seats of the labor side – at least in Germany – are filled directly by trade unions and most of the other employee representatives are trade union members. The labor constituency and the trade unions expect to be informed by their representatives.[621]

Third, codetermination is said to have contributed to a more peaceful climate between capital and labor, fewer strikes and better cooperation of both sides in the interest of the economy as a whole.[622] In Germany, management and shareholders' representatives who have sought to avoid confrontations with the powerful German trade unions – which could have provoked strikes – have generally been reluctant to openly challenge the legitimacy and usefulness of parity codetermination. From the viewpoint of the enterprise, the merit of codetermination is that it has proven to be an early warning system for social conflicts and that it helps to keep down strikes. It further triggers the networking and interest-balancing powers of the supervisory board.[623] Moreover, foreign businessmen – who until recently just could not

---

the specific form of ownership are asset specificity, information asymmetries, risk preferences, and transaction and agency costs." Boatright, John R.: "Employee Governance and the Ownership of the Firm". *Business Ethics Quarterly*, Vol. 14, No. 1, 1.2004, pp. 1–21, 16.

620 "While there is a mandatory rule on boardroom secrecy, in practice this is often not respected. Even inside information slips out to employees and trade unions, the European Court of Justice has clearly stated that codetermination cannot justify such a leak." Boatright, John R.: "Employee Governance and the Ownership of the Firm". *Business Ethics Quarterly*, Vol. 14, No. 1, 1.2004, pp. 1–21, 17.

621 "The danger of such leaks may make the management reluctant to inform the (supervisory) board of inside information. Whether an increased flow of (non-inside) information about corporate strategy to trade unions reduces the likelihood of management and union misunderstanding their respective positions in collective bargaining is rather speculative." Davies, Paul L. / Hopt, Klaus J.: "Corporate Boards in Europe – Accountability and Convergence". *American Journal Comparative Law*, Vol. 61, No. 2, 2013, pp. 301–375, 343.

622 See Hopt, Klaus J.: "Labor Representation on Corporate Boards: Impacts and Problems for Corporate Governance and Economic Integration in Europe". *International Review of Law and Economics*, Vol. 14, No. 2, 6.1994, pp. 203–214, 212.

623 On the case of Franz Bsirske – head of the United Services Union and member of the supervisory board of Lufthansa – who organised a strike of the union members at the expense of the airline in 2002, see Hopt, Klaus J.: „Interessenwahrung

comprehend the concept of codetermination and who were astounded by the complex and extensive German rules – are embedded in a more comprehensive system of mostly friendly labor relations – relations that have helped Germany to recover quickly and thoroughly from the GFC of 2007–2008 and the European financial crisis of 2009–2011.[624] In an interview from 26 October 2009, Siemens chief executive Peter Löscher stated: "In my view codetermination is an advantage of Germany as a business location."[625] Within the context of the social norms that make up the fabric of Germany's post-war capitalist system, empowering shareholders via procedural devices is unlikely to transform the system into a shareholder-centered model.[626]

In sum, the shareholder primacy theory definitely has some strong points, such as the focus on a single objective that can facilitate more certain management,[627]

---

und Interessenkonflikte im Aktien-, Bank- und Berufsrecht – Zur Dogmatik des modernen Geschäftsbesorgungsrechts". *Zeitschrift für Unternehmens- und Gesellschaftsrecht*, Vol. 3, No. 1, 2.2004, pp. 1–184, 4.

624 "Foreign investment companies and foreign hedge funds are now coming to the German markets in unexpected numbers and buying up companies which, they think, are poorly managed. They show less consideration for the employees' interests when reorganizing those companies in their search for more profitability. Following an expression used by a former German top politician these foreign investment companies and hedge funds are now called 'locusts'. That expression reflects apprehensions in Germany that such 'Locusts' will carve up the companies acquired by them and will suck them dry with no regard for the interests of their employees before reselling them at huge profits to somebody else. In many cases this is a distorted picture of the role of investment companies and hedge funds." A. Sorkin: "Germany's Blackstone Deal Swats Down "Locust" Talk". *New York Times*, April 24th, 2006; Dougherty C.: "The Buzz on German Private Equity". *The Economist International Herald Tribune* 20.10.2006; Benoit, Bertrand: "German Deputy Still Targets "Locusts"". *Financial Times* 14.2.2007; Gow D.: "Germany fears the New "Locusts"", *Guardian*, 4.6.2008; Plessis J.J. Du / Großfeld B. / Luttermann C. / Saenger I. / Sandrock O.: *German Corporate Governance in International and European Context.* Springer: 2nd Edition, 2012, pp. 172, 191.

625 *Berliner Morgen post* 26.10.2009.

626 Milhaupt, Curtis J. / Pistor, Katharina: *Law and Capitalism: What Corporate Crises Reveal about Legal Systems and Economic Development around the World.* University of Chicago Press: 2008, p. 84.

627 "It was noted earlier that the theory relies on the argument that it fosters efficiency, particularly so as to produce social wealth. It is more efficient for the managers to run the business to benefit the shareholders because they have the greatest incentive to monitor the directors' managing role and this will lead to increased benefits for all. Furthermore, it is argued that it is more efficient if directors operate on the basis of maximizing shareholder wealth, because the least cost is expended in doing this." van der Weide M.: "Against Fiduciary Duties to Corporate Stakeholders". *Delaware Journal of Corporate Law*, Vol. 21, No. 1, 1996, pp. 27–86, 56–57; Smith, Thomas A.: "The Efficient Norm for Corporate Law: A Neo-traditional Interpretation of Fiduciary Duty". *Michigan Law Review*, Vol. 98, No.1, 1999, pp. 214–269, 215.

although it clearly has some major shortcomings and its foundations are questionable. While not forgotten, the continuing creation of shareholder value – the primary goal of the venture capitalist – must take its place alongside a host of other considerations. The problem lies not so much in finding weaknesses in shareholder primacy but, rather, in the desperate need for a new approach to replace the theory.[628]

C. The Third Road of Corporate Governance in the US

The rise of independent directors and the decline of cumulative voting show that the US corporate law has adopted a neutral way of protecting minorities by providing independent directors on the board rather than minority representation, which is regarded by opponents as a system inconsistent with the notion that a director should properly represent all interest groups rather than the interests of a special constituency within a corporation.[629] The independent directors may add independent, critical scrutiny of management action to the board[630] and provide a means for virtual representation of majority interests by a well-motivated minority,[631] rather than minority representation. More to the point, the independent directors may prevent the misuse of cumulative voting, which makes the directors solely responsible for ensuring the minority shareholders' benefit rather than that of the whole corporation. On the other hand, independent directors can protect small shareholders against large shareholders, who use their voting power to select directors and managers who will do their bidding at the expense of the powerless minority.

This paper questions whether the goal of shareholder maximization is efficient: "the directors can work more efficiently if they are focused only on one objective and the interests of one type of stakeholder. If managers owed duties to various constituencies, then it would be impossible for directors to balance all of the divergent interests, with the result that managers would make poor decisions."; Committee on Corporate Law, Other Constituency Statutes: "Potential for Confusion". *The Business Lawyer*, Vol. 45, No. 4, 1990, pp. 2253–2271, 2269.

628 See Keay, Andrew: "Shareholder Primacy in Corporate Law: Can it Survive? Should it Survive?". *European Company and Financial Law Review*, Vol. 7, No. 3, 2010, pp. 369–413, 413.

629 "The corporate governance reforms that followed in the wake of the 2001–2002 corporate failures were mainly initiated to align the interests between managers and the often-passive investors by focusing on the independence and composition of the board of directors, auditing and remuneration processes, risk management systems and strict disclosure rules." Kraakman, Reinier / Armour, John / Davies, Paul / Enriques, Luca / Hansmann, Henry B. / Hertig, Gérard / Hopt, Klaus J. / Kanda, Hideki / Rock, Edward B.: *The anatomy of corporate law – A Comparative and Functional Approach*. Oxford University Press: 2nd Edition, 2009, p. 66.

630 See Gordon, Jeffrey N.: "Institutions as Relational Investors: A New Look at Cumulative Voting". *Columbia Law Review*, Vol. 94, No. 1, 1.1994, pp. 124–192, 170.

631 See Gordon, Jeffrey N.: "Institutions as Relational Investors: A New Look at Cumulative Voting". *Columbia Law Review*, Vol. 94, No. 1, 1.1994, pp. 124–192, 171.

It is also suggested that the value of cumulative voting as a safeguard of minority rights has probably been overestimated and its absence is compensated by an increased measure of responsibility placed on the directors regardless of whether they are elected by minority shareholders. On the one side, fiduciary duties are originated to protect stockholders, who own the corporation – in the sense that they own equity investments in the corporate entity – but have limited control over it.[632] "It is well established that the directors owe their fiduciary obligation to the corporation and its shareholders."[633] According to the prevailing agency theory,[634] managers are the agents of the shareholders, being employed to run the public corporation's business for the shareholders who do not have the time or ability to do so. The upshot is that shareholder primacy means that both the managers and the independent directors are fully accountable to shareholders for what they do in running the corporation's business.[635] Under the DGCL, the duties of care and loyalty that directors owe to their corporation translate for practical purposes into a duty to serve the interests of the shareholders,[636] although a duty to creditors arises as the company approaches insolvency.[637] The statement that the directors should act "in the best interests of the corporation" has been interpreted to "represent a fiduciary duty to a company and its shareholders"[638] and to express a duty "to promote

---

632 See N. Am. Catholic Educ. Programming Found., Inc. v. Gheewalla, 930 A.2d 101 ("Delaware corporate law provides for a separation of control and ownership. The directors of Delaware corporations have 'the legal responsibility to manage the business of a corporation for the benefit of its shareholders owners.' Accordingly, fiduciary duties are imposed upon the directors to regulate their conduct when they perform that function.").

633 N. Am. Catholic Educ. Programming Found., Inc. v. Gheewalla, 930 A.2d 92, 99 (Del. 2007) (holding that creditors of a corporation in the zone of insolvency may not assert direct claims for breach of fiduciary duty because they are protected by contract terms, fraudulent conveyance law, and other law, while fiduciary duties exist to protect stockholders).

634 This is based on a large number of influential works: Jensen M.C. / Mecklin W.H.: "Theory of the firm: Managerial behavior, agency costs and ownership structure". *Journal of Financial Economics*, Vol. 3, No. 4, 1976, pp. 305–360; Fama, Eugene: "Agency Problems and the Theory of the Firm". *The Journal of Political Economy*, Vol. 88, No. 2, 1980, pp. 288–307; Fama, E.F. / Jensen M.C.: "The separation of ownership and control". *Journal of Law and Economics*, Vol. 26, No. 2, 1983, pp. 301–328; Easterbrook, Frank H. / Fischel, Daniel R.: *The Economic Structure of Corporation Law*. Harvard University Press: Cambridge, Mass, 1991, pp. 36–39.

635 See Keay, Andrew: "Shareholder Primacy in Corporate Law: Can it Survive? Should it Survive?". *European Company and Financial Law Review*, Vol. 7, No. 3, 2010, pp. 369–413, 381.

636 See Aronson, et al v. Lewis, 473 A 2d 805 (Del 1984).

637 See e.g. Credit Lyonnais Bank Nederland NV v. Pathe Communications Corp., 1991 WL 277, 613 (Del. Ch. 1991).

638 See Central Iowa Power Co-op. v. Consumers Energy, 741 NW 2d 822 (2007).

the interest of the shareholders"[639]. The decision-makers entrusted by shareholders must act out of loyalty to those shareholders and in good faith act to make informed decisions on behalf of the shareholders, untainted by self-interest. Where they fail to do so, this court stands ready to remedy breaches of fiduciary duty. Put briefly, shareholder voting rights are supplemented by an affirmative duty of loyalty of the managers to shareholders as the bottom line of minority shareholders' protection.

On the other side, fiduciary duty can prevent the abuse of rights by minority shareholders. An increasingly common factual scenario that raises such questions is that involving the responsibilities of individuals who may be elected to the board by – and thus may seemingly "represent" – particular constituencies of the corporation.[640] The directors elected by majority shareholders is supposed to represent all of the shareholders, while in practice a board elected in its entirety by the controlling shareholders without the concurrence of the minority or in opposition to them certainly is not the alter ego of the minority. A board elected by cumulative voting and consequently comprising minority as well as majority representatives qualifies as the alter ego of all of the shareholders, except of course in transactions where the interests of the majority and minority shareholders are in conflict. In those situations, the directors are fiduciaries of the minority.[641] There remains truth in the words of Louis D. Brandeis, stating that everyone should know that the denial of minority representation on boards of directors has resulted in the domination of most corporations by one or two men and in practically banishing all criticism of the dominant power. Indeed, even where the board is not so dominated, there is too often that "harmonious cooperation" among directors, which secures for each – in his own line – a due share of the corporation's favors.[642] In fairness, all of the directors should bear a share of the responsibility associated with the prerogatives

639 See Storetrax.com. Inc. v. Gurland, 915 A. 2d 991, 1000 (Md. Ct. Spec. App.2007).

640 "They may be called "constituency directors" or "representative directors." Examples include directors designated by creditors, venture capitalists, labor unions, controlling or other substantial stockholders, or preferred stockholders; directors elected by a particular class of stockholders or by a minority interest under a cumulative voting scheme; or directors representing other constituencies." See, e.g. , Cyril Moscow, The Representative Director Problem, Insights, June 2002, p. 6 (noting many of these categories of representative directors); Terence Woolf, The Venture Capitalist's Corporate Opportunity Problem, Columbia Business Law Review, Vol. 2001, No. 2, pp. 473–508 (suggesting that the application of the traditional duty of loyalty rubric and corporate opportunity test in the venture capital context "has the potential to harm capital formation and business development" because they are based on an "anachronistic and ineffectual" "notion that directors and officers owe their undivided loyalty to a single company and its shareholders").

641 Jones v. H. F. Ahmanson & Co., 1 Cal. 3d 93, 460 P.2d 464, 81 Cal. Rptr. 592 (1969).

642 See Baird, Douglas G. / Henderson, M. Todd: "Other People's Money". *Stanford Law Review*, Vol. 60, No. 5, 2008, pp. 1309–1343.

of the office.[643] The idea is that directors supported by institutional investors or other qualified minorities would be subversive elements of disruption discounts, including the role of fiduciary duties in constraining directors' actions.[644] To the extent that constituency directors confront real tensions between their fiduciary duties and the expectations of their sponsors, fiduciary duties require directors to generally be responsible for protecting the best interests of the corporation and all its stockholders, despite the directors' designation by some particular constituency.[645] "The directors owe their fiduciary duties to the corporation and directors may be permitted to take into account the interests of other constituencies – or the corporation itself to the extent that the corporation's interest differs from that of the stockholders – when making board decisions. Directors will generally be responsible for protecting the best interests of the corporation and all its stockholders, despite the directors' designation by some particular constituency, because fiduciary duties generally will trump contractual expectations in the corporate context. Constituency directors may face greater risks of liability for breach of fiduciary duty if constituency directors constitute a majority of the board than if they are only a minority of the board."[646] Even if the minority shareholders elect the board, directors need not necessarily represent their interests.[647]

Legally speaking, the managers are employed by the corporation rather than the shareholders, whereby they are not the agents of the shareholders and they make contracts on behalf of the corporate entity. Even if one can argue that the managers and directors owe fiduciary duties to the shareholders as a group and that is highly debatable, there is nothing suggesting that fiduciary duties impose a demand that

643 See Hans A. Mattes, The Burden of the Corporate Director Elected Noncumulatively, California Law Review, Vol. 63, No. 2, March, 1975, pp. 463–470, 467.

644 See Ventoruzzo, Marco: "Empowering Shareholders in Directors' Elections: A Revolution in the Making". *European Company and Financial Law Review*, Vol. 8, No. 2, 6.2011, pp. 105–144, 143.

645 See Veasey, E. Norman / Di Guglielmo, Christine T.: "How Many Masters Can a Director Serve? A Look at the Tensions Facing Constituency Directors". *The Business Lawyer*, Vol. 63, No. 3, 5.2008, pp. 761–775, 775.

646 Veasey, E. Norman / Di Guglielmo, Christine T.: "How Many Masters Can a Director Serve? A Look at the Tensions Facing Constituency Directors". *The Business Lawyer*, Vol. 63, No. 3, 5.2008, pp. 761–775, 775.

647 See Shleifer, Andrei / Vishny, Robert W.: "A Survey of Corporate Governance". *Journal of Finance*, Vol. 52, No. 2, 1997, pp. 737–783, 751; N. Am. Catholic Educ. Programming Found., Inc. v. Gheewalla, 930 A.2d 103 (describing the fiduciary duties of directors of an insolvent corporation as a "duty to maximize the value of the insolvent corporation for the benefit of all those having an interest in it"); Unocal Corp. v. Mesa Petroleum Co., 493 A.2d 946, 954 ("[T]the boards power to act derives from its fundamental duty and obligation to protect the corporate enterprise, which includes stockholders. ...").

the corporation's business is to be run in a particular way[648] and certainly not purely based upon shareholder maximization. As the managers work for the corporation, at best the responsibilities owed to shareholders are only indirect.[649] Under the law of agency, principals are entitled to control their agents, although the managers and independent directors who make up the board are usually empowered to manage the corporation and they cannot be ordered what to do by the shareholders at the general meeting, given that the directors have the exclusive right to manage the corporation.[650] When discharging their functions, the directors are not agents of the shareholders but, rather, agents of the corporation.

This is the reality that if American corporate law makes all constituencies an end of corporate governance, American corporate lawmakers chose a decidedly unusual way to enable that equality. According to the view of Leo E. Strine, Jr, "there is any way to bridge the great divide between Bebchuk, on the one extreme, and those like Lynn Stout, on the other, as their positions are so starkly divergent". On the one hand, stockholders have formidable power under our system of corporate governance. In American corporate law, only stockholders get to elect directors, vote on corporate transactions and charter amendments and sue to enforce the corporation's compliance with the corporate law and the directors' compliance with their fiduciary duties. On the other hand, all fiduciaries within the accountability system for productive corporations should themselves be accountable for acting with fidelity to the best interests of the end-user investors, whose money is ultimately at stake. It might be possible to improve the system as it actually exists whereby it works better for both investors and society more generally.[651]

Therefore, the US has followed the third road of corporate governance, namely long governance, which, as a legal concept, is close to bedrock Delaware case law, stating that "directors, when acting deliberately, in an informed way, and in the good faith pursuit of corporate interests, may follow a course designed to achieve long-term value even at the cost of immediate value maximization" or that "directors of a Delaware corporation have the prerogative to determine that the market undervalues its stock and to protect its stockholders form offers that do not reflect the

648 See Marens, Richard / Wicks, Andrew: "Getting Real: Stakeholder Theory, Managerial Practice and the General Irrelevance of Fiduciary Duties Owed to Shareholders". *Business Ethics Quarterly*, Vol. 9, No. 2, 4.1999, pp. 273–293, 277.

649 See Millon, David: "Theories of the Corporation". *Duke Law Journal*, Vol. 1990, No. 2, 1995, pp. 201–262, 218.

650 See McDonnell, Breit H.: "Professor Bainbridge and the Arrowian Moment: A Review of the New Corporate Governance in Theory and Practice". *Delaware Journal of Corporate Law*, Vol. 34, No. 1, 2009, pp. 139–190, 165.

651 See Strine, Leo E. Jr.: "Can We Do Better by Ordinary Investors? A Pragmatic Reaction to the Dueling Ideological Mythologists of Corporate Law". *Columbia Law Review*, Vol. 114, No. 2, 3.2014, pp. 449–502, 474.

long-term value of the corporation under its present management plans".[652] Where there is a long-term approach involving capital being committed to the corporation indefinitely and the facilitation of the long-term capital growth of the corporation, it would seem that there is more possibility of enhancing social wealth.[653] The American Law Institute in its Principles of Corporate Governance explicitly recognizes that directors may focus on long-term profitability rather than short-term gain and that the interests or expectations of a corporation's various constituencies influence long-term profitability:

> *That the objective of the corporation is to conduct business activities with a view to enhancing corporate profit and shareholder gain does not mean that the objective of the corporation must be to realize corporate profit and shareholder gain in the short run. Indeed, the contrary is true: long-run profitability and shareholder gain are at the core of the economic objective. Activity that entails a short-run cost to achieve an appropriately greater long-run profit is therefore not a departure from the economic objective. An orientation toward lawful, ethical, and public-spirited activity will normally fall within this description. The modern corporation by its nature creates interdependencies with a variety of groups with whom the corporation has a legitimate concern, such as employees, customers, suppliers, and members of the communities in which the corporation operates. The long-term profitability of the corporation generally depends on meeting the fair expectations of such groups. Short-term profits may properly be subordinated to recognition that responsible maintenance of these interdependencies is likely to contribute to long-term corporate profit and shareholder gain. The corporation's business may be conducted accordingly.*[654]

This approach would tend to emphasize long-term value over short-term gain, even if certain constituencies would prefer a short-term gain, while leaving room for the board to decide how to allocate value when circumstances require a trade-off among constituencies. Fundamentally speaking, the American model of corporate governance is based on the fiduciary relationship of independent directors by frequently linking the business judgment rule to the decisions made by them.[655] The

---

652 See Unitrin v. American General Corp., 651 A.2d 1361, 1376 (Del. 1995). "The content long governance lends to directors' duties is the maximization of long-term corporate welfare, which is most diligently achieved through the pursuance of growth, i.e. business capital accumulation through the reinvestment of profits." Masouros, Pavlos E.: *Corporate Law and Economic Stagnation: How Shareholder Value and Short-Termism Contribute to the Decline of the Western Economies.* Eleven International Publishing: 28.1.2013, p. 277.

653 See Allen W.: "Ambiguity in Corporation Law". *Delaware Journal of Corporate Law,* Vol. 22, 1997, pp. 894–903, 896.

654 ALI Principles of Corporate Governance: Analysis and Recommendations § 2.01 cmt. f (1994).

655 Allen, William T.: "Independent Directors in MBO Transactions: Are They Fact or Fantasy?" *The Business Lawyer,* Vol. 45, No. 4, 8.1990, pp. 2055–2063, 2057; "As Chancellor Allen writes: Our statutory corporation law has long assumed

relationship between the far-reaching, always-applicable director duty of due care and the more finely drawn policy of non-review housed in the business judgment rule is one of the most important relationships in corporate law.[656] As Jill E. Fisch and Caroline M. Gentile proposed: "so long as adherence to procedural standards, coupled with the retention of outside professionals, is sufficient to insulate directors from personal accountability, there is little reason to expect directors to monitor management closely."[657] In this respect, I have to point out that in the US long governance, independent directors as well as fiduciary duty are designed to preserve the power of directors and managers in controlling the corporation.

D. Long-term Shareholder Engagement in the European Union

In terms of the European company law, Article 50(2)(g) of the Treaty on the Functioning of the European Union (hereinafter "TFEU") – which is the legal basis for Directive 2007/36/EC, providing competence to act in the area of corporate governance in the EU – provides in particular coordination measures concerning the protection of interests of companies' members and other stakeholders such as creditors with a view to making such protection equivalent throughout the union. According to the proposal, "effective and sustainable shareholder engagement is one of the cornerstones of listed companies' corporate governance model, which depends on checks and balances between the different organs and different stakeholders"[658]. "Appropriate standards ensuring a well-functioning corporate governance of these companies with a view to their long-term sustainability are thus in the interest not only of

---

that disinterested directors can exercise a business judgment unaffected by the fact that the CEO of the firm may be self-interested. Indeed, one of the principal threads in the development of corporation law over the past 20 years has been the emphasis on bringing more outside directors onto boards, and the creation of more board committees comprised of outside directors."; Cernat, Lucian: "The Emerging European Corporate Governance Model: Anglo-Saxon, Continental, or still the Century of Diversity?". *Journal of European Public Policy*, Vol. 11, No. 1, 2004, pp. 147–166, 150; Cede & Co. v. Technicolor, Inc., 634 A.2d 345, 360 (Del. 1993), modified, 636 A.2d 956 (Del. 1994); Citron v. Fairchild Camera & Instrument Corp., 569 A.2d 53, 64 (Del. 1989).

656 Johnson, Lyman: "The Modest Business Judgment Rule". *The Business Lawyer*, Vol. 55, No. 2, 2.2000, pp. 625–652, 636; Balotti, R. Franklin / Hanks, James J. Jr.: "Rejudging the Business Judgment Rule". *The Business Lawyer*, Vol. 48, No. 4, 1993, pp. 1337–1353, 1345.

657 Fisch, Jill E. / Gentile, Caroline M.: "The Qualified Legal Comp liance Committee: Using the Attorney Conduct Rules to Restructure the Board of Directors". *Duke Law Journal*, Vol. 53, No. 2003, p p. 517–584, 567.

658 The Proposal, (8).

Member States where these companies are based but also of those Member States where they operate. Only common EU action can ensure such common standards."[659]

The GCGC provides that "all members of the supervisory board are bound by the enterprise's interests".[660] The code "clarifies" the obligation of the management and supervisory boards to ensure the continued existence of the enterprise, as well as its sustainable creation of value in conformity with the principles of the social market economy".[661] The management board is responsible for independently managing the enterprise in its own best interest,[662] thus taking into account the interests of shareholders, employees and other stakeholders, with the objective of sustainable creation of value. Article 3.1 provides that the management board and supervisory board cooperate closely to the benefit of the enterprise. Networking with stakeholders and business partners and the balancing of interests within the corporation have been rated as indispensably valuable, particularly for resolving desperate situations. The meaning of "the benefit of the enterprise" has become clear despite the long term discussions concerning this.[663] According to the draft of the commission in the meeting on June 18, 2009, pursuing the benefit of the enterprise is regarded as a general principle and consistent with the principle of social market economy, which concerns the existence of the corporation and sustainable growth of corporate value and the interests of shareholders, employees and the other stakeholders of the company. The complete application of this concept – which always accompanies many reasonable alternatives from the crises – has not yet been successful (perhaps it is not feasible either). Nonetheless, the concept of "the benefit of the enterprise" can serve as a guiding idea for corporate governance. Therefore, corporate governance cannot ignore the stakeholder debate and the concept of corporate governance encompasses more than simply the creation of legal structures for decision-making and supervising the corporation.[664]

---

659 The Proposal, p. 3.

660 GCGC, Article 5.5.1.

661 GCGC, Foreword (2012).

662 GCGC, Foreword (2012), Article 4.1.1.

663 See Jungein FS v. Caemmerer, 1978, 547 ff.; Laske, Stephan: „Unternehmensinteresse und Mitbestimmung". *ZGR*, Vol. 8, No. 2, 1.1979, pp. 173–200, 175 ff.; Hopt, Klaus J.: "New Ways in Corporate Governance: European Experiments with Labor Representation on Corporate Boards". *Michigan Law Review*, Vol. 82, No. 5/6, Festschrift in Honor of Eric Stein (April – May, 1984), pp. 1338–1363, 1360; Kort, Michael: *Vorstandshandeln im Spannungsverhältnis zwischen Unternehmensinteresse und Aktionärsinteressen.* AG 2012, pp. 605–610, 605.

664 About the definitions of the whole benefit of corporations, see Cleland, Alan S. / Bruno, Albert V.: "Building value: Customer and shareholder". *Strategy & Leadership*, Vol. 25, No. 3, 1997, pp. 22–28, 24; Schmidt, Reinhard H. / Maßmann, Jens: *Drei Mißverständnisse zum Thema "Shareholder Value".* (Working Paper Series: Finance and Accounting 31) Goethe University Frankfurt am Main, Department of Finance: 2.1999, p. 149; Charreaux, Gerard / Desbrières, Philippe: „Corporate Governance: Stakeholder Value Versus Shareholder Value". *Journal of Management and*

In the view of the EU Action Plan: "Effective, sustainable shareholder engagement is one of the cornerstones of listed companies' corporate governance model, which depends inter alia on checks and balances between the different organs and different stakeholders. If the majority of shareholders remains passive, do not seek interaction with the company and do not vote, the functioning of the current corporate governance system is less effective. In such circumstances, no corrective action can be expected from the shareholders' side and supervision of management rests entirely on the shoulders of the (supervisory) board."[665] Modern European company law objectives as presented by the Commission in its Action Plan focus on two particular goals: to foster the efficiency and competitiveness of business; and in function of the first goal, to strengthen shareholders' rights and protection for employees, creditors and the other parties with which companies deal. The EU Green Paper 2011 refers to the possibility of giving further consideration to a number of specific proposals suggested by the Reflection Group in 2011 aimed at encouraging greater long-term shareholder engagement. These include granting increased voting rights or dividends to long-term investors.[666]

The objective of the proposal is the long-term sustainability of EU companies, to create an attractive environment for shareholders and enhance cross-border voting by improving the efficiency of the equity investment chain to contribute to growth, jobcreation and EU competitiveness. It also delivers on the commitment of the renewed strategy on the long-term financing of the European economy,[667]

Governance, Vol. 5, No. 2, 2001, pp. 107–128, 109; Schneider, Uwe H. / Strenger, Christian: „Corporate Governance -Grundsätze" (German Panel on Corporate Governance). *Die Aktiengesellschaft: AG*; Zeitschrift für das gesamte Aktienwesen, für deutsches, europäisches und internationales Unternehmens- und Kapitalmarktrecht, Vol. 45, No. 3, 2000, p. 106–113, 106–107; Berliner, Martin Peltzer / von Werder, Axel: „Der "German Code of Corporate Governance (GCCG)" des Berliner Initiativkreises". *Die Aktiengesellschaft: AG*, Vol. 46, 2001, pp. 1–15, 1–2; Grundmann, Stefan / Mülbert, Peter: "Corporate Governance – Europäische Perspektiven". *ZGR*, Vol. 30, No. 2, 2001, pp. 215–223, 215; Claussen, Carsten P. / Bröcker, Norbert: „Corporate-Governance-Grundsätze in Deutschland – nützliche Orientierungshilfe oder regulatorisches Übermass?". *Die Aktiengesellschaft: AG*, Vol. 45, No. 11, 2000, pp. 481–491.

665 EU Action Plan, Article 3.

666 See European Commission: *EU Green Paper on Long-Term Financing of the European Economy*, 25.3.2013, p. 14 ("Ideas have also been advanced to encourage greater long-term shareholder engagement, which could be subject to further consideration, such as analyzing the possibility of options around granting increased voting rights or dividends to long-term investors").

667 See European Commission: *Communication from the Commission to the European Parliament and the Council on Long-Term Financing of the European Economy*, 27.3.2014.

contributing to a more long-term perspective of shareholders, which ensures better operating conditions for listed companies.[668]

When governments propose deeper shareholder engagement with companies – for example the UK and the Netherland, as well as the EU[669] – they are probably thinking about engagement by long-only institutional shareholders, whose interests in the long-term success of the company broadly coincide with those of other stakeholders.[670] The emphasis on the engagement of shareholders is caused by the serious doubt of the independent directors in improving the corporate governance. The Report of the Reflection Group on the Future of EU Company Law[671] proposes that the widespread use of independent directors does not appear to have mitigated the crisis. This might be because they were never really "independent", given that they lacked the necessary expertise or experience or because of behavioral issues, such as "group think". A major problem might be the too much focus on independence at the expense of core business expertise. Furthermore, the issue of incentives must be addressed. In some jurisdictions, independent directors may be poorly paid but bear the same risk as any other director, whereas in some other jurisdictions there

668 The Proposal, p. 2.

669 EU Green Paper of 2011, p. 11.

670 "Activist shareholders, it can be argued, provide the mechanism whereby long-only investors overcome their collective action problems. Nevertheless, whilst long-only shareholders typically engage with investee company management in a reactive way, in order to preserve the value of investments made for non-activist reasons, activist hedge funds are proactive, i.e. they invest in order to reap benefits from changing the policies of the incumbent management. They tend to concentrate on proposing immediate and fairly radical changes to existing corporate strategy in order to increase the value of the company, with aim of exiting it after the changes have borne fruit. Interventions by activist shareholders can thus be seen a qualitatively different from interventions undertaken by long-only shareholders, even if the former type of intervention is dependent upon the support of the institutions. Activists' interventions are more likely to be resisted not only by incumbent management but also by other stakeholders, especially employees. Governments tend not to welcome such forms of engagement, because they are politically unpopular, but it is difficult to craft laws which facilitate long-term but not short-term engagement. Incentives to long-termism are an alternative approach which has been adopted in France and in the Netherlands." See for a general proposal Bolton, Patrick / Samama, Frédéric: "L-Shares: Rewarding Long-term Investors". *ECGI Finance Working Paper* No. 342/2013; "A similar but less extreme story can be told about France where reforms of 2001 promoting shareholder activism were supplemented by reforms in 2010 prohibiting opaque 'empty voting' and restricting activism by hedge funds." See Davies, Paul L. / Hopt, Klaus J.: "Corporate Boards in Europe – Accountability and Convergence". *American Journal Comparative Law*, Vol. 61, No. 2, 2013, pp. 301–375, 363.

671 See European Commission: *Report of the Reflection Group on the Future of EU Company Law*, 4.2011, chapter 3.1.6 (ii) pp. 51–52.

is no difference between the remuneration of independent and non-independent directors. Their compensation should be more attractive to better incentivize them, while also leading them to reduce the number of positions held.[672] Therefore, the European Commission gives broader focus not only to the role of proxy advisors and the transparency of their actions, but also the composition, functioning and evaluation of the board of directors and the long-term engagement of shareholders. It rests upon the assumption that if shareholders were infused with incentives that would allow them to develop long-term horizons, then their interests could be significantly aligned with those of the various stakeholders and predominantly the employees.[673] Put differently, in a world where an increasing percentage of a public firm's shareholder base would be long-termist, the de facto or de jure orientation of modern corporate governance towards shareholder value would not necessarily be at odds with the interests of the other stakeholders.[674]

E. The Combination of Shareholder-centered and Stakeholder-centered Model in China

To cope with the corporate governance problems in PLCs of China and promote the development of capital market, Company Law of 2005 adopted both cumulative voting (which is not popular in its motherland) and independent director system (which is the most significant system of corporate governance in the US). Consequently, both the supervisory board from the German model and independent directors from the American model have been brought into China's corporate governance system[675]

672 See The former Reflection Group on the Future of EU Company Law: "Response to the European Commission's Action Plan on Company Law and Corporate Governance". *European Company and Financial Law Review*, 2013, pp. 304–327, 316.

673 See McCahery, Joseph A. / Vermeulen, Erik P.M. / Hisatake, Masato: "The Present and Future of Corporate Governance: Re-examining the Role of the Board of Directors and Investor Relations in Listed Companies". *European Company and Financial Law Review*, 2013, pp. 117–163, 130.

674 See Masouros, Pavlos E.: *Corporate Law and Economic Stagnation: How Shareholder Value and Short-Termism Contribute to the Decline of the Western Economies.* Eleven International Publishing: 28.1.2013, p. 272.

675 In summary, the American and the German systems set their priorities in different areas. The American model focuses on the protection of shareholders, while the German model tends to equally protect the stakeholders of the companies by giving representations on the supervisory board to both of shareholders and employees. The German model is stakeholder-centered, under which the firm is an integral component of the social fabric and characterized by the intersecting interests of various stakeholders, including not only shareholders and managers but also employees, banks and the surrounding community. Regarding the differences between German model and American model, see generally Schneper, William D. / Guillén, Mauro F.: "Stakeholder Rights and Corporate Governance: A Cross-National Study of Hostile Takeovers". *Administrative Science Quarterly*, Vol. 49,

and the minority representatives elected through cumulative voting could be not only directors but also supervisors. In terms of the corporate governance value, the acceptance of independent directors does not definitely mean pursuing the maximization of shareholders' interests but, rather, trying to reach the long-term benefits of the whole corporations. In the Code, Article 81 stipulates that a listed company shall respect the legal rights of banks and other creditors, employees, consumers, suppliers, the community and other stakeholders. Specifically speaking, Article 82 provides that a listed company shall actively cooperate with its stakeholders and jointly advance the company's sustained and healthy development. Furthermore, according to Article 83, a company shall provide the necessary means to ensure the legal rights of stakeholders. Stakeholders shall have opportunities and channels for redress for infringement of rights. Article 84 provides that a company shall provide necessary information to banks and other creditors, enabling them to make judgments and decisions about the company's operating and financial situation. Article 85 stipulates that a company shall encourage employees' feedback regarding the company's operating and financial situations and important decisions affecting employees' benefits through direct communications with the board of directors, the supervisory board and the management personnel. Finally, Article 86 provides that besides maintaining the listed company's development and maximizing the benefits of shareholders, the company shall be concerned with the welfare, environmental protection and public interests of the community in which it resides, as well as shall pay attention to the company's social responsibilities.

No. 2, 2004, pp. 263–295; The stakeholder-centered view of the firm has been defined as the belief that "each group of stakeholders merits consideration for its own sake and not merely because of its ability to further the interests of some other group, such as shareowners". Donaldson, T., Preston L.E.: "The stakeholder theory of the corporation Concepts, evidence and implications". *Academy of Management Review*, Vol. 20, No. 1, 1995, pp. 65–91; See also Mitchell R.K. / Agle B.R. / Wood D.J.: "Toward a theory of stakeholder identification and salience Defining the principle of who and what really counts". *Academy of Management Review*, Vol. 22, No. 4, 1997, pp. 853–886; Blair, Margaret M.: *Ownership and Control: Rethinking Corporate Governance for the Twenty-first Century*. Washington, D.C.: Brookings Institution: 1995, pp. 62–64; Aguilera R. / Jackson G.: "The cross-national diversity of corporate governance Dimensions and determinants". *Academy of Management Review*, Vol. 28, No. 3, 2003, pp. 447–465; Roe, Mark J.: "Political preconditions to separating ownership from corporate control". *Stanford Law Review*, Vol. 53, No. 3, 2000, pp. 539–606.

I. Adoption of Independent Directors in Addition to the Board of Supervisors

In China, the adoption of the system of independent directors is due to the supervisory board, who played a minimal role as a watchdog, but served as a "rubber stamp" and fell short of the expectations of investors and legislators.[676] China has adopted the two-tier board structure comprising a board of directors and a supervisory board in the Company Law of 1993. The supervisory board comprises at least three members and includes representatives of shareholders and an appropriate percentage of representatives of the firm's employees.[677] Unlike the supervisory board in the German model, in China it has only a loosely defined monitoring role over the board of directors and managers.

First, the supervisors in China are not involved in the selection of directors and managers and have no means of disciplining them because the supervisory board and the board of directors are legally on the same hierarchical level.[678] In light of the insider corporate governance structure designed by the Company Law of 1993, the shareholders' meeting serves as the organ of super power. In such a corporate governance system, the shareholders can directly perform their rights to manage the corporation and monitor the management board through making decisions on major issues in general meetings, whereas the supervisory board only takes on part of the responsibility to monitor and control the board of directors and does not have the power to appoint and dismiss executive board directors. The shareholders' meeting can directly control the board of directors through making decisions on major issues, while the board of supervisors simply performs part of the task of monitoring and controlling and does not have strategic decision-making powers. Nonetheless, the board of supervisors in Germany has some power in management through Article 111 (4) of AktG, which provides that management responsibilities may not be conferred on the supervisory board. However, the articles or the supervisory board have

---

676 See Li Yanbing: "Gufen Youxian Gongsi Jianshihui Zhidu zhi Bijiao Yanjiu" [A Comparative Study on the Supervisory Board System of the Stock Corporation]. In: Shen Sibao (ed.): *International Business Law Review*, 2000, p. 264; On Kit Tam: "Ethical Issues in the Evolution of Corporate Governance in China". *Journal of Business Ethics*, May 2002, Vol. 37, No. 3, pp. 303–320, 307; Schipani, Cindy A. / Liu, Junhai: "Corporate Governance in China: Then and Now". *Columbia Business Law Review*, Vol. 2002, No. 1, 2002, pp. 1–69, 6–8; Lin, Thomas W.: "Corporate Governance in China: Recent Developments, Key Problems, and Solutions". *Journal of Accounting and Corporate Governance*, Vol. 1, No. 1, 6.2004, pp. 1–23, 7; Shan, Yuan G. / Taylor, Dennis W.: "Related-party disclosures in the two-tier board system in China: Influences of ownership structure and board composition". *Corporate Board: Role, Duties and Composition*, Vol. 4, No. 1, 2008, pp. 37–49, 40.

677 Company Law, Article 51.

678 See Lin, Thomas W.: "Corporate Governance in China: Recent Developments, Key Problems, and Solutions". *Journal of Accounting and Corporate Governance*, Vol. 1, No. 1, 6.2004, pp. 1–23, 7.

to determine that specific types of transactions may be entered into only with the consent of the supervisory board. The major powers of the supervisory board are representing shareholders to appoint and dismiss members of the managing board and the power to represent the company in its dealings with members of the management board.[679]

Second, the supervisory board, including employee representatives, is designed based on the view of stakeholder theory rather than protecting minority shareholders.[680] Article 51 provides that a limited liability company may set up a board of supervisors, which shall comprise at least three persons. A limited liability company that has relatively fewer shareholders or is relatively small in scale may have one or two supervisors, and does not have to establish a board of supervisors. The board of supervisors shall include representatives of shareholders and representatives of the employees of the company at an appropriate ratio, which shall be specifically stimulated in the articles of association. The employees' representatives – who are to serve as members of the board of supervisors – shall be democratically elected by the employees of the company through the assembly of the employees' representatives or the assembly of employees, or by any other means.

Third, in terms of the nomination of supervisors, Article 102 of the Company Law stipulates that "the shareholders separately or aggregately holding 3% or more of the shares of the company may put forward a written temporary proposal to the board of directors 10 days before a shareholders' assembly is held". The proposal includes the nomination of a candidate for the election of supervisors. However, separately or aggregately holding 3% or more of the shares is too much for many medium and small shareholders, who can barely reach it. It means that minority shareholders rarely have the chance to propose their candidates, not to mention successfully elect their supervisors by cumulative voting. Accordingly, Article 2.2.12 of the Guidelines of the Shenzhen Stock Exchange for Standardized Operation of Companies Listed on the Small and Medium-Sized Enterprise Board[681] provides that the "Shenzhen Stock Exchange encourages companies to adopt multi-candidate election and provide that the shareholders who alone or jointly hold 1% shares of the company can nominate

679 AktG 111(1) rules that the supervisory board shall supervise the management of the company. AktG 84 (1) rules that the supervisory board shall appoint the members of the management board for a period not exceeding five years.

680 See On Kit Tam: "Ethical Issues in the Evolution of Corporate Governance in China". *Journal of Business Ethics*, May 2002, Vol. 37, No. 3, pp. 303–320, 307; Dahya, Jay / Karbhari, Yusuf / Xiao, Jason Zezong / Yang, Mei: "The Usefulness of the Supervisory Board Report in China". *Corporate Governance: An International Review*, Vol. 11, No.4, 2003, pp. 308–321; Lin, Thomas W.: "Corporate Governance in China: Recent Developments, Key Problems, and Solutions". *Journal of Accounting and Corporate Governance*, Vol. 1, No. 1, 6.2004, pp. 1–23, 7.

681 Shenzhen Stock Exchange: *Guidelines of the Shenzhen Stock Exchange for Standardized Operation of Companies Listed on the Small and Medium-Sized Enterprise Board*, 28.7.2010.

the candidate of directors and supervisors before the convening of general meeting in their articles". Thus, the shareholders who, alone or jointly, hold 1% shares only have the right to nominate supervisors in the companies listed on the Small and Medium-Sized Enterprise Board of Shenzhen Stock Exchange.

According to Article 103, supervisors elected by the shareholders generally should be elected by the shareholders' meeting through straight voting in public companies, which may also lead to a majority-controlled board of supervisors.[682] Since there is no legal requirement that supervisors are independent, the controlling shareholder has good reasons to appoint "insiders" to the supervisory board to ensure its loyalty.[683] Shareholder representatives sitting on the supervisory board tend to lack independence from the controlling shareholders and the directors.

Thus, both directors and supervisors may be nominees of the controlling shareholder.[684] Normally, they are former colleagues in the controlling company and the relations between them are usually close and collegial in nature. What makes it worse is that supervisors are always administratively subordinate to the directors, in either the company's party committee or the controlling company. Many supervisors may owe their position and remuneration to the chair of the board or other senior executives.[685]

All these disincentives deter supervisors from actively carrying out their monitoring responsibilities. The Chinese legislation intended to add some independence to the board and provide an insider monitor for the board of directors, hoping that independent directors would be able to play the monitoring role that the board of supervisors had been unable to play. Academics also show a positive attitude towards the introduction of an independent director mechanism and believe that it will help to alleviate the problem of concentrated ownership structure (i.e., the mistreatment of minority shareholders from a controlling shareholder) and the prevailing "insider-dominance" by providing a better check-and-balance mechanism within the board, as well as facilitating a board of directors' monitoring function.[686] In other words,

682 See Feinerman, James V.: "New Hope for Corporate Governance in China?". *The China Quarterly*, No. 191, 9.2007, pp. 590–612, 607.

683 See Li Yanbing: "Gufen Youxian Gongsi Jianshihui Zhidu zhi Bijiao Yanjiu" [A Comparative Study on the Supervisory Board System of the Stock Corporation]. In: Shen Sibao (ed.): *International Business Law Review*, 2000, p. 272.

684 See Li Yanbing: "Gufen Youxian Gongsi Jianshihui Zhidu zhi Bijiao Yanjiu" [A Comparative Study on the Supervisory Board System of the Stock Corporation]. In: Shen Sibao (ed.): *International Business Law Review*, 2000, p. 264.

685 See Shanghai Stock Exchange: *The Results and Analysis of the Questionnaire Survey on Corporate Governance of Listed Companies*. Shangshi Gongsi [Listed Companies], 12.2000, pp. 11–25, 23.

686 See Zhu Ciyun: "Xinde Linian yu Xinde Shijiao-Ping Dalu "Gongsifa" de Xiugai" [New Ideas and Perspectives-Discussions on the amendment of "Company Law"]. *Study on Yue Dan Civil and Business Law*, Vol. 10. Qinghua University Press: 2006, pp. 40, 53.

independent directors are expected to be able to play the monitoring role that the board of supervisors has been unable to play. As a result, how to coordinate the relationship between directors and supervisors has become the central issue of Chinese corporate governance.

II. Functions of Independent Directors and Supervisors

The problem concerning whether independent directors can work within the dual-board structure as an effective addition to Chinese corporate governance has become the center of debates among academics. In discussing the conflicting role of supervisors and independent directors, some Chinese academics consider these two institutions as serving different purposes, whereby they can successfully co-exist while functioning in a supplementary fashion.[687] In opposition to this opinion, some commentators fear that having two monitoring institutions will lead to conflicts and duplication of functions. They attack independent directors for being redundant and believe that corporate law should revert to the supervisory board and enhance its monitoring authority.[688] As Professor Jiang Ping has pointed out, many independent directors do not play their role in corporate governance and they know nothing about the company, meaning that they are futile and affect the role of supervisors.[689] Other than these two opinions, there are also opinions positing that the provisions about independent director mechanism are too simple and probably some revisions are needed for it to perform its function. The independent director mechanism needs more time to fit itself into the Chinese corporate environment.[690]

---

687 See Jiangyu Wang: "The Strange Role of Independent Directors in a Two-Tier Board Structure of China's Listed Companies". *Compliance and Regulatory Journal*, Vol. 3, No. 3, 2008, pp. 47–55, 47; Li Jianwei: *Gongsi Zhidu, Gongsi Zhili yu Gongsi Guanli* [Corporate System, Corporate Governance and Management]. The People's Court Press: 2005, p. 161; Zhong, Gan Pei: "Lun Wan shan Wo guo Shang shi Gong si Zhi li Jie gou zhong de Jian shi Zhi du" [Comment on Improving Supervisors Mechanism in the Governance Structure in Chinese Listed Companies]. *China Legal Science*, 5.2001, p. 84; Lay Hong Tan / Jiangyu Wang: "Modelling an Effective Corporate Governance System for China's Listed State-Owned Enterprises: Issues and Challenges in a Transitional Economy". *Journal of Corporate Law Studies*, Vol. 7, No. 1, 2007, pp. 143–183, 147.

688 See Li Jianwei: *Gongsi Zhidu, Gongsi Zhili yu Gongsi Guanli* [Corporate System, Corporate Governance and Management]. The People's Court Press: 2005, p. 161; Kuang, Duan: *Gongsi Zhili Moshi Lun* [Discussions on the Model of Corporate Governance]. Law Press China: 2007, p. 205; Jiang Daxing: "Duli Dongshi: zai Chuangtong Kuangjia zhong Xingdong (Xia)?" [Independent Directors: perform in the traditional System?]. *Law Review*, No. 3, 2003, p. 47.

689 See Kuang, Duan: *Gongsi Zhili Moshi Lun* [Discussions on the Model of Corporate Governance]. Law Press China: 2007, p. 205.

690 See Yun, Gu Gong / Luo, Pei Xin: "Lun Wo guo Jian li Du li Dong shi Zhi du de Ji ge Fa lu Wen ti" [On Several Legal Issues of the Establishment of Independent Director

Furthermore, supervisors in China face similar challenges regarding their ability to perform their function adequately.[691] Generally speaking, the uncertainty created by the power overlap between the supervisors and independent directors in China may create an obstacle for furthering the implementation of independent directors in China. However, the legal systems that have been established should not be easily changed and the conflicts shall be resolved by the interpretation of legal provisions. Consequently, for final settlement of the disagreement, it requires a detailed analysis and comparison of how both institutions function.

1. *Similar Powers*

On the one side, the independent directors and supervisors have similar powers with respect to some corporate affairs. First, according to Article 53 para.1 of the Company Law, the board of directors can investigate the company's financial affairs and Article 5 para.4 of Independent Directors Opinion rules that the independent directors shall make up more than half of the members of the auditing committee,[692] which is responsible for recommending the engagement or replacement of the company's external auditing institutions, reviewing the internal audit system and its execution, overseeing the interaction between the company's internal and external auditing institutions and inspecting the company's financial information and its disclosure, as well as monitoring the company's internal control system.[693] Second, both the supervisory board and independent directors can propose to convene temporary shareholders' meeting according to Article 53 para.4 of the Company Law and Article 5 para.1 (3) of the Independent Directors Opinion. Third, they also have the power to independently engage external auditing institutions and consultancies in terms of Article 60 in the Code, which provides that the supervisory board may independently hire intermediary institutions to provide professional opinions and Article 5 para.1 (5) in the Independent Directors Opinion. Fourth, based on Article 54 of the Company Law, the supervisors – where necessary – may hire an accounting firm to help with the relevant expenses being borne by the company. Similarly, Article 5 para.1 (2) of the Independent Directors Opinion rules that independent directors can propose the engagement or dismissal of an accounting firm to the board of directors. Finally, both supervisors and directors have the power of representing the company and filing lawsuits against each other based on the

in China]. *China Legal Science*, June, 2001, p. 75; Zhu Ciyun: "Xinde Linian yu Xinde Shijiao-Ping Dalu "Gongsifa" de Xiugai" [New Ideas and Perspectives-Discussions on the amendment of "Company Law"]. *Study on Yue Dan Civil and Business Law*, Vol. 10. Qinghua University Press: 2006, p. 62.

691 Zhong, Gan Pei: "Lun Wan shan Wo guo Shang shi Gong si Zhi li Jie gou zhong de Jian shi Zhi du" [Comment on Improving Supervisors Mechanism in the Governance Structure in Chinese Listed Companies]. *China Legal Science*, 5.2001, p. 79.

692 Independent Directors Opinion, Article 5 para.4.

693 The Code, Article 54.

requirement of shareholders. Article 151 of the Company Law rules that where a director or senior manager is under the circumstance as stated in Article 149 of this Law, the shareholders of the limited liability company or joint stock limited company separately or aggregately holding 1% or more of the total shares of the company may require the board of supervisors or the supervisor of the limited liability company with no board of supervisors in writing to file a lawsuit in the people's court. If the supervisor is under the circumstance as stated in Article 149 of this Law, the aforesaid shareholder(s) may require the board of directors or the executive director of the limited liability company with no board of directors in writing to file a lawsuit in the people's court.

Finally, the hybrid model of China's corporate governance, with some Chinese specialties and a combination of stakeholder- and shareholder-centered models, shows the intention of making all constituencies including shareholders and employees an end of corporate governance.[694] Article 147 of the Company Law also provides that the directors (including independent directors), supervisors and senior managers shall bear the duty of loyalty and duty of care to the company and no director, supervisor or senior manager may take any bribe or other illegal gains by taking the advantage of his authorities or encroach upon the properties of the company. In the code, Article 33 provides that directors shall faithfully, honestly and diligently perform their duties for the best interests of the company and all the shareholders. Article 50 rules that the independent directors shall bear the duties of good faith and due diligence towards the listed company and all the shareholders. They shall earnestly perform their duties in accordance with laws, regulations and the company's articles of association, protect the overall interests of the company and be especially concerned with protecting the interests of minority shareholders from being infringed. The independent directors shall carry out their duties independently and not subject themselves to the influence of the company's major shareholders, actual controllers or other entities or persons who are interested parties of the listed company. Article 1 (2) in the Independent Directors Opinion provides that an independent director has a fiduciary obligation and an obligation of diligence towards the listed company and all its shareholders. An independent director should – pursuant to the requirements of the relevant laws and regulations, these Guiding Opinions and the company's articles of association – conscientiously perform his duties and responsibilities, safeguard the company's overall interests and particularly pay attention to ensure that the lawful rights and interests of small and medium shareholders are not prejudiced. In terms of the supervisors, Article 59 of the Code provides that the supervisory board of a listed company shall be accountable to all shareholders. The supervisory board shall supervise the corporate finance, the legitimacy of directors, managers and other senior management personnel's performance of duties, as well as protect the company's and the shareholders' legal rights and interests.

694 See Peerenboom R.: *China Modernizes: Threat to the West or Model for the* Rest. Oxford University Press: 2008, pp. 36–43.

2. *Different Powers*

On the other side, the independent directors possess some power that supervisors cannot perform. First, the independent directors can constitute insider supervision of executive directors and participate in the decision-making process of some important issues. For example, Article 6 para.1 provides that an independent director should express his independent opinion to the board of directors or the shareholders' general meeting on matters such as the nomination, appointment and removal and remuneration of directors and senior management personnel as well as matters that may – in an independent director's opinion – prejudice the rights and interests of small and medium shareholders.[695] The independent directors shall offer important information to supervisors to enhance the role of the board of supervisors based on the provisions of Article 98 para.3, para.4 and para.5 in the Guidelines for Articles of Listed Companies, which rules that directors shall investigate the performance of the company and report regularly to the company, signing confirmation opinion in written form to ensure the sincerity, preciseness and integrity of the information revealed by the company and provide genuinely the relevant information and material to the board of supervisors, as well as not impede the board of supervisors from exercising its functions and powers.

Second, the independent directors serve as an ex-ante supervision system[696] by performing more functions of management such as delivering independent opinions on major connected transactions based on Article 5 para.1 of the Independent Director Opinion, which stipulates that in listed companies major connected transactions should be submitted to the board of directors for deliberation after the approval of the independent directors,[697] while the supervisors perform ex-post control[698] by

695 Independent Directors Opinion, Article 6 para.1–6.

696 See Gan Peizhong: "Lun Wanshan Woguo Shangshi Gongsi Zhili Jiegou zhong de Jianshi Zhidu" [Discussions on Improving the Supervisory Board in the Corporate Governance System of China]. *China Legal Science*, 2001, No. 5, p. 84.

697 Independent Directors Opinion, Article 5 (1) also provides some specific power to guarantee the function of independent directors in major connected transactions: (1) before rendering their judgment, Independent Directors may engage an intermediary organization to issue an independent financial consultant report for use as a basis for rendering their judgment; (2) proposing the engagement or dismissal of an accounting firm to the board of directors; (3) proposing to the board of directors the convening of an extraordinary shareholders' general meeting; (4) proposing the convening of a meeting of the board of directors; (5) independently engaging external auditing institutions and consultancies; and (6) openly soliciting shareholders' voting rights before the holding of a shareholders' general meeting.

698 See Liu Heping: "Shangshi Gongsi Duli Dongshi yu Jianshihui Gaunxi Lun – Jianlun Duli Dongshi Gongneng Dingwei" [Discussions on the Relationship between Independent directors and Supervisory Board – the role of Independent Directors]. In: Wang Baoshu (ed.): *Essays of Business Law.* Law Press China: Vol. 6, 2000, p. 54.

supervising acts undertaken by directors and managers during the performance of their duties and proposing to remove directors or managers when a serious breach occurs,[699] as well as requesting directors or managers to rectify conduct that is harmful to the interests of the company[700] and filing lawsuits against directors when a director breaches his or her duty to abide by the law, administrative rules or articles of corporate charter.[701]

Third, independent directors focus on the protection of shareholders, while supervisors tend to equally protect shareholders and employees because Article 118 of the Company Law rules that the board of supervisors shall include not only representatives of shareholders but also an appropriate percentage of representatives of the company's employees. The percentage of the representatives of employees shall account for not less than one-third of all the supervisors, although the concrete percentage shall be specified in the articles of association. The representatives of employees who serve as members of the board of supervisors shall be democratically elected through the assembly of representatives of the company's employees, the assembly of employees or by other means.

Further, the supervisors are responsible for monitoring the legality of directors' action, while independent directors check whether the decisions of the board are reasonable for the business of corporations. Article 53 para. 2 and 3 stipulate that the board of supervisors may exercise the authorities of supervising the duty-related acts of the directors and senior managers, as well as bring forward proposals on the removal of any director or senior manager who violates any law, administrative regulation, the articles of association or any resolution of the shareholders' meeting and demand any director or senior manager to make rectifications if his act has injured the interests of the company. While Article 6 of the Independent Directors Opinion provides that independent directors should express independent opinions on material matters of the listed company, such as the nomination, appointment and removal of directors and the engagement or dismissal of senior management personnel as well as the remuneration of the company's directors and senior management personnel.

Finally, the independent directors apparently have the power to propose to the board of directors the convening of an extraordinary shareholders' general meeting, rather than actually calling a meeting of shareholders or the board, while the board of supervisors may exercise the authorities of proposing to convene a temporary shareholders' meeting, as well as convene and preside over a shareholders' meeting when the board of directors does not exercise the functions of convening and presiding over the shareholders' meeting as prescribed in this Law according to the Article 53 para.4 of the Company Law. More importantly, the Independent Directors Opinion does not actually confer these powers on independent directors, although

699 Company Law, Article 54, para.2
700 Company Law, Article 54, para.3.
701 Company Law, Article 151.

it calls upon companies to confer these powers, presumably through provisions in their articles of incorporation or other internal rules.[702]

Based on the provisions of the Company Law and the Independent Directors Opinion, I conclude that the functions of independent directors and supervisors can coordinate with each other and the role of independent directors may not necessarily be affected by supervisors. China's pursuit of long-term corporate development relies on the combination of shareholder-centered and stakeholder-centered model. At present, the merits of the American and the German systems do not dominate – either separately or jointly – in the Chinese corporate governance. It is unclear which system is better for corporate governance of China. The formation and selection of a corporate governance model suitable to the Chinese situation remain to be further refined. The further improvement of China's corporate governance system – in particular, coordinating the functions of supervisors and independent directors – relies on the governance practice of every PLC, because the enterprises would choose the most suitable governance system for themselves.

702 Clarke, Donald C.: "The Independent Director in Chinese Corporate Governance". *Delaware Journal of Corporate Law*, Vol. 31, No. 1, 2006, pp. 125–228, 194.

Conclusion: Convergence of the Value and Diversity of the Approaches for Protecting Minority Shareholders

Based on the different attitudes among the three economy giants for cumulative voting – which is a small yet impossible-to-be-ignored system designed for minority shareholders' protection in PLCs – this dissertation concludes that despite the importance of minority shareholders' protection, the means for this purpose in terms of the insider corporate governance system is regulating RPTs, which is limited by the long-term development of corporations because both the stakeholder- and shareholder-centered models have been modified and come to converge into the long governance model. Moreover, there is a persistence of diversity in the ways of controlling self-dealing and realizing the long governance.

The entire US corporate governance system relies on the independence and the fiduciary duty of directors to find a happy medium that carefully balances two competing values, namely the authority and accountability of the directors, rather than purely pursuing maximization of shareholder' interests by business judgment rule. This approach would tend to emphasize long-term value over short-term gain, even if certain constituencies would prefer a short-term gain, while leaving room for the board to decide how to allocate value when circumstances require a trade-off among constituencies. In this respect, these arrangements are beneficial to the professional managers and designed to preserve the power of directors and managers in controlling corporation. At the level of European corporate law, the (supervisory) board includes employee representatives and independent directors without minority representatives. Regarding minority shareholders' protection, the EU relies on the approval of shareholders and advice from independent directors to control the RPTs and foster the engagement of shareholders in the corporate governance. Therefore, in the US, we can say that the officers' primacy still triumphs and the system of internal governance becomes distant from its common historical roots because the economic and financial development started to accelerate in the US, whereby increasingly more power was attributed to managers and increasingly more control was eroded from the shareholders, while Europe is confirming and strengthening the shareholder-oriented model of corporation (albeit for those countries adopting two-tier boards).[703]

In terms of China, to cope with the corporate governance problems in PLCs, the Company Law of 2005 adopted cumulative voting, which is not popular in its motherland. There is no doubt that the decline of cumulative voting in American

703 See Bruno, Sabrina: "Directors' Versus Shareholders' Primacy in U.S. Corporations Through the Eyes of History: Is Directors' Power "Inherent"?". *European Company and Financial Law Review*, 2012, pp. 421–445, 445.

corporate governance is partly the result of the unique political history of this country. While these historic conditions – including misuse in a hostile takeover in the US – do not exist in China, where the governance system has only been established for little more than ten years and has been integrated in several institutions in Germany and the US, its improvement requires the experience and practice of corporations to prove whether those institutions can work towards improving corporate governance and how effective the system would be in practice. Moreover, Chinese legislation does not simply transplant the institutions from the US but, rather, transforms the foreign systems to adapt to the conditions of Chinese corporate governance such as the legislative form of cumulative voting.

On the other hand, the feature of the coexistence of a supervisory board and a board of independent directors as well as the adoption of cumulative voting demonstrate an important characteristic of China's economic and corporate reform, namely its cultural and philosophical approach of "crossing the river by touching stones" (mozhe shitou guohe). First, China differs from many European countries in as much as the latter have their own corporate governance model, which has worked for a long time and has made the adoption of a system contradicting their own traditions or one with the same functions as their current system difficult, whereby its corporate governance system combines the shareholder- and stakeholder-centered models. Second, China's political leaders and policy-makers have faced the challenges of globalization, transition and development. There are no textbooks to guide China along this path simply because no country has ever faced such a set of challenges. Under such circumstances, China's policy-makers and regulators were eager to learn from and introduce foreign experience, albeit this caused the conflicts among institutions for corporate governance. Accordingly, the state should pay more attention to the formulation often repeated in the official media: considering China's particular conditions and develop a system of "corporate governance with Chinese characteristics" to build its own best pathway.[704] Increasingly more scholars have realized that China should not blindly adopt foreign corporate governance systems without considering the real problems.[705]

As La Porta, Lopez-de-Silanes, Shleifer and Vishny hold, "where laws are protective of outside investors and well enforced, investors are willing to finance

---

704 See Nolan, Peter H.: "China at the crossroads". *Polity Press*, 1st Edition, 2004, p. 1.

705 See Clarke, Donald C.: "The Independent Director in Chinese Corporate Governance". *Delaware Journal of Corporate Law*, Vol. 31, No. 1, 2006, pp. 125–228; Xu Xiaosong: "Gongsi Zhili: "Jiegou" yihuo "Wenti"" [Corporate Governance: "Structure" or "Problem"]. *Zhengfa Luntan* [Tribune of Political Science and Law], Vol. 31, No. 6, 11.2013, pp. 61–68, 68; Zhu Ciyun / Lin Kai: "Gongsi Zhidu Qutong Lilun Jianshi Xia de Zhonguo Gongsi Zhili Pingxi" [Analysis of Chinese Corporate Governance under the Theory of Converge of Corporate Governance], *Law Research*, Vol. 5, 2013, pp. 24–41, 41.

corporations, and financial markets are both broader and more valuable"[706]. However, according to John C. Coffee, rather than creating developed capital market, the law was triggered by it, whereby the massive dispersed investors formed an economic interest group, which promoted legislations to draft law for protecting them.[707] It seems like the "chicken-and-egg question". Subsequently, Curtis J. Milhaupt and Katharina Pistor regard the relationship between law and economy as a "rolling relationship".[708] In the 1980s, the rapid development of the economy in Japan and Germany promoted the research of their corporate governance system and some scholars even though that their bank-centered system was better than the US market-centered model.[709] In the mid-1990s, the US dependence of the development of high-technology and the information technology reform regained great economic growth while Japan encountered an economic bubble burst. Consequently, the US corporate governance system became the focus of studies and was regarded as the most developed system around the world.[710] However, from 2001 to 2002 the exposure of corporate governance scandals and the financial crisis in 2008 highlighted serious corporate governance shortcomings, mainly related to internal controls, executive remuneration

706 See La Porta, Rafael / Lopez-de-Silanes, Florencio / Shleifer, Anderei / Vishny, Robert W.: "Investor Protection and Corporate Valuation". *Journal of Finance*, Vol. 57, No. 3, 2002, pp. 1147–1170, 1147; Kamar, Ehud: "Beyond Competition for Incorporations". *Georgetown Law Journal*, Vol. 94, No. 6, 2006, pp. 1725–1772, 1725.

707 See Coffee, John C.: "The Rise of Dispersed Ownership: The Roles of Law and the State in the Separation of Ownership and Control". *Yale Law Journal*, Vol. 111, No. 1, 10.2001, pp. 1–82, 80–81; Choi, Stephen J.: "Law, Finance and Path Dependence: Developing Strong Securities Markets". *Texas Law Review*, Vol. 80, No. 7, 2002, pp. 1657–1728, 1680.

708 See Milhaupt, Curtis J. / Pistor, Katharina: *Law and Capitalism: What Corporate Crises Reveal about Legal Systems and Economic Development around the World.* University of Chicago Press: 2008, p. 16.

709 See Grundfest, Joseph A.: "Subordination of American Capital". *Journal of Finance Economics*, Vol. 27, No. 1, 1990, pp. 89–114; Gilson, Ronald: "Globalizing corporate governance: convergence of form or function". *The American Journal of Comparative Law*, Vol. 49, No. 2, Spring 2001, pp. 329–357; Gilson, Ronald J. / Roe, Mark J.: "Understanding the Japanese Keiretsu: Overlaps Between Corporate Governance and Industrial Organization and Industrial Organization". *Yale Law Journal*, Vol. 102, No. 4, 1.1993, pp. 871–906; Berglof, Eric / Peroti, Enrico: "The Governance Structure of the Japanese Financial". *Keiretsu*, Vol. 36, No. 2, 10.1994, pp. 259–284.

710 See Macey, Jonathan R. / Miller, Geoffrey: "Corporate Governance and Commercial Banking: A Comparative Examination of Germany, Japan, and the United States". *Stanford Law Review*, Vol. 48, No. 1, 11.1995, pp. 73–112; Milhaupt, Curtis J.: "The Market for Innovation in the United States and Japan: Venture Capital and the Comparative Corporate Governance Debate". *Northwestern University Law Review*, Vol. 91, No. 3, 1997, pp. 865–898.

and external auditors.[711] Corporate frauds and accounting failures had been made easier by the lack of appropriate internal controls for which the firm's managers and directors were generally responsible. Furthermore, stock options and other incentives aggressively promoted managers to manipulate share prices through false information relative to their firms' financial performance. The auditors and other gatekeepers – such as investment bankers, business lawyers and rating agencies – largely contributed to the first crisis of this century by covering frauds and aiding insolvent companies to conceal their true financial conditions.[712] At the same time, during a slow "end of US hegemony" twenty-year period, the US share of world trade has fallen whereas Asia has become the world's fastest-growing region.

Therefore, we cannot look for solutions in other countries' corporate governance systems simply because their economies are doing well in the current phase of an economic cycle.[713] As Paul Davies points out, it is unwise to look for solutions in other countries' corporate governance systems simply because one's own economy is performing poorly in the current phase of an economic cycle.[714] A strong economy is also as likely (if not more) to be the consequence of many other legal, economic, political and other factors.[715] Although lawmakers were concerned about economic efficiency in designing the corporate decision-making structure, they had no clear criterion by which to achieve this goal.[716] Indeed, there is no "global best corporate governance system". Due to the differences of corporate governance issues among countries, a system working well in one country does not mean it can also solve the problem in others. As a result, every country has to develop its own corporate governance measures based on its particular conditions.[717]

---

711 See Coffee, John C.: "A Theory of Corporate Scandals: Why the US and Europe Differ". *Oxford Rev of Economic Policy*, Vol. 21, No.2, 2005, pp. 198–211.

712 See Coffee, John C.: "Racing towards the Top: The Impact of Cross-Listings and Stock Market Competition on International Corporate Governance". *Columbia Law Review*, Vol. 102, No. 7, 11.2002, pp. 1757–1831; Dunn, William: "Pattern Recognition Receptors: Doubling Up for the Innate Immune Response". *Cell Press*, Vol. 111, No. 7, 12.2002, pp. 927–930.

713 See Huang Hui: "Lvlun Gongsi Fa Yitihua: Zhongguo Shijiao ji Qishi" [General Analysis of Converge of Corporate Law: in the Perspective of China]. *Journal of Comparative Law*, Vol. 5, 2013, pp. 61–76, 71.

714 See Davies, Paul: "Employee Representation and Corporate Law Reform: A Comment from the United Kingdom". *Comparative Labor Law and Policy Journal*, Vol. 22, No. 1, 2000, pp. 135–148, 135–136.

715 See Bebchuk, Lucian A.: "Letting Shareholders Set the Rules". *Harvard Law Review*, Vol. 119, No. 6, 2006, pp. 1784–1813, 1791–1792.

716 See Cools, Sofie: "The Dividing Line Between Shareholder Democracy and Board Autonomy: Inherent Conflicts of Interest as Normative Criterion". *European Company and Financial Law Review*, Vol. 11, No. 2, 2014, pp. 258–296, 269.

717 See Huang Hui: "Lvlun Gongsi Fa Yitihua: Zhongguo Shijiao ji Qishi" [General Analysis of Converge of Corporate Law: in the Perspective of China]. *Journal of Comparative Law*, Vol. 5, 2013, pp. 61–76, 65.

The simple reality is that despite the well-recognized purpose of protecting minority shareholders due to the pressure on the developing capital market, there will always be corporate law systems that differ from country to country and we should be skeptical of the so-called "convergence theory" stating that any one structure or even a class of structures is best.[718] There remains a persistence of diversity in corporate governance and it is unclear what type of convergence may result, as well as whether convergence is either desirable or inevitable. In this world, there are many cultures, many types of economies and six billion persons whom the global convergence advocates ignore. For many of those cultures and those economies, US style capitalism or corporate governance – or many other Westernizing influences for that matter – will never penetrate the social and governmental barriers against them.[719]

On the other hand, the diversity of approaches for protecting minority shareholders in the US, the EU and China supports the argument that legal rules are often the product of political processes that combine public-regarding features with interest group politics. To the extent that interest groups play a role, each interest group will seek to push for rules that favor it. "Interest groups differ in their ability to mobilize and then exert pressure in favor of legal rules that favor them or against rules that disfavor them. The more resources and power a group has, the more influence the group will tend to have in the political process."[720] As a result, the corporate rules that will actually be chosen and maintained might depend on the relative strength of the relevant interest groups. When a certain set of rules leads corporate control to be at the hands of one group of players, their control of existing structures will make these players more influential in subsequent interest group politics, thus making it more likely that the country will have these or similar rules in the future. Their power within corporations will translate into power in the political process and influence on corporate rules.[721] Those who have on-share corporate control – whether controlling shareholders (in the EU), professional managers (in the US) or other players – are likely to have an influence owing to the resources that they command. These resources will enable them to lobby, make campaign contributions

718 See Jacoby, Sanford M.: "Corporate Governance in Comparative Perspective: Prospects for Convergence". *Comparative Labor Law and Policy Journal*, Vol. 22, No. 1, 2000, pp. 5–32.

719 See Branson, Douglas M.: "The Very Uncertain Prospect of "Global" Convergence in Corporate Governance". *Cornell International Law Journal*, Vol. 34, No. 2, 2001, p. 321–362, 327.

720 Bebchuk, Lucian A. / Roe, Mark J.: "A Theory of Path Dependence in Corporate Ownership and Governance". *Stanford Law Review*, Vol. 52, No. 1, 11.1999, pp. 127–170, 158.

721 See Bebchuk, Lucian A. / Roe, Mark J.: "A Theory of Path Dependence in Corporate Ownership and Governance". *Stanford Law Review*, Vol. 52, No. 1, 11.1999, pp. 127–170, 158.

and otherwise gain political influence.[722] Put simply, although the corporate governance value has converged on pursuing the entire benefit of corporations and long-term development among the US, EU and China, there is and will remain a persistence of diversity in the ways of protecting minority shareholders and realizing long governance.

722 "These resources also provide them with visibility, access to media, high social status, and access to elite and influential groups, all of which can be helpful in influencing the corporate rules system." See Bebchuk, Lucian A. / Roe, Mark J.: "A Theory of Path Dependence in Corporate Ownership and Governance". *Stanford Law Review*, Vol. 52, No. 1, 11.1999, pp. 127–170, 159–160.

www.ingramcontent.com/pod-product-compliance
Ingram Content Group UK Ltd.
Pitfield, Milton Keynes, MK11 3LW, UK
UKHW021842100926
8556IPUK00019B/1003

9 783631 700051